Using Eudora

Quick Start to Eudora Success!

Essential Windows in Eudora for Windows

If you use Eudora for Windows on a regular basis, you'll need to be familiar with the Mailbox and Message windows shown here.

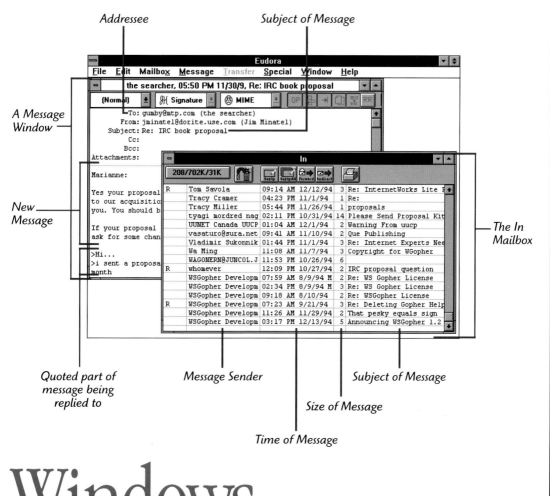

Addressee

Subject of Message

A Message Window

New Message

The In Mailbox

Quoted part of message being replied to

Message Sender

Subject of Message

Size of Message

Time of Message

Windows

® 201 W. 103rd Street • Indianapolis, IN 46290 • (317) 581-3500
Copyright© 1994 Que Corporation

Shortcut Keys for Macintosh Users

Moving and Copying	Shortcut
Copy selection	F3 or ⌘+C
Cut selection	F2 or ⌘+X
Paste	F4 or ⌘+V
Paste as Quotation	⌘+'

Editing	Shortcut
Undo last action	F1 or ⌘+Z
Select all of the message	⌘+A

Managing Mail	Shortcut
Attach file to mail	⌘+H
Check your mail	⌘+M
Close a message	⌘+W
Create a new message	⌘+N
Delete the current message	⌘+D
Filter messages (version 2 only)	⌘+J
Open the In Mailbox	⌘+I
Queue the current message	⌘+E
Reply to the current message	⌘+R
Save the current message	⌘+S
Send message	⌘+E
Send queued messages	⌘+T

Finding Messages and Text	Shortcut
Find a message or text in a message	⌘+F
Find again	⌘+G
Find selected text	⌘+=
Find next message with given text	⌘+;

Moving in and between messages	Shortcut
Go to the previous message	↑ or ←
Go to the next message	↓ or →
Move to the beginning of the current window	Home
Move to the end of the current window	End
Move up one "screen" in current window	PgUp
Move down one "screen" in current window	PgDn

Moving between messages from message window	Shortcut
Go to the previous message	⌘+↑ or ⌘+←
Go to the next message	⌘+↓ or ⌘+→

Nicknames	Shortcut
Open the Nickname window	⌘+L
Make a new Nickname	⌘+K
Finish a Nickname	⌘+,

Other Shortcuts	Shortcut
Help	Help
Move the current window behind another window	⌘+B
Open the Ph Window	⌘+U
Open a file	⌘+O
Print a message	⌘+P
Quit Eudora	⌘+Q
Stop what Eudora is doing	Esc or ⌘+.

Macintosh

Using

Eudora

Using

Eudora

Dee-Ann and Robert LeBlanc

que

Using Eudora

Library of Congress Catalog No.: 95-67128

ISBN: 0-7897-0178-2

98 97 96 95   6 5 4 3 2 1

Interpretation of the printing code: the rightmost double-digit number is the year of the book's printing; the rightmost single-digit number, the number of the book's printing. For example, a printing code of 95-1 shows that the first printing of the book occurred in 1995.

Publisher: *David P. Ewing*

Associate Publisher: *Stacy Hiquet*

Associate Publisher—Operations: *Corinne Walls*

Director of Product Series: *Charles O. Stewart III*

Publishing Director: *Brad R. Koch*

Managing Editor: *Sandra Doell*

Credits

Acquisitions Editor
Beverly Eppink

Product Director
Jim Minatel

Production Editor
Mitzi Foster Gianakos

Editors
Noelle Gasco
Heather Kaufman

Technical Editor
Richard M. Donnelly
Alfonso Hermida
Jim Mann

Figure Specialist
Cari Ohm

Book Designers
Amy Peppler Adams
Sandra Stevenson

Cover Designer
Jay Corpus

Acquisitions Assistant
Ruth Slates

Operations Coordinator
Patty Brooks

Editorial Assistant
Andrea Duvall

Production Team
Maxine Dillingham
Lorell Fleming
Daryl Kessler
Steph Mineart
Kris Simmons

Composed in *ITC Century*, *ITC Highlander*, and *MCPdigital* by Que Corporation.

Dedication

We dedicate this book to our families for their support and for putting up with a pair of workaholics who can't get it through their heads that one doesn't work during one's "vacation."

About the Authors

Robert and Dee-Ann LeBlanc are the co-owners of Renaissoft Enterprises, a computer services firm that specializes in Internet consulting and training, and custom software development.

Dee-Ann has been using UseNet since 1988, when she got her first computer account with Internet access. She wears several hats for Renaissoft Enterprises as a computer consultant, technical writer, and manager.

Robert is a systems programmer and site administrator for Renaissoft Enterprises' site, renaissoft.com. He has a background in aerospace engineering and computing science. He is also the author of several publicly released software packages for UNIX systems, such as the Qfax Utility Suite, a fax server/ spooler for use with major e-mail packages.

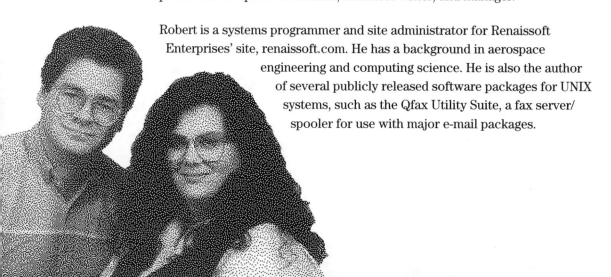

Acknowledgments

We would like to thank David Lawrence, Sonja Kueppers, and Mike Strainic for coming through for us on short notice and Hank van Dyk for being there when we really, really need some pictures done. Last, but certainly not least, a huge thanks to Beverly Eppink, Jim Minatel, and Mitzi Foster Gianakos for helping us through our first book and not panicking as we wandered across the continent in the middle of it all.

Trademarks

Contents at a Glance

{Table of Contents}

Introduction

Part I: Welcome to the World of Electronic Mail

Chapter 1: An Introduction to E-mail

Why do I need Eudora?

see page 15

Chapter 2: The Power of E-mail

Chapter 3: How Internet E-mail Works

Where did my e-mail disappear to?

see page 39

Chapter 4: E-mail Writing Style

Part II: Getting Started

Chapter 5: Installing Eudora on a Macintosh

*Getting
the free
version of
Eudora*

see page 61

Chapter 6: Installing Eudora on Windows

Getting the free version of Eudora

see page 91

*Testing,
testing,
...1,2,3...*

see page 121

Chapter 7: Connecting with Eudora

Chapter 8: Staying Informed

Part III: Using Eudora

Chapter 9: Sending E-mail

*The composition window
see page 134*

Chapter 10: Receiving E-mail

What is a nickname?

see page 143

Chapter 11: Answering E-mail

What mail forwarding does

see page 168

Chapter 12: Accessing FTP and Gopher through E-mail

All the world loves a MIME

see page 208

Chapter 13: Sending and Receiving Files

What makes up a mailbox window? see page 224

Part IV: Maintenance

Chapter 14: Mailboxes and Folders

*All I ever
wanted
to know
about sav-
ing mail*

see page 242

Chapter 15: Working with Mail

*Filtering
messages*

see page 257

Part V: New Features of Commercial Eudora

Chapter 16: Special Features of Eudora 2.1 for Macintosh

Chapter 17: Spell-checking E-mail with Spellswell

Chapter 18: Special Features of Eudora 2.0 for Windows

Using Multi-purpose Internet Mail Extension (MIME)

see page 299

Introduction

Electronic mail is fast becoming the medium of choice for communicating with others around the world. The world-spanning Internet has made it possible for people on opposite sides of the globe to send letters, programs, pictures, sounds, and more to each other in a matter of seconds.

It's a stark contrast from the days when people used to wait weeks or months for mail from abroad. When American author Eudora Welty wrote a short story called "Why I Live at the P.O.", she could hardly have known that her name would one day come to be synonymous with electronic mail in the Information Age.

The Internet, for all its wonderful potential, can be complicated to use. Even something as "simple" as sending electronic mail (e-mail) can be daunting without the right tools. It's thanks in part to user-friendly programs such as Eudora that it's possible for people from all walks of life to use e-mail today.

Eudora brings the post office to where you live, to turn a phrase on Ms. Welty. Whether you're interested in swapping letters with a pen pal or keeping in touch with a distant friend, Eudora lets you do all this and things you might not have even thought of—through e-mail you can tap into resources like UseNet news, program archives, and much more.

Let *Using Eudora* be your guidebook as you explore the world of electronic mail and put this powerful program to work for you.

What this book is

This is a book about Qualcomm's popular electronic mail program Eudora, which is available for Apple Macintosh and Microsoft Windows systems. Both the freeware and commercial versions of Eudora are covered for both platforms.

We've designed this book with the busy professional in mind; it's nice to be able to find out what you need to know without having to wade through text that's either insultingly introductory or intimidatingly technical. We've tried to fill that void in-between.

Here's a brief look at what you have in store for you in the pages ahead:

Part I: Welcome to the World of Electronic Mail

These chapters provide an introduction to electronic mail for those who need or want more background to bring them up to speed.

Chapter 1, "An Introduction to E-mail," eases you into the book by refreshing your memory with some background material you'll need later in the book.

Chapter 2, "The Power of E-mail," illustrates some of the many neat things you can do with e-mail.

Chapter 3, "How Internet E-mail Works," is designed to give you a better picture of how e-mail works, and points out both its strengths and weaknesses.

Chapter 4, "E-mail Writing Style," points out the importance of "netiquette" and the peculiarities of communicating in a world without body language.

Part II: Getting Started

These chapters cover the installation and configuration of Eudora, and how to get connected to the Internet.

Chapter 5, "Installing Eudora on a Macintosh," takes you through the installation and configuration process on your Apple Macintosh.

Chapter 6, "Installing Eudora on Windows," shows Microsoft Windows users how to install and configure Eudora.

Chapter 7, "Connecting with Eudora," deals with the business of connecting Eudora to the Internet.

Chapter 8, "Staying Informed," explains how you can get in touch with Qualcomm, and how to find out about the latest versions of Eudora.

Part III: Using Eudora

Here you'll learn how to do day-to-day tasks such as writing, sending, and replying to e-mail with Eudora. You'll also get a glimpse at some of the more useful (and often obscure) things you can do with e-mail.

Chapter 9, "Sending E-mail," illustrates, step-by-step, how to compose and send a letter.

Chapter 10, "Receiving E-mail," shows you how to have Eudora check for mail and retrieve it for you.

Chapter 11, "Answering E-mail," points out the differences between replying to a letter and composing an original letter, and illustrates how to forward and redirect e-mail you receive.

Chapter 12, "Accessing FTP and Gopher through E-mail," shows you how to tap into resources like FTP mailservers, mailing lists, Gopher, Archie, and UseNet news by e-mail.

Chapter 13, "Sending and Receiving Files," shows you how you can encode programs, graphics, and sound files to send by e-mail.

Part IV: Maintenance

These chapters teach you the essentials of managing your e-mail and point out some useful ways you can manipulate your mail.

Chapter 14, "Mailboxes and Folders," goes into more detail about Eudora's mailboxes and folders, and how you can use them to organize your e-mail.

Chapter 15, "Working with Mail," shows you how to save, move, copy, and delete mail from your mailboxes.

Part V: New Features of Commercial Eudora

You'll discover the many new and powerful features found only the commercial versions of Eudora.

Chapter 16, "Special Features of Eudora 2.1 for Macintosh," describes the new features found in Eudora 2.1 for the Macintosh.

Chapter 17, "Spell-checking E-mail with Spellswell," covers how to incorporate and use Working Software's Spellswell spell-checker with Eudora for the Macintosh.

Chapter 18, "Special Features of Eudora 2.0 for Windows," illustrates the new features of Eudora 2.0 for Windows.

Also you'll find a tear-out reference card at the beginning of this book with some keyboard shortcuts for all versions of Eudora.

What this book is not

This book assumes that you know the basics about the Internet, what it is, and what you can do with it. While we do repeat a few essential points, you won't find a comprehensive Internet primer between these covers.

This focuses on e-mail, specifically Eudora. In focusing on Eudora and keeping the coverage here concise and to the point, we have not covered topics such as how you get connected to the Internet. This is covered in many other books that don't have the depth of coverage you'll find here on Eudora.

If you're looking for an introductory-level book about the Internet, you might have a look at some other books in Que's lineup, including Easy Internet and Using the Internet. Hayden's Internet Starter Kit for Macintosh, 2nd Edition is a good choice for Mac users.

Conventions used in this book

Throughout this book you'll see a number of different highlighted sections designed to present different kinds of information to you in an easy-to-follow style.

In the many examples you'll find in this book, you'll see that when we want you to type something, we'll set that in **bold type**. On-screen text is in special `mono type`. Electronic mail addresses also are distinguished by **bold type**.

For Windows users, we've underlined the hotkeys in menu commands. For instance, if you see <u>M</u>essage, <u>N</u>ew Message that means that pressing Alt+M and then N will do the same thing as opening the Message menu with the mouse and choosing New Message. Mac users can ignore this difference between the Windows and Mac versions.

(!) (Tip)

Keep your eyes open for Tips like this; they can show you clever shortcuts or point out interesting but obscure features that can make your life easier.

(∗) {Note}

A Note often points out something subtle, yet important, that you should know. Even if you skip over Tips, you should always read Notes.

(?) Q&A

What's a Q&A section?

Just as it sounds, a Q&A poses a specific question that you may have, and then provides the answer to that question. This is also a troubleshooting section. Reading Q&As can help you avoid getting into trouble.

(X) <Caution>

If you don't heed Cautions, you may do something harmful without knowing it. They're *very* important!

Sidebars

Sidebars take you aside for a moment and follow tangents that aren't strictly necessary for the topic at hand, but might be inspired by it. They let us share personal anecdotes or touch on something relevant but not crucial to the subject matter.

Part I:

Welcome to the World of Electronic Mail

An Introduction to E-mail

One of the most popular uses of the Internet is sending electronic mail, or e-mail. It's like going to the post office except that it's faster and you don't have to leave your chair.

By choosing to buy this book, you've taken the first step toward "getting connected" to a new world. The problem is that the media never tells you what you can do on the Internet. Like everything else that deals with computers, all that you hear about it is hype and you don't get any feeling for the practical, everyday uses.

Welcome to the Internet

You are in the process of joining the millions of people in the world who have access to the "wonders of the Internet." Let's take some time to get to know the world you're entering.

What is the Internet?

The **Internet** is a worldwide network of computers. Many of these computers are permanently connected to the Internet using fiber optics or "leased lines." Others only connect part of the time using phone lines. Rarely are any of the computers on the Internet connected to one another using a single wire that runs between them.

Brief history of the Net

The Internet, often referred to as just "the Net," was not always a sprawling, globe-spanning network. It had humble beginnings.

The Internet was born in 1969. The Defense Advanced Research Projects Agency (DARPA) developed a computer network they called ARPANET. Why? To study methods of data communications that were reliable but didn't rely on any particular computer software type. They wanted data communications software that was so general that they could use any kind of computer and all sorts of different computer programs to access and use it. They were so successful that many of the data communication techniques they developed are still used today.

Even then, computer networks were addictive. The people and divisions of ARPANET began using it for daily data communications instead of just experimentation. In 1975, ARPANET reached puberty as it was expanded to a fully operational network. DARPA handed it over to its new mentor, the Defense Communications Agency (DCA), which is known today as the Defense Information Systems Agency (DISA). Of course, that didn't stop development work on ARPANET.

In 1983, that development work bore fruit and a standard file transfer protocol was adopted by Military Standards (MIL STD). The new file transfer protocol (FTP) standard made the network easy to use by people on different kinds of computers all at the same time, boosting the number of people adding to the network.

The term "Internet" was becoming popular around this time, but it was really two separate networks. ARPANET was now a new, smaller network, and the rest was split into MILNET, which was the unclassified part of the Defense Data Network (DDN). Both of these networks, combined, were the Internet.

⊛ {Note} A **protocol** is a language used by computers when they communicate with one another. Using a standard protocol means that no matter how similar or different the computers themselves are, each knows how to tell the other one what it wants. When a "file transfer protocol" is mentioned, that just means that the computers are able to transfer information to one another easily because they're using the same protocol.

In 1990, ARPANET finally reached adulthood by, well, ceasing to exist. All that's left of the original ARPANET is the DDN, which is still connected to the Internet. The Internet itself has grown and continues to grow by leaps and bounds, with more and more networks connecting to it.

See table 1.1 for a chart of the evolution of ARPANET into the Internet.

⊛ {Note} The word "Internet" has two meanings, depending on whether or not you capitalize the first letter.

The lowercase "internet" actually refers to any general collection of computer networks that form one large network because they use a common protocol.

"Internet" refers to one particular computer network, the adult version of ARPANET. All of the networks talk to each other through the Internet with a specific protocol, the Internet Protocol (IP).

Table 1.1   Evolution of ARPANET into the Internet

Year	Network	Event
1969	ARPANET	DARPA was developed
1975	ARPANET	ARPANET now supervised by DCA
1983	ARPANET & MILNET/DDN	File Transfer Protocol developed by MIL STD, Internet becomes common term
1990	Internet & DDN	Internet on its own. DDN all that's left of ARPANET. They're both still linked.

How big is it?

It's difficult to determine how large the Internet is, but many have tried. Way back in 1986, ARPANET connected less than 6,000 computers. By 1991, there were over 600,000. Now? The number changes on a daily basis and you can't ask someone from every computer connected to the Internet to stand up and be counted, so it's hard to get a correct count. As of July 1994, the number of computers on the Internet was 3,212,000 according to InterNIC, the people who assign Internet addresses.

What can I use it for?

There are a great number of things you can use the Internet for. Figure 1.1 illustrates the point.

Fig. 1.1
The Internet and its
uses...the possibilities!

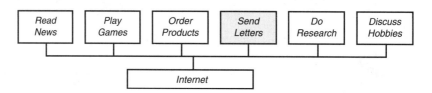

The topic of interest in this book is communication; that's what e-mail is all about.

Internet Growth

6,000 to 600,000 means that the size of the Internet from 1986, when it was ARPANET, to 1991 increased 100 times!

600,000 to 3,212,000 means that the size of the Internet from 1991 to the end of 1994 increased almost 5.5 times. As more computers get into households around the world, the number of the computers will increase on the Internet, but the number of people will increase faster, because multiple people can have accounts through the same computer on many systems.

Imagine, the conservative estimate of people on the Internet around the end of 1994 is 20,000,000 people! Keep in mind that with world population figures in the billions this is still just a small fraction, but at the current growth rate, who knows where it'll end?

E-mail

One of the most popular uses of the Internet is sending electronic mail, or e-mail. It's like going to the post office except that it's faster, you don't need a stamp, and you don't have to worry about trying to read anyone's handwriting—it's written with a keyboard instead of a pen. It's also something you don't have to go anywhere to do, so it's a great thing to have available to you when you're sick and stuck inside.

E-mail is also inexpensive and very, very fast—even if you're writing to someone on another continent.

What is e-mail?

A piece of **e-mail** is a letter that is written on and delivered by computers. A piece of e-mail is often referred to as a "note."

Who can use it?

Anyone who has a computer on a network that is Internet-connected can use Eudora. Also, if you have a modem, a phone line to attach the modem to, and an account that meets the proper requirements, you can use e-mail. People who don't have these things can still use e-mail if they know someone who will let them use their equipment. Figure 1.2 illustrates these requirements and combines them with the possibilities listed earlier.

Fig. 1.2
What do you need to use e-mail? This is it.

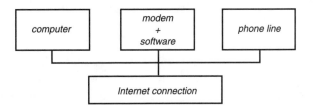

Electronic mail is not something that's only available on the Internet. There are a lot of offices with setups that allow employees to send e-mail to other employees and management just within the company. There are also pay services such as Prodigy, America Online (AOL), CompuServe, GEnie, and

Delphi. Most of these networks have been around for years, allowing people to send e-mail to others who subscribe to the same service, as well as offering other handy features. Lately, these services have been adding ways for people to get to the Internet as well, seeing the value of being connected to the popular world-wide network.

What can it be used for?

E-mail has many uses. The main limits on those uses involve the capabilities of today's technology and your imagination.

Using e-mail, you can trade information almost instantaneously with other people around the world. Physical location becomes less and less important. And, boy, does it save on the long distance bill! After all, no matter where you send your e-mail, your computer just calls your service provider—which is hopefully a local call. Forget a recipe? Send e-mail to your mom. Curious about a product from a particular company? They've got an e-mail address in their ad. Just got those pictures of your new baby developed? If you have access to a scanner, you can have the pictures copied into a file computers can read and send electronic copies to family and friends. On vacation and don't want to give the phone number to your boss? Promise you'll check your e-mail every few days in case she needs to contact you.

E-mail certainly won't replace the post office even if everyone in the world gets connected to the Internet. After all, you may be able to send cookie recipes to someone over e-mail, or pictures of cookies, but you can't send real cookies. No doubt there are few people who want to give up the occasional care package or the ability to have catalog purchases delivered to their doors.

The main differences between going to the post office and sending e-mail are that you don't have to go anywhere to do it (if your computer is in your home), and you don't have to handle anything except your computer and keyboard. No licking, folding, or messing up someone's address on an envelope and having to start all over again. Sure, you can make a mistake with e-mail too, but it's easy to fix and doesn't require you to trash the entire note and start all over again. Suddenly, it doesn't matter how bad your handwriting is either. Wouldn't you be more likely to keep up with people if you didn't actually have to go out and do it? Having access to e-mail removes the excuse that you're just too lazy to go to the post office or a mailbox.

Eudora

To fetch and read your e-mail you need software that knows how to do it. Eudora is an excellent choice for many people.

Where does Eudora come in?

Eudora is a program that calls your service provider—or connects to your network—and sends/fetches your mail for you. It also has many features that help you to manage your e-mail and keep track of people's e-mail addresses.

There are several different versions of Eudora. There are versions for the Macintosh and Microsoft Windows. There are also freeware and shareware versions for both platforms.

 *{Note}*

Freeware programs are free of charge. However, the author generally does have a copyright on the program. The programmer who wrote the freeware actually owns it; she's just letting you use it for free.

Commercial programs are programs you purchase. Each comes with a license agreement that says what you can and can't do as far as making backups and buying the program once but using it on more than one computer. In the case of the commercial version of Eudora, you cannot install it on more than one machine as you can with the freeware version. However, there are special rates available from Qualcomm for those who want to install Eudora on a group of computers.

Why do I need Eudora?

There are plenty of different kinds of computer accounts available from all sorts of service providers. Table 1.2 lists some popular types of accounts and what makes them different from other accounts.

Table 1.2   Popular Computer Accounts and Their Features

Account Type	Characteristics
menu	A menu account is on a service provider that you use menus to get around in. Examples are many BBSs (Bulletin Board Systems) and many large commercial providers (CompuServe, AOL). In a menu account, you read your mail online using their menu-driven software. Sometimes you can shut the menus off and just use a prompt, but you still have to use their specialized commands.
dialup/shell	With a shell account, you dial up by modem and you have access to an operating system, usually UNIX or VM (rarely DOS). You can execute commands (which means running programs, unlike the menu accounts), have storage space, and may have access to a compiler so you can write your own programs.
SLIP/PPP	With a SLIP or PPP account, you are connecting directly to a TCP/IP network (a network using Internet Protocol). There are no menus. You use different programs that know the proper Internet Protocol instructions to do different things. This is the most direct way to connect to the Internet with a modem, as it simulates being at a terminal wired straight to a network, making your computer a part of the Internet.
UUCP	With a UUCP account everything is done offline. Your computer calls up your service provider at regular intervals to pick up and deliver news and mail. It's like being part of the Internet without being permanently connected.

The type of account you would use Eudora with is a dialup (in special cases), a SLIP/PPP, or dedicated hookup to a network with Internet access (for example, at work). For these you need access to a POP server to receive the mail and an SMTP server to send the mail. You can also use Eudora with a UUCP account and don't need POP or SMTP because UUCP takes care of all of that, though you need to get a UUCP program for your computer that Eudora can get its instructions from.

Our account choice ...

At the moment, we use UUCP for our e-mail and news. It has a way of making you feel "connected" to the Net because you can read the news and mail through your system. In a way, it's a "budget Internet connection" and the ultimate offline reader because you can usually get a UUCP feed through a service provider for a reasonable rate. It's also fun because you can arrange for your own site name.

Why are we telling you this? Eudora lets you use UUCP!

❶ *(Tip)*

> If you're unsure of what a particular service provider offers, it's best to call or send them e-mail and tell them what you need. They'll let you know if they can provide it.

Once you have the right kind of account, and there are plenty out there, you can get set up and then sit back and relax, letting your e-mail come to you at home or in your office.

✱ *{Note}*

Most modem programs are **online readers.** You dial into your service provider, log in, read your mail, reply, and manage your mail as well (for example, deleting old mail). When you're finished with all of this, you log out and hang up. Your service provider sends your e-mail to the Internet when you're finished sending and replying, regardless of whether you've logged out or you are still logged in.

Programs such as Eudora are **offline readers** (when you're using Eudora in its dialup mode). With offline readers, your computer dials into your service provider, logs in, downloads your mail, logs out, and hangs up. You then read and answer your mail on your own computer. When you're finished, your computer dials back into your service provider and logs in. It then uploads your outgoing mail and gets any new mail you may have waiting. Your computer logs out and hangs up and your service provider sends your outgoing e-mail to the Internet.

What can it do for me?

Eudora can do a lot of things for you. It can

- send your e-mail

- receive your e-mail

- enable you to compose your e-mail

- let you forward e-mail to other people

- let you get files from the Internet

- let you send/receive compressed files—files that were shrunk because they were too large to send as they were

Eudora also helps you manage your mail. It helps you

- create mailboxes to keep mail in

- create folders to keep mailboxes in

- sort mail in mailboxes in several ways

Eudora has advanced features too. It

- lets you assign nicknames so you don't have to keep track of long e-mail addresses

- lets you just click to send mail to nicknames you frequently write to

- attaches files like word processing documents, sounds, or pictures to e-mail—**attaching** a file is like paper-clipping it to your e-mail

Not all mailer programs know how to deal with attachments, though most do. If you're going to send an attachment to someone and it's important he gets it right away, check with him first to see if his program knows what to do with attachments.

And these are just the things you can do with the freeware version of Eudora! In this book, we'll show you how to use the freeware version and also how to use the extra features of the commercial version.

2 The Power of E-mail

In this chapter:

- Using e-mail to talk to friends
- What is a mailing list?
- E-mail in business advertisements
- Keeping in touch with customers
- Government e-mail addresses
- Sending programs and files to others
- Requesting files from remote FTP servers

You may have never met in person, but you can get to know someone very well through your computer.

We've already discussed a bit of what you can do with e-mail. Now, we'll get more specific to give you a feel for just how much is waiting for you out there.

Friends

A great use for electronic mail is keeping in touch with relatives and friends. It's also a way to meet and keep in touch with new friends around the world. After all, since your computer calls your service provider to send your mail— no matter where that e-mail is going—every note costs the same amount. That's a lot different from the telephone or post office! Plus, if you call someone, she may not be home, and if you write her via postal mail—

affectionately called "snail mail" by those on the Internet—the letter could take weeks to get there. With e-mail, though, the note gets anywhere in the world almost immediately and the person you sent it to can check it whenever she gets the chance.

Mailing lists

There are mailing lists on the Internet just like there are mailing lists in the real world. While real life mailing lists are sometimes used to keep track of people to send advertisements to, they're also used to keep track of magazine subscribers, alumni to send newsletters to, and more. Mailing lists on the Internet are sometimes things people sign up for so they can talk about shared interests, and are also used for sending out newsletters or holding discussions about work projects. Anything you may want or need to discuss with a group of people, large or small, or just keep people informed about, can be the topic of an electronic mailing list.

Each list is dedicated to a specific topic, and there are all sorts of them. There are lists dedicated to professional subjects, hobbies, topics of regional or world interest, or even just personal mailing lists to allow a group of friends to discuss things.

E-mail and our lives

We, the authors of this book, use e-mail to keep in touch with friends and family in several countries. We also make new friends regularly, and meet with them when we're traveling through their areas. In fact, we met each other over the Internet.

We used to live about 3,000 miles apart. This gets difficult when you're dating. Using e-mail though, we were able to keep in touch every day, keeping up with what was happening in each other's lives and generally not growing apart.

E-mail is a great way to save a long distance relationship (though seeing <<<HUG>>> on your screen isn't always enough).

One of the groomsmen at our wedding was the gent who introduced us over the Internet. Neither of us had ever met him in person before we picked him up at the airport two days before the wedding. When he later told our story at the wedding reception, several of the people there decided that they were going to go out to buy computers and get themselves e-mail accounts!

How do mailing lists work over e-mail? It's simple, actually. You subscribe to the list through e-mail. Then, every time someone sends e-mail to the list, you and everyone else on the list gets a copy of that mail. The important thing about Internet mailing lists is that you can unsubscribe from them. After all, your interests are constantly changing. You may subscribe to a mailing list dedicated to your favorite hobby and then become bored with it a few months later. You just unsubscribe from the list, and maybe join another list that deals with your new favorite hobby.

Internet mailing lists are sort of like conference calls in the real world except for a few key differences. Mailing lists exist as long as someone is willing to maintain them. In fact, they'll exist longer than that because they can survive okay on their own for a while. Also, mailing lists constantly have people joining and leaving. The major difference between mailing lists and conference calls is that response to what people say in conference calls happens in **real-time** and response in e-mail and mailing lists are delayed. (Real-time, as used on the Internet, usually means methods of communication that allow people to see what's being said and reply almost immediately. Although e-mail is fast, it's not a real-time method of communication. Phone and in-person conversations are examples of real-time communication in everyday life.)

While it looks like no one is really in control of a mailing list, that's actually not the case. Every mailing list has a maintainer, the person who is actually in charge of making sure the list works and helping people with problems they may have. This maintainer is often the person who created the list, but sometimes the list has been around for years and passed to someone else to watch over.

Depending on what kind of software the list maintainer's using, she has different ways of making sure no one abuses the list. After all, because it's so easy to just send e-mail to everyone who has subscribed, some people like to waltz in and try to make life uncomfortable for everyone else. It's especially important to read the list rules that you receive when you subscribe. If subscribers violate these rules to the point where the list maintainer decides they're only on the list to cause trouble, the violators can be removed and even permanently banned from coming back.

There are also **moderated** lists. To post to a list like this, your mail to the list goes to the moderator first. If the moderator feels your mail is acceptable, he sends it out to the rest of the list. If your mail is considered inappropriate for the list, the moderator will usually notify you of why this is, and perhaps offer suggestions of what to remove from it before he'll put it through to everyone else. Some lists are more moderated than others, meaning that some moderators rule with an iron fist while others interfere so little that you almost forget they're there. Table 2.1 lists different kinds of lists and why they might be moderated.

Table 2.1   Reasons a List Might Be Moderated

List Type	Moderation Reason
Scientific	Conversation on a mailing list often strays off of the list's topic. The moderator's job on a scientific list is to allow mail to go to the list only if it's related to the scientific topic of the list.
Controversial	Controversial topics attract people who want to join to insult and hassle those who disagree with their views. A moderator's job on a list with a controversial topic is to keep the serious discussion in and insults out.
Recovery	There are mailing lists dedicated to helping people recover from all sorts of problems. The job of a moderator for this kind of list is to make sure that people feel comfortable and safe so they can discuss their situations. This can include banning known trouble-makers from the list, and keeping the insults and arguments down to a minimum or blocking them completely.
Instructional	There are mailing lists that exist only to teach or inform people about specific things. The moderators of these lists make sure that only mail asking questions or answering them, or containing information that covers the list topic, goes out to the list.

An **archive** for a group or mailing list is a group of files containing mail that was sent to that group or mailing list in the past.

Business

More and more businesses are waking up to the fact that a lot of their potential customers have access to electronic mail.

Using e-mail to advertise

Businesses have gotten smart and started putting e-mail addresses in their ads. After all, they're small, so they don't take up much space for the value the advertiser gets out of them. People who don't have access to e-mail just ignore that part of the ad. People who do have access to e-mail definitely notice the address in the ad. Plus, people are more likely to send a quick piece of e-mail asking about a product than they are to call an 800 number. Why call a handy phone number when you know you're just going to end up on hold for a half hour? With e-mail, you can just send it off and eventually get a reply. No muss, no fuss, no wasting your time listening to bad music.

 *{Note}*

For those of you out there thinking of actually using e-mail for your business, here's something important for you to consider. A request for information is not an invitation to constantly send product updates. If you want to make a list of people to send product updates to, then you add a simple statement at the end of the information they originally requested:

If you wish to be notified of further product updates, please respond to this note and tell us you want to be put on our mailing list.

The people who do want to be on your list will say so and you can add them. The ones who don't, won't. It's very easy to offend an experienced Internet user by sending junk e-mail. It's not worth the loss of business you'll suffer if your company automatically sends junk e-mail to everyone who asks you for information about your products. Word travels fast on the Internet and it's easy to get a bad reputation within a few days or even hours. Reputation is really all you have on the Internet, and it's hard to win back.

Keeping in touch with customers

Another growing business use for e-mail is having a customer service e-mail address. Customers appreciate not having to wait on hold, and it allows businesses to free up staff who were previously tied to the phone. After all, e-mail doesn't have to be dealt with the moment it arrives.

Also, more and more television programs are displaying Internet e-mail addresses in the same section they display the address or phone number to contact for questions or comments. Maybe soon you can use your e-mail to answer those TV news polls instead of using the phone.

Newspaper reporters, as well, are beginning to print their e-mail addresses. It's nice to be able to tell them what you think about their articles.

General correspondence

One of the best business uses for e-mail is simple correspondence. Rather than making long-distance phone calls or using an overnight courier service, you can send e-mail with those important questions or that urgent form.

Even routine correspondence is better through e-mail. You can send news-letters to project managers all over the world almost instantaneously and cheaply, or announce the yearly staff party without having to print up fliers.

Government officials

You'd be amazed at who's on the Internet.

President and Vice President

The President and Vice President of the United States actually have electronic mail addresses. While this mail is answered by a form letter, it's a way

TV e-mail addresses

In Canada, the CBC (Canadian Broadcasting Company) has e-mail addresses for almost all of its news programs. Even CBC radio stations are getting e-mail addresses. Several shows on the FOX network are advertising e-mail addresses as well.

of speaking your mind to the powers that be. The question is, does anyone read them?

⊛ {Note} | The e-mail address of the President is **president@whitehouse.gov**.

The e-mail address of the Vice President is **vice-president@whitehouse.gov**.

Also, if you send e-mail to **congress@hr.house.gov**, you'll get a listing of congressional e-mail addresses. You don't need anything in the subject or body of the note. The computer at the other end knows to send you the list if it gets any e-mail from you.

Other officials and offices

Politicians and government offices in various countries are also jumping on the electronic mail bandwagon. More and more fliers about things like getting government contracts or getting information about this or that service are giving e-mail addresses. Once again, better than being put on hold on the phone.

Transferring data

You can send more than just plain letters through electronic mail. In fact, you can use e-mail to send anything you can put into a format a computer can understand.

Sending programs and files to others

Have some shareware or freeware you want to send to someone? How about some pictures, or even digitized sounds? It's possible to send all of these and more.

FYI...

We kept in touch with our publishers through e-mail while working on this book. We even submitted parts of the book itself through e-mail!

Requesting remote files through an FTP mail-server

There are programs, pictures, sounds, and text files of all sorts available on the Internet, put there by people who figured other people would like them. While using FTP is very different from using e-mail, there are a few FTP servers on the Internet that do allow you to request files through e-mail. Some FTP servers even allow you to request files from other servers, fetch them for you, and send them back to you through e-mail. Fetching files over the Internet is covered in detail in chapter 13, "Sending and Receiving Files."

 **{Note}** An **FTP server** is a computer that has a collection of files that people from all over the Internet are allowed to download.

3 How Internet E-mail Works

Most users don't know what happens to their e-mail once they send it, except that it eventually ends up where it's supposed to go. But how?

Most of us haven't got a clue as to what happens to our letters and packages once we drop them into a mailbox or take them to a post office. We're more than content, most of the time, to just trust the postal system and treat it as a magical "black box" whose workings are dark and mysterious. We don't tend to think about how the mail system works—until something goes wrong, of course. Why is it that two letters mailed to the same person on the same day from the same mailbox can arrive days or weeks apart? Why does mail sometimes not even get there at all? (And where does it go?)

In the electronic world it's not much different. There are still a lot of people convinced that computers are perfect, and that machines don't lose mail (though it's often far more tempting to blame computers for our mistakes—they take criticism much better than most of us). In this chapter, we'll explain how electronic mail works, and maybe put to rest the theory that the rings of Saturn are composed of lost mail.

How to make sense of e-mail addresses

When you want to send a postal letter to someone, you need to address the envelope in a particular format that the postal service requires. For instance, you might send mail to your rich Uncle Mike (owner of the fictitious Nowhere Industries) by addressing your letters to:

Michael J. Smith

123 Maple Avenue

Beverly Hills, CA 90210

U.S.A.

This format gives the postal service all the information it needs to deliver your mail to us. Notice how the information is structured from most to least specific. Reading from bottom-to-top and right-to-left, the postal sorters can narrow things down one step at a time:

U.S.A.	All people in the United States
CA	All people in the state of California
Beverly Hills	All people in the city of Beverly Hills
Maple Avenue	All people living on Maple Avenue
123	All people living at 123 Maple Avenue
Michael J. Smith	The specific person Michael J. Smith

You'll notice we omitted the ZIP code (90210). While the ZIP code (*postal code* elsewhere in the world) can help the postal service break down a large metropolitan area into manageable zones, it can also serve as a kind of double-check code for the address. When the post office computers scan the other parts of the address, they compare this information to make sure it makes sense. This lets them quickly detect things like spelling mistakes and incomplete addresses, and can even help them guess at what the right address might be.

Electronic mail has a lot in common with postal mail. Every e-mail user has an address of his own, and it has its own structure. To take up our last example, Uncle Mike's electronic mail address at his office looks like:

mike@nowhere.com

Just like a postal address, this address can be taken apart backwards to provide more and more detail:

com	All commercial machines on the Internet
nowhere	All users of Nowhere Industries' computers
mike	The specific user Mike

The period (.) is used as a separator in e-mail addresses, just as you'd use a comma in a postal address. In more complicated addresses, you may see several periods.

> The simplest way to take apart an e-mail address is to look for the @ ("at") symbol. Everything to the left is used to figure out WHO to send the mail to, and everything on the right determines WHERE to send it.

The example we've worked with so far has been pretty simple, as e-mail addresses go. As another example, let's suppose Uncle Mike was located at the fictitious University of Nowhere where he's in charge of a biomedical facility. His address might then look something like:

mike@biomed.nowhere.edu

Taking that address apart, we get:

edu	All users at educational institutions
nowhere	All users at the University of Nowhere

| biomed | All users at the university's biomedical facility |
| mike | The specific user Mike |

You may have noticed that we've used lowercase for all of our e-mail addresses. We could as easily have sent mail to **MIKE@BioMed.Nowhere.EDU**, but the mail delivery programs aren't case-sensitive, so both addresses are equivalent.

You can also run into some strange ways to name users. "mike" is pretty self-explanatory, but "uncle-mike" is perfectly all right as well, as is "uncle.mike". In fact, some systems like to refer to their users by their first and last names, as in "michael.smith". A middle initial might be added, to make "michael.j.smith". As you can imagine, this can lead to some pretty long and hard-to-type addresses, so a lot of systems shorten this down to initials, such as "mjs". To guard against there being more than one "mjs" at your site, the system may add a number to those initials, for example, "mjs123". Kind of looks like a license plate, doesn't it?

The future of e-mail addresses

The way the Internet is growing, it won't be too long before everyone in the world has a unique e-mail address, just as we're all reachable by postal mail. There has already been some discussion about ways to handle this virtual population explosion, and it's beginning to look like we may soon see addresses like:

michael.j.smith@123.maple_avenue.beverly_hills.ca.us

If that looks ugly to you, you're not alone. That's not only a mouthful, it's far more likely to be mistyped or remembered incorrectly.

To its credit, say the advocates of this system, it's patterned after the user's postal address, which should be easy enough to remember, and most mail programs (including Eudora) allow you to store complicated addresses in a kind of "phonebook," which lets you create a simple alias (for example, "mike") to use when you want to send out mail to your uncle.

To others, it's an issue of privacy. The proposed address format shows everyone your postal address, which you might not care to do. This also opens the way for unscrupulous advertisers to put Internet users onto mailing lists (postal and e-mail) without the users' knowledge or consent.

It's clear, however, that something has to be done to deal with the fact that the Internet population is doubling each year. It should be interesting to see how this problem gets solved; stay tuned.

What's an Internet domain?

Just as the world is divided into continents and countries, the Internet can be broken down into smaller divisions called **domains**. Every country in the world has its own domain, which is simply a two-letter code, as illustrated in the following table.

ISO Country Codes

aq	Antarctica	ar	Argentina	at	Austria
au	Australia	az	Azerbaijan	be	Belgium
bg	Bulgaria	br	Brazil	ca	Canada
ch	Switzerland	cl	Chile	cm	Cameroon
cn	China	co	Colombia	cr	Costa Rica
cs	Czechoslovakia	cy	Cyprus	cz	Czech Republic
de	Germany	dk	Denmark	dz	Algeria
ec	Ecuador	ee	Estonia	eg	Egypt
es	Spain	fi	Finland	fj	Fiji
fr	France	gr	Greece	gu	Guam
hk	Hong Kong	hr	Croatia	hu	Hungary
id	Indonesia	ie	Ireland	il	Israel
in	India	ir	Iran	is	Iceland
it	Italy	jp	Japan	kr	South Korea
kw	Kuwait	lb	Lebanon	li	Liechtenstein
lt	Lithuania	lu	Luxembourg	lv	Latvia
md	Moldavia	mo	Macau	mx	Mexico
my	Malaysia	ni	Nicaragua	nl	Netherlands
no	Norway	nz	New Zealand	pa	Panama
pe	Peru	ph	Philippines	pl	Poland
pr	Puerto Rico	pt	Portugal	re	Reunion
ro	Romania	ru	Russia	sa	Saudi Arabia
se	Sweden	sg	Singapore	si	Slovenia
sk	Slovakia	su	Soviet Union	th	Thailand
tn	Tunisia	tr	Turkey	tw	Taiwan
ua	Ukraine	uk	United Kingdom	us	United States
uy	Uruguay	ve	Venezuela	yu	Yugoslavia
za	South Africa				

In addition, the "continents" of the Internet can be thought of as the "Big Six" domains:

com	commercial/business institutions
edu	educational institutions
gov	government institutions
mil	U.S. military institutions
net	network (Internet) service providers
org	non-profit organizations

The Big Six domains are older, used mainly in the United States (particularly mil and gov), but this is for historic reasons; a Big Six domain doesn't automatically imply a U.S. address anymore. A domain is just a convenient way to group addresses by associating the ones that have something in common. This can be based on geography (for example, by country), or by purpose (such as the Big Six). Sites are usually only registered in one domain, even if two or more might apply. As an example, a university in the United States might fall under both the "edu" and "us" domains, but "edu" is more likely to be chosen because it's more descriptive. On the other hand, a university in Australia might prefer to register itself under the "au" domain to distinguish itself from its American counterparts, because many people still think of the Big Six as U.S. domains.

The domain of an e-mail address always appears at the far right, separated from the rest of the address by a period. Here are a few examples of different kinds of addresses and their domains:

mike@nowhere.com	Business institution
msmith@somewhere.nowhere.gov	Government institution
michael_smith@nowhere.edu	Educational institution
mjs@nowhere.fi	Finland
mike@nowhere.fl.us	Florida, U.S.A.
michael@nowhere.edu.au	School in Australia
mjs@nowhere.ac.at	School in Austria

Note from the example that in countries other than the U.S., "edu" and "ac" (academic) are often treated as subdomains of the country domain. This uses the best of both classification schemes—the address is defined by geography and purpose. While most U.S. addresses still belong to one of the Big Six domains, there's a movement afoot to add the "us" domain to these addresses as well.

Anatomy of a mail header

Your letter to Uncle Mike has to include more than just his address on the envelope; you have to add your return address as well (along with sufficient postage, of course). By the time the letter reaches him, it's also postmarked with a date and certain other mystical machine symbols it acquired along the way.

E-mail has many of the same bits of information packaged with it, so that when Uncle Mike checks his e-mail he can find out who sent it, when it was sent, when it was received, where it was sent from, and even some hints about the route the mail took to get to him. This veritable storehouse of information is found at the very beginning of every piece of e-mail, so it's aptly called a **mail header** (see fig. 3.1).

Fig. 3.1
A sample mail header.

```
Return-Path: <mike@nowhere.com>

Received: from mailhost.nowhere.com by davinci.renaissoft.com
(Sendmail 8.6.9/8.6.9) id OAA29770; Sun, 6 Nov 1994 13:18:55 -0800

Received: from venus.nowhere.com by mailhost.nowhere.com
(Smail3.1.28.1 #5) id m0r4EwD-0003KbC; Sun, 6 Nov 94 13:15 PST

Date: Sun, 06 Nov 1994 13:15:51 -0800 (PST)

From: mike@nowhere.com (Michael J. Smith)

Subject: Hi there, Nephew!

To: rjl@renaissoft.com (Robert J. LeBlanc)

Message-id: <01HJ24Y693389N6K5R@nowhere.com>

MIME-version: 1.0

Content-type: TEXT/PLAIN; CHARSET=US-ASCII

Content-transfer-encoding: 7BIT
```

Let's dissect the mail header in figure 3.1 one item at a time.

```
Return-Path: <mike@nowhere.com>
```

The Return-Path: header tells the mail program what path to use to send your reply to Uncle Mike. Usually this is just the sender's e-mail address, but not always; if the letter had to follow a convoluted path to get to you, it may look ugly and confusing. As an example, let's suppose the letter from Uncle Mike had come to us with the following header:

```
Return-Path: <nowhere.com!mike@libra.somewhere.edu>
```

In this example, **nowhere.com!mike** is just another way of writing **mike@nowhere.com**; because an e-mail address should only have one @ symbol in it, this avoids a potentially confusing situation. What this return path means is that our reply should go to a machine called **libra.somewhere.edu**, but instead of delivering it to an ordinary user this machine will re-mail the message to **mike@nowhere.com**.

```
Received: from mailhost.nowhere.com
by davinci.renaissoft.com (Sendmail 8.6.9/8.6.9) id OAA29770;
Sun, 6 Nov 1994 13:18:55 -0800

Received: from venus.nowhere.com by mailhost.nowhere.com
(Smail3.1.28.1) id m0r4EwD-0003KbC; Sun, 6 Nov 94 13:15 PST
```

The Received: lines in the mail header show you the path the mail took on its way to reaching you. The names you see here are the machines that passed the mail along, and the times give you a rough idea of where your mail was at a given moment in time. You can use this information to determine how mail is getting to you, and where it's spending most of its time.

The easy way to read these headers is backwards—or rather from the bottom up. Looking at the last of these lines, it seems that Uncle Mike sent his mail from a machine called **venus.nowhere.com**, which then passed it along to a machine called **mailhost.nowhere.com**, which is presumably the machine that handles mail at his site. This was at 1:15 p.m. PST. Moving up one line, we see that the letter was then passed along to our machine, **davinci.renaissoft.com**, at about 1:19 p.m. PST, for a total travel time of about four minutes.

There's more information packed into these headers than most people care about, including the mail transport programs that were used (Smail and Sendmail in our example), their version numbers, and a message ID string that's designed to be read by mail programs, not humans.

✱ *{Note}*___ It's always a good idea to take time stamps with a grain of salt when they're reported by machines you don't know about. Computers are notorious for having inaccurate clocks at best, and if their administrators fail to correct for things like Daylight Savings Time, the results you get aren't going to be worth much. You can sometimes even receive a piece of mail several minutes before it was sent—if you believe the time stamps, that is.

```
Date: Sun, 06 Nov 1994 13:15:51 -0800 (PST)
```

This shows you the time and date the letter was sent, according to the computer it was sent from. The time is local to the sender, but a time zone adjustment shows you how many hours to add or subtract to convert that to Greenwich Mean Time (GMT). Some particularly smart mail programs will do this conversion for you.

In our example, -0800 implies that the machine Uncle Mike sent his note from was set to a time eight hours earlier than GMT, which is also commonly known as Pacific Standard Time (PST).

```
From: mike@nowhere.com (Michael J. Smith)
```

The From: header shows you the e-mail address of the person who sent the mail, and usually the sender's full name. On some systems the user can specify the text that will appear as his "full name", so you'll occasionally see nicknames and other aliases here. You should also be a bit suspicious of people with "full names" like "Elvis A. Presley".

As we mentioned when we discussed the Return-Path: header, it's often just a copy of the From: header, but not always. Sometimes you want people to reply to a different address than the one you sent the message from, but you still want them to know who wrote the message. As an example, if you post to a mailing list, you want people to know you wrote the message, but you want their replies to go out to the list, not just to you.

```
Subject: Hi there, Nephew!
```

This is just a short note about the subject of your letter, for the receiver to see at a glance. If you don't include any subject information, most mail programs will fill this in with (none) or something similar. You don't have to specify a subject, but it's usually a good idea, because a lot of people have to wade through a lot of mail messages and can't be bothered to read all of them to see what they're about.

```
To: rjl@renaissoft.com (Robert J. LeBlanc)
```

This is the e-mail address of the person the mail is for, often with a full name added to make it more legible.

```
Message-id: <01HJ24Y693389N6K5R@nowhere.com>
```

The Message-id: header is created by the sender's mail program as a kind of postmark for the message. If there's ever a dispute about where a message came from, or whether two messages are identical, you can have a look at this header.

```
MIME-version: 1.0
```

This header tells us that Uncle Mike's computer supports MIME encoding, which means that we can send him mail in MIME format, including attachments such as graphics, sounds, and binary files (see chapter 13 for more about MIME). By looking through the headers of mail from the people you write to, you can see whether they can receive MIME-encoded mail from you.

```
Content-type: TEXT/PLAIN; CHARSET=US-ASCII
```

Uncle Mike's note contains plain text that uses the US-ASCII character set. This is the most widely readable kind of e-mail, because it doesn't contain any international characters or graphics, and doesn't have any accompanying attachments. If the character set were anything else, such as the popular international set ISO-8859-1 (ISO Latin-1), you'd need a mail program that understands MIME to be able to read it. A smart mail program such as Eudora can use this header to figure out how to display the message on your computer.

```
Content-transfer-encoding: 7BIT
```

Content-transfer-encoding tells us that Uncle Mike's mail is in 7-bit format, which is standard for the US-ASCII character set. If this were a MIME message, you'd see "8BIT" here instead. This header and the Content-type header are really just two different ways to say the same thing. Because some mail programs look for one header while others look for the other one, it's common practice to include the information both ways to keep everybody happy.

Other headers

You may find that your mail contains some headers we haven't mentioned here. Beyond the "standard" mail headers, there are a number of system-dependent headers that show up from time to time. In particular, you'll come across headers that begin with X- (for example, X-Sender, X-Reply-to, X-Password, and so on). These are custom headers that are ignored by your mailer, but are meaningful to some remote system for a special purpose.

How does my e-mail get there?

The e-mail process starts with your mail program (in this case, Eudora), which lets you compose the message and give it an address. After sending off the mail, most users haven't got the foggiest idea what happens to their messages, except that it eventually arrives where it's supposed to. It's a tribute to the integrity of the e-mail system that we can put that much trust in it. But where does it go? It's not a question anyone should be ashamed for asking because it's far from intuitive.

Once your mail to Uncle Mike leaves your mail program, it falls into the hands of a **mail transport program** that your service provider runs. Virtually every computer on the Internet runs a mail transport program in one form or another to do two things:

- deliver the mail, if it's for a user on this machine

- pass along the mail, if it's for a user on another machine

It would be awfully nice if we could simply have mail go directly to Uncle Mike, but it's just not practical; it would be like asking for a telephone cable running directly between you and your Uncle Mike. Like the phone system, the Internet works on a system of **hub-based routing,** which is just a fancy way to describe a switchboard, really. Your service provider may have direct connections to a few other service providers nearby (using a protocol called

SMTP—the Simple Mail Transfer Protocol), which in turn have connections to still other providers, and so on; your mail reaches each site, where the mail transport programs decide whether they should deliver the mail (if it's for someone at that site), or pass it along to another nearby site.

Your letter can hop across quite a number of different sites on its way to Uncle Mike, but there's a limit on this to keep mail from bouncing around the Internet indefinitely. Most mail transport programs will stop relaying a mail message after a relatively small "hop count", such as 10 or 20.

Once your letter reaches Uncle Mike's computer, his mail program allows him to read it and reply to it; mission accomplished.

Why does e-mail seem slow today?

As you travel the much-touted Information Superhighway, you're bound to discover that some sections of the road are faster than others. You'll find that you can send e-mail halfway around the world and get a reply in a few minutes, and then send e-mail across town that won't arrive for hours. These delays are either **transient** or **constant**.

Transient delays

During "rush hour" on the Superhighway, when everyone seems to want to use the Internet to read news, check and send mail, transfer files, and chat, things tend to slow down. Even the fastest computers can get bogged down when too many people try to use them at once, or when they're running programs that hog most of their computing power. This can make a computer have to wait minutes or even hours before processing the mail it receives or wants to send out. If a machine goes down for maintenance for a few hours, it delays mail processing for that whole length of time. Fortunately, these problems all go away eventually, so they're usually only a minor annoyance.

Constant delays

E-mail has to pass through a number of different machines between you and your Uncle Mike, and this puts your mail in the hands of virtual strangers.

If all of these intermediate machines quickly pass things along, your mail will get to your uncle in the blink of an eye. Unfortunately, not all Internet sites consider mail a very high priority. In particular, a lot of machines on the Internet are connected by UUCP, which is a non-permanent kind of link; they dial up their service providers at regular intervals (say, once an hour) to pick up and deliver news and mail without having to be connected all the time. As you can imagine, if your mail has to pass through a UUCP site along its route, it can get delayed for hours, depending on how often the site connects to its provider.

Where did my e-mail disappear to?

As reliable as e-mail is, you'll likely find that once in a fairly blue moon your mail will just vanish on its way to the receiver. To make matters worse, you generally don't get any messages from your mail program to tell you that something went wrong, so you're left apologizing weeks later for not sending that birthday note to your sister, even though you know you sent it on time.

Mail can vanish for a number of reasons:

- non-existent address

- wrong address

- your letter is too long

- technical problems

Non-existent address

Most of the time, if you send out mail to an address that doesn't exist, or to a user that doesn't exist, you'll get a brief note back telling you what went wrong (see fig. 3.2). If your mail ends up exceeding the "maximum hop count" as it bounces from site to site trying to find the address, however, it may die a silent death.

Fig. 3.2
A non-existent address
message.

```
From mike@nowhere.com Sat Oct  8 23:04:44 1994
Return-Path: <mike@nowhere.com>
Received: from deep.UUCP by davinci.renaissoft.com with UUCP
    (Smail3.1.28.1 #6) id mOqtrNC-0003KpC; Sat, 8 Oct 94 23:04 PDT
Received: from mailhost.nowhere.com by deep.rsoft.bc.ca with smtp
    (Smail3.1.28.1 #5) id mOqtrEu-0002A9C; Sat, 8 Oct 94 22:56 PDT
Received: from venus (venus.nowhere.com) by mailhost.nowhere.com
(4.1/SMI-4.1)
    id AA19060; Sat, 8 Oct 94 22:53:12 PDT
To: rjl@davinci.renaissoft.com
Subject: Forwarded Mail from: Mailer-Daemon (Mail Delivery Subsystem)
From: mike@nowhere.com (Michael J. Smith)
Message-Id: <OXZwTc4w165v@venus.nowhere.com>
Date: Sat, 08 Oct 94 22:53:08 PDT
In-Reply-To: <9410090619.AB19010@mailhost.nowhere.com>
Status: RO

    ----- Transcript of session follows -----
<rjk@davinci.renaissoft.com>... User unknown

    ----- Unsent message follows -----
Return-Path: <mike@nowhere.com>
Received: from venus (venus.nowhere.com) by mailhost.nowhere.com
(4.1/SMI-4.1)
    id AA19007; Sat, 8 Oct 94 22:46:18 PDT
To: rjk@davinci.renaissoft.com
Subject: hi!
From: mike@nowhere.com (Michael J. Smith)
Message-Id: <wkZwTc2w165v@venus.nowhere.com>
Date: Sat, 08 Oct 94 22:45:46 PDT

Hi Rob...just wanted to say hi and ask how the proposal was coming.
```

Wrong address

This is perhaps the most annoying cause of vanishing mail, especially when you're dealing with people whose user names involve numbers. All it takes is a little sloppiness at the keyboard and suddenly **a1027737@nowhere.com** turns into **a1072737@nowhere.com**. Your mail goes to some user named "a1072737", who may actually exist! If you're lucky and she's a kind-hearted soul, she may reply to you and let you know what happened, but a lot of people aren't that considerate and just ignore the misdirected note. The intended recipient doesn't get your message, and you have no idea what went wrong.

If, on the other hand, "a1072737" doesn't exist at **nowhere.com**, you'll get an automated reply from the postmaster there, explaining that user a1072737 is unknown.

Your letter is too long

You've been sending mail back and forth to Uncle Mike for years without a problem, but this time when you decide to pour your heart out in a long letter, he never gets it! Most e-mail programs don't set any limits on the length of a letter, so why all of a sudden did this 200-line letter to Uncle Mike disappear? You're even more mystified by the fact that you've always been able to send 400-line notes to your Aunt Zelda. What's going on here?

The problem lies with the mail transport programs that your mail has to pass through on its way to Uncle Mike. Each mail transport program can be set to ignore mail that it determines is too big, as set by its administrators. Most sites on the Internet define "too big" to be a reasonably large number, such as 100,000 bytes or more, but some sites that are more concerned with conserving disk space limit this to much smaller figures, sometimes as low as 10,000 bytes. If your lengthy letter has to pass through one of these sites along its route, it will simply vanish without a trace.

Because this maximum size definition varies from site to site, it's quite possible that you can send enormous letters to your Aunt Zelda, and yet be limited to a mere tenth of that length in your letters to Uncle Mike. It all depends on the path your mail takes on its way to the receiver. If you want to play it safe, keep your messages to about 100 lines or less in length, which most sites should gladly relay.

Technical problems

With all the computers, disk drives, modems, and routers working around the clock to provide the service we call the Internet, it's amazing that we don't have more problems than we do. Still, foul-ups are inevitable, whether it's a router that gets its addressing tables messed up, a hard disk that decides to crash—taking all of its precious e-mail data with it, a malicious hacker messing with the system, or just a novice system administrator who accidentally deletes all the mail files passing through his site. There's not much you can do about this kind of problem, unfortunately, but it's nerve-calming to know that sometimes it just isn't your fault.

Is my e-mail safe from prying eyes?

With all the hopping around that mail goes through across the Internet, it only makes sense to wonder whether people might be snooping into your private mail. In a sense, e-mail is no more secure than postal mail is; anyone handling your postal mail can steam open the envelope, read your letter, and then reseal it, if they want to badly enough. In the e-mail world, that process involves uncompressing the mail data, reading it, then compressing it again.

The text of your message itself is not encoded or hidden in any way, other than the standard compression it undergoes to make it easier to transmit. Your trade secrets and credit card numbers are not terribly secure, and it really isn't advisable to send anything that sensitive by regular e-mail; there are known to be a number of criminally minded techies out there scanning e-mail for patterns that look like credit card numbers, so be careful. If a company advertises on the Internet and asks you to send them your credit card information for payment, write to them and express your concerns, and offer to give them this information over the phone instead.

Of course, the same concerns apply to the use of cordless and cellular phones—it's equally likely that someone with a radio scanner can eavesdrop on your phone calls if they're placed this way. To be honest, there's no reason to be paranoid about using e-mail for most purposes; the sheer volume of traffic on the Internet makes it highly unlikely that *your* message will get singled out for anyone's snooping. You should just be aware that e-mail has this vulnerability.

There are ways to use e-mail to send sensitive information, if you're concerned about security. Public-key encryption programs such as PGP (Pretty Good Privacy) are widely available from BBSs and FTP sites around the world (PGP is free) and do an extremely good job of making your mail readable only by the intended receiver. Several companies that do business on the Internet have begun using PGP as a means of accepting credit card and validation information by e-mail.

How do I join the e-mail system?

To get yourself hooked up to the Internet is to be a member of the e-mail community. You'll need a computer of just about any kind—processing speed and fancy graphics won't make any real difference for e-mail purposes. On the other hand, if you're a Windows 3.1 user you'll want a 386 with at least 2 megabytes of memory to be comfortable, and Macintosh System 7 users will probably want about 4 megabytes of RAM.

If you're connecting from a home or business computer, you'll probably also need a modem; again, the speed isn't a big factor for mail, unless you're sending a lot of large messages or files, in which case it can become tedious otherwise.

You'll also need a mail program—this is where Eudora comes in.

Lastly, you'll need to make arrangements with a local Internet service provider. If you're already connected to the Internet, you can skip this step, but most likely if you're using a modem, you'll need to arrange some kind of Internet account. This can range from a simple dial-up account to a SLIP/PPP account to a UUCP account, or some form of dedicated connection, as your budget dictates. To use Eudora, you'll have to ensure that your service provider offers POP3 service as well.

4

E-mail Writing Style

The Internet is a world-wide network. So you have the chance to talk to people from all sorts of cultures. This fact also means there are plenty of chances to be misunderstood or to misunderstand others.

In this chapter:

- What are those weird symbols?
- You mean that's really a word?
- What about body language?
- These people use some strange words
- Why spelling is important
- Internet etiquette or "netiquette"
- Unwanted e-mail
- What are those quotes and drawings at the end of people's e-mail?

Writing style is as important on the Internet as speaking style, tone of voice, and body language combined are when communicating in person. When the only way people have to get to know you is through what you type on a keyboard, they have no way of knowing whether you're being serious, sarcastic, funny, or insulting. They can't see a smirk, a smile, or clenched fists. All they see are words. That's why it's very important to try to give people a feel for what you really mean when you type something.

What follow are tips and suggestions on how to avoid having people misread what you write. Following these suggestions will help you to avoid accidentally upsetting people with what was meant to be funny, and will help you to figure out whether people writing to you are being serious or not. These tips and suggestions will also help you to avoid a lot of common **newbie** (someone who's new, or acts like they're new, to the Internet) mistakes involving spelling and grammar, and the various strange terms and symbols used in Internet circles.

Getting your point across

The Internet has developed a language all its own. It consists of strange symbols, acronyms, and terms aimed at showing emotion to avoid misunderstandings, removing the need to type commonly used phrases over and over again, defining types of people, and referring to things that happen a lot.

How do I show emotion, and what are those strange symbols?

Symbols called **emoticons** are mostly used to show emotions and facial expressions. They are often referred to as smileys even though they don't always show happiness—perhaps the people on the Internet are optimists. Emoticons are read left to right, but some people who like to be different put them backwards on occasion. The most basic emoticon looks a little like a happy face turned on its side, as in :). Think of the colon as a pair of eyes and the parenthesis as a smiling mouth. (You may need to tilt your head sideways to the left to understand them at first.) Table 4.1 describes the various parts of emoticons, and table 4.2 lists examples of how emoticons are used in text.

Table 4.1   The Anatomy of an Emoticon

Face Part	Symbol	Represents
Eyebrows: (optional)	>	Clever
Eyes:	:	Normal
	;	Winking
	.	Only One
	,	Only One, Winking
	8	With Glasses
Nose: (optional)	-	Straight
	^	Crooked
Mustache: (optional)	{	Mustache
Mouth:	)	Smile
	]	Smile
	>	Smile
	(	Frown
	[	Frown
	<	Frown
	/	Neutral Expression, Dismay/Discomfort
Tongue: (optional)	p	Silly or Taunting, Sticking out your tongue
Beard: (optional)	}	Beard
	>	Goatee

Table 4.2   Emoticon Examples and Translations

Phrase with Emoticons	What the Emoticons Show
I just won the lottery. : -) : -) : -)	This person is probably joking!
You're too serious. :)	This phrase would probably upset someone if the emoticon didn't point out that the comment wasn't a criticism.
I'm sorry to hear that. : (	The frown here adds a note of sincerity.
I knew that! : - p	This person's sticking out her tongue at people.
Sounds like a lot of fun. : - /	This person is being sarcastic.
Like my new glasses? 8 -)	It's sort of hard to show off your new glasses on the Internet, so this is the next best thing. :)
It was his kind of party, if you know what I mean. ;)	The winking emoticon here adds a "nudge nudge, wink wink."
I grew a mustache. It itches! : -{	When a mustache is added, the smile or frown isn't usually shown. It looks, well...silly. : -{)

There are a number of other symbols you may run into as you talk to other people. Table 4.3 illustrates some of these.

Table 4.3   Some Other Symbols

Symbol	What it Means
@>–>–––	A rose. Yes, there's romance even on the Internet.
––––>	An arrow pointing to something.
==	Equal. You may find people using this symbol instead of = to show that two things are equivalent; it's an old programming convention that's made its way into Internet jargon.
!=	Not Equal. This means that the two items being compared are not equal to one another. Example: "Blue != Green" It's another little programming convention to get used to.
important	Underscores (_) are used to mark a word as important.
important	Asterisks (*) are also used to highlight a word.
IMPORTANT	Capital letters are yet another way of highlighting a word. Doing an entire letter in all capital letters is like shouting, so this is a technique to use sparingly.

You mean that's really a word?

When your main way of "talking" is typing things, you get tired of typing the same things over and over and over again. Over the years, various common phrases have been reduced to acronyms. Table 4.4 lists acronyms you are likely to see.

Table 4.4   Common Acronyms and Translations

Acronym	Meaning
AFAIK	As Far As I Know
BTW	By The Way
FAQ	Frequently Asked Question
IMHO	In My Humble Opinion
IMNSHO	In My Not-So-Humble Opinion
IMO	In My Opinion
ISO	In Search Of
OTOH	On The Other Hand
pbbfth	a raspberry
RL	Real Life
ROFL (ROTFL)	Rolling On The Floor Laughing
RTFM	Read The "Full" Manual
FWIW	For What It's Worth

The Internet is a great place for coining new terms. Table 4.5 lists some common examples.

Table 4.5 Commonly Used Terms

Term	Definition
flame	E-mail containing mostly personal attacks and insults.
flame war	Ongoing exchange of flames.
newbie	Person new to the Internet.
smiley	A group of characters representing a smile, such as :).
spam	Nuisance traffic on the Internet because there are many, many copies sent (junk e-mail, for example).
bandwidth	Amount of messages.

Spelling

What and how you write on the Internet reflects who you are. Bad spelling can make you look sloppy and uneducated, whether you really are or not. Therefore, it's important to try to avoid at least the most common mistakes. Poor spelling can make someone with a Ph.D. look like a high school student, and you can't show your diplomas to people over the Internet.

If you have the Macintosh commercial version of Eudora, you can purchase the Spellswell spell-checker to doublecheck your work. There are easy ways around that, too. You can cut and paste the body of your e-mail over to your favorite word processor, spell-check it, and then cut and paste it back.

Netiquette

The Internet is a world-wide network. Because of this, you have the chance to talk to people from all sorts of cultures. This fact also means there are plenty of chances to be misunderstood or to misunderstand others.

Quoting people

It's important to remember when responding to people over the Internet that it may be days between when they wrote to you and when they read your reply. Therefore, it's important that you quote at least the parts of the message you're responding to rather than just writing back saying, "Yes, that's a great idea," because you might confuse them and get another piece of e-mail back asking what their great idea was.

Here are several important rules to consider when it comes to quoting text:

- Clearly label who said what.
- Delete the parts of the letter you're not commenting on.
- Don't delete too much; keep the context of the discussion.
- Be careful of quoting people who are quoting people who are quoting people.

It's important to clearly label who said what mainly because people get annoyed when they're quoted as saying something they didn't say. Also, if you're holding a discussion with one person, then copy that to someone else, that third person needs to know who said what to understand what's going on.

It's also important to delete what you're not referring to because, if you don't, letters will get longer and longer. These longer and longer letters will contain less and less of what you're actually talking about and more and more of what you talked about before that's now old news. You and the person you're talking with are now forced to wade through this mess of text to get to your discussion. This gets annoying very quickly and easily kills a conversation.

On the other hand, if you delete too much of what you're quoting, you lose the context of the conversation. The person you're talking to loses track of what you were talking about and you spend the next part of your conversation reminding him of why it was important that you said X, Y, and Z in your previous note. Once again, this gets very annoying.

Finally, it's important to be careful of **nested quoting**. You get nested quoting as the conversation continues when neither you nor the person you're talking with delete particular old parts of the conversation. It starts as, "You said: X." Then it goes to, "I said you said X." It continues to, "You said I said you said X." I don't think I need to go any further to show you how annoying and difficult this gets to read after a while.

✱ {Note} _____ Notice all of the times we've used the word "annoying" in this section. E-mail is a quick, efficient way of talking to people, but it's awful if people don't take a little time to clean up their replies and only leave in the relevant parts.

To better illustrate these points, follow figures 4.1 through 4.5 as we discuss some things about this book.

In this short exchange (figures 4.1 and 4.2), who wrote what is not labeled and it's not necessary to quote the entire note in the reply.

Fig. 4.1
Original note.

Fig. 4.2
Bad response to note.

 Notice the > before some of the lines in the note? That's what Eudora uses to show which part of the message is being quoted.

A better way to respond to this note is shown in figure 4.3.

Fig. 4.3
Better response to
note.

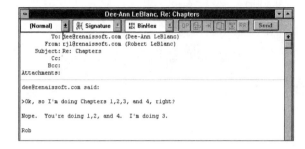

Now, the conversation continues.

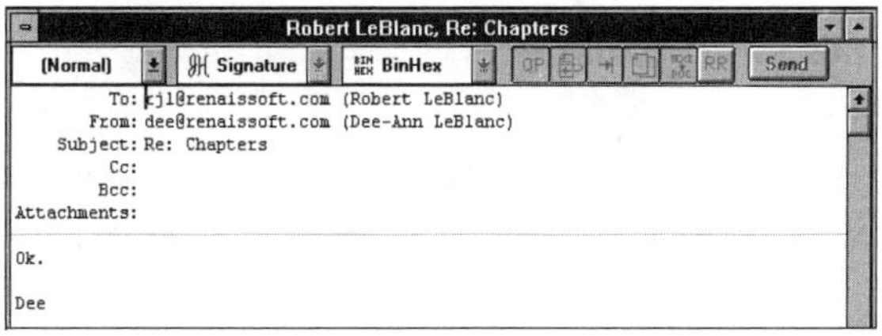

Fig. 4.4
Poorly formatted
response to response.

The reason this response doesn't work very well is that the whole context is lost. If Rob looks back on that note later to remind himself about what they'd agreed on, he'll be lost. A better reply from Dee can be found in figure 4.5.

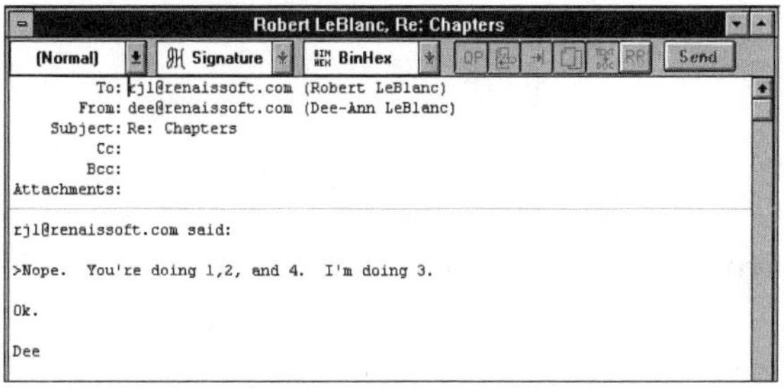

Fig. 4.5
A better continuation.

This reply is better than the other because it's in context. No confusion is left over who said what, and what was agreed upon. Also, only the part of the conversation that's necessary to keep the context is there.

Figure 4.6 shows you how ugly things get if nothing is deleted and no one puts in lines saying who said what.

Fig. 4.6
Example of very poor response style.

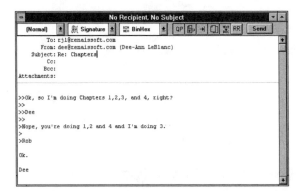

Just imagine if the notes had been longer, or the conversation had gone on for a few more passes back and forth. It gets almost impossible to read!

Now, be nice

On the Internet, many people fall into the trap of feeling there's no need to be polite. After all, you'll probably never meet the people you're talking to, right? Maybe so, but it's certainly possible. Also remember, you're dealing with people from different cultures, some of whom will seem excessively polite to you, and others will seem coarse or rude.

It's easy to be misinterpreted, so your choice of words is that much more important. It's worth the extra few seconds to pause and consider how the person you're writing to may interpret what you're saying. Sarcasm is especially hard to get across in a written note. People often assume you're serious unless emoticons or such popular statements as, "For the humor impaired, this is sarcasm" are included.

Take a deep breath

There is no way to get a piece of mail back after you've sent it. Once it's out there in the Internet, it's gone and the damage is done.

If you're offended or angry about something, don't just type up a quick angry response and send it out. Stop. Breathe. Read it twice, even three times. Take a walk. The beauty of e-mail is that you don't have to respond to it immediately. Make absolutely certain that you're not reading too much into things. If, after doing all of these things, you're still offended, send a calm, rational note in response. Point out what you think the person is saying, and explain why it upsets you. The person may have meant it, but it may also turn out that he hadn't considered the implications of what he was saying. Your calm, rational response will allow the conversation to continue with either the two of you discussing your differences, or your correspondent explaining what he really meant. If the reply you receive is hostile, then you can ignore it or explain that you refuse to engage in a yelling match. After all, why should you let your blood pressure go up just because someone else is a hothead?

Exchanges involving nothing but yelling (done by typing in ALL CAPITAL LETTERS) and/or insults are called flames. There is a way to tell the difference between an argument and a flame. Attack the point, it's an argument. Attack the person, it's a flame. Long lasting flame exchanges are called flame wars. Avoid these. They're not worth it.

 Typing in ALL CAPITAL LETTERS is also considered very, very rude on the Internet. Partially because it's hard on the eyes, and partially because it makes people feel like you're yelling at them.

Habitual flamers

There are people on the Internet who love baiting people into flame wars. Those who are experienced on the Internet spot them quickly and often already know the person by reputation. Newbies, however, are often caught up in frustrating battles with these people. If someone seems to be trying to get you angry, he probably is. If you don't want to get involved, ignore him. If you want to play with him, respond calmly and rationally. It annoys flamers.

Unwanted e-mail

You may check your e-mail one day and find that you have something from some business that wants to sell you some product. That's called **unsolicited e-mail** unless you wrote to that business and asked them to send you information about their products and updates. Unsolicited e-mail is a big, big no-no on the Internet when it's business-related.

There are several things you can do. First, respond to the e-mail saying you never asked for that information and you want your name off their list immediately. Second, send e-mail to the postmaster at the site the mail came from, which is something you can determine by looking at the headers as discussed in chapter 3 (for example, if the mail came from **sellit@generic.com**, then you would send your e-mail to **postmaster@generic.com**) with a copy of the unsolicited note and your response to it. If the company sends you more unsolicited e-mail, do the same thing again, pointing out to the postmaster that this is the second time and you've previously asked to be removed from the list. Many postmasters will do their best to deal with the situation when these things are reported.

The reason unsolicited e-mail is bad form is that it's like sending someone junk mail by C.O.D. for anyone who has to pay for how long they're online. It's also considered an invasion of privacy because you never asked to be placed on their list. Unlike the real world where you get on mailing lists by putting yourself on other mailing lists, it's simple for a company to go onto the Internet and gather e-mail addresses from all sorts of places. If companies are allowed to function this way, then doing almost anything on the Internet will be just like to inviting them to send junk mail to your account. This doesn't make for a pleasant environment.

Signature files

Many people have little quotes that appear at the end of every piece of e-mail they send. These are called .signatures, or .sigs. Sometimes they're quotes, sometimes they're business information, and what they all have in common is that they contain some piece of information you'd like to share with other people. See figures 4.7 and 4.8 for example .signatures.

Fig. 4.7
Example of a "quoting" .signature file.

Fig. 4.8
Example of a "business card" .signature file.

The following are a few basic guidelines to use when creating your .sig file:

- Keep it short.
- Keep it simple.
- Be careful with personal information.
- Keep the "--" at the beginning of your .sig.

It's important to keep your .sig short. After all, some of your e-mail may only be a few lines long, and it looks awful when your .sig is three times longer than your letter. A good guideline to follow is a maximum of five lines. A lot of news and mail programs will delete any .sig that's longer than that, so if you keep it to five or below, you're okay.

It's also important to keep it simple. If you get too fancy, (for example, using ASCII art, which are drawing pictures using the normal keys on the keyboard) it gets messed up when people start quoting you. It can also look childish, and rarely fits in only five lines. Just try to keep it to either quotes you're fond of or something similar to a business card.

Remember that people you don't know all over the world could be seeing your .sig, so be careful with your personal information. Unfortunately, this is especially true if you're female, because you're more likely to receive prank or obscene phone calls if you let your phone number get out.

Finally, it's important that you have "--" on the line before your .sig. Many mail and news programs use that line to determine where your .signature begins.

Part II:

Getting Started

5

Installing Eudora on a Macintosh

Installing Eudora is really quite easy. There's no complicated Installer. Once you have the files, it's time to get down to business and install Eudora.

In this chapter:

- Where to download the latest release of the free version of Eudora
- Install the free or commercial versions of Eudora
- Set up Eudora to know your e-mail account
- Configure Eudora for the way you work

Now that you are convinced how wonderful electronic mail is, you're probably ready to install Eudora. We're going to cover the installation and configuration for both the free and commercial versions for the Mac here. In spots where the instructions are different for the freeware and commercial versions, we'll tell you how to do both.

Getting the free version of Eudora

If you are just starting with Eudora and are planning to use the free version for a while before purchasing the retail version (or instead of purchasing it), you'll need to download this from the Internet before you can proceed. If you purchased the retail version—which you can do by calling 1-800-2-EUDORA or by sending e-mail to **eudora-rep@qualcomm.com**—you can skip over this section and go to the section "Installing Eudora."

Where to get free Eudora

The best place to get the current freeware version (1.5.1) of Eudora is on
Qualcomm's own FTP site. The information you need to get the program is:

FTP Site: **ftp.qualcomm.com**

Directory: /quest/mac/eudora/1.5

File: eudora151.hqx

To get the manual for the current freeware version you will use:

FTP Site: **ftp.qualcomm.com**

Directory: /quest/mac/eudora/documentation

File: man151-word.sea.hqx

✱ {Note}_____| This manual is huge, almost 2 megs!

Downloading Eudora

❓Q&A_____ **I'm using a dialup shell account.**
Do I have to do anything extra to get connected?

You'll need some extra files to make Eudora work with your shell account. The
/quest/mac/eudora/dialup/providers directory contains navigation files—files
that Eudora uses to get and send your e-mail through shell accounts.

You'll need to be sure to get the right files for the particular provider that you
use. The providers directory has files for several popular service providers. The
/quest/mac/eudora/dialup/servers directory contains navigation files for types of
servers other providers are probably using.

Tables 5.1 and 5.2 list the contents of these two directories and what each file
is for. If your provider is listed in table 5.3, just fetch the appropriate file. If
not, you'll have to ask your provider which of the servers in table 5.4 they use.

Table 5.1 Contents of /quest/mac/eudora/dialup/providers directory

File	Purpose
echo-nyc.hqx	Navigation file for Echo provider
holonet.hqx	Navigation file for Holonet provider
netcom-unix.hqx	Navigation file for Netcom provider
portal.hqx	Navigation file for Portal provider
well.hqx	Navigation file for Well provider

Table 5.2 Contents of /quest/mac/eudora/dialup/servers directory

File	Purpose
annex-nopass.hqx	Navigation file for providers using annex servers that are set not to require an extra password
annex-pass.hqx	Navigation file for providers using annex servers that are set to require an extra password
cisco-optional.hqx	Navigation file for providers using cisco servers that don't require a password
cisco-pass.hqx	Navigation file for providers using cisco servers that are set to require an extra password
srialpop.shar	Program to be installed by UNIX sysadmins to ensure that those using Eudora for direct UNIX dialins have proper tty modes
unix.hqx	Navigation file for providers using a general UNIX server
xyplex-script.hqx	Navigation file for use with Xyplex servers. These servers have many different options, so if this one doesn't work for you, try the other
xyplex-setport.hqx	Navigation file for use with Xyplex servers. These servers have many different options, so if this one doesn't work for you, try the other

❶ (Tip)

If you have a file with ".sea.hqx" on the end, you can also use the program Stuffit Expander to make the file usable. Stuffit Expander will uncode and uncompress the file for you all at once.

⊛ **{Note}**_____

The files that have "hqx" after them are encoded using a program called BinHex. This keeps all of the parts of the file your Macintosh needs together even when the file is not stored on a Macintosh computer.

The files that have "sea" after them are **Self-Extracting Archives**. This means that all you have to do is double-click on them and they uncompress themselves.

Read the filenames and extensions from right to left. For example, the program itself is just "eudora151.hqx" so you use BinHex to uncode it and you're ready to go on. The documentation is "man151-word.sea.hqx" so you first use BinHex to uncode it and then double-click on it to uncompress it.

Installing Eudora

Installing Eudora is really quite easy. There's no complicated Installer. Once you have the files, it's time to get down to business and install Eudora.

With the commercial version, all you need to do is drag the program file Eudora 2.1 from disk 1 to a folder on your hard drive.

If you are using the free version, there is nothing to do to install Eudora. Once you have uncoded it (as described in the previous section) you are ready to go.

⊛ **{Note}**_____

Eudora creates a folder in your System Folder that contains your preferences and mailboxes.

❶ **(Tip)**_____

Consider adding Eudora to your Apple Menu, or creating an alias for it to keep on your Desktop. It's a great way to avoid wading through folders when you want to check or send mail.

 **<Caution>** If you don't have MacTCP and your connection set up, you need to do this before going any further with Eudora.

Installing extras

You can install extra files called **plug-ins** to customize Eudora even more. These files are located in /quest/mac/eudora/plugins. Table 5.3 lists the files available in this directory and what you might use each one for.

Table 5.3 Contents of /quest/mac/eudora/plugins directory

File	Use
1%hex.hqx	Sets attachment detection threshold to 1%. Useful if Eudora isn't converting BinHex files for you for some reason.
2min–recv.hqx	Sets Eudora's timeout to 2 minutes instead of 45 seconds. Useful for people with slow servers or connections.
3min–open.hqx	Sets Eudora's open connection timeout to 3 minutes. Useful again for people with slow servers.
90margins.hqx	Tells Eudora to keep its windows 90 pixels (dots on your screen) from the right and bottom edge of your screen. Useful for keeping rows of icons from getting covered up.
934-forward.hqx	Tells Eudora to use RFC 934-style forwarding.
POPSend.hqx	Tells Eudora to use the XTND XMIT command in POP3 to send mail instead of SMTP. XTND SMIT is a little more secure than STMP and is required by some sites.
README	Contains up-to-date information on the contents of the directory. Useful for finding possible new information or instructions not in your manuals or this book.
apop.hqx	Tells Eudora to use the APOP authentication protocol.
nq-charset.hqx	Stops Eudora from quoting MIME character set parameters. Useful if you're sending mail to certain UNIX mailers that implement MIME improperly.
plus-minus.hqx	Changes Eudora's priority icons to ++, +, nothing, -, and —. Useful if the other icons don't mean much to you at a glance.
turbo-scroll.hqx	Makes Eudora scroll a lot faster than before. Useful if you find Eudora's scrolling just too slow.

To install these files, follow these steps:

1 Make sure Eudora isn't running.

2 Drag the file(s) into your System Folder.

3 Drag the file(s) into either your Preferences or Eudora folder, whichever you prefer.

4 Start Eudora.

Installing dial-up files

If you are going to be using Eudora with a command line shell account, there are some additional files you need to dial up to your account.

As mentioned before, you can find these files at:

FTP Site: **ftp.qualcomm.com**

Directory: /quest/mac/eudora/dialup/providers

A dial-up navigation file is basically a plug-in. To install, follow the same procedure as you would for a plug-in file:

1 Make sure Eudora isn't running.

2 Drag into your System Folder.

MacTCP and SLIP/PPP connections

In order to use Eudora with a SLIP/PPP service provider or on a network connected to the Internet, you will need MacTCP. MacTCP comes on disk 2 of the commercial version of Eudora. It also comes standard with System 7.5. Several books that get you started on the Internet, such as *Internet Starter Kit for Macintosh, Second Edition,* include this software on disk.

If you are using a SLIP/PPP connection, you'll also need connection software like InterSLIP or MacPPP. Again, a good place to get these if you don't have them is *Internet Starter Kit for Macintosh, Second Edition.*

3 Drag into either your Preferences or Eudora folder, whichever you prefer.

4 Start Eudora.

To use these navigation files, you'll need to use ResEdit to make a few changes to set the exact phone number and so on. See your manual for more details on how to do this.

Configuring Eudora

 *{Note}* | Early copies of Eudora 2.1 were shipped with documentation for version 2.0.3 plus an addendum to the manual. Current copies of Eudora 2.1 are shipped with documentation for this version.

Now that you've got Eudora installed, it's time to tell it how to actually get and send your mail, and to personalize it for your use. If yours is a SLIP/PPP account, all of the instructions in this chapter apply. If your account uses UUCP, see chapter 7 for instructions on setting up a few other things.

All of the configuration options discussed in the rest of the chapter are accessed through the same menu command. To change any configuration settings choose Special, Settings. This will open the dialog box shown in figure 5.1.

Fig. 5.1
The main Eudora configuration dialog box.

```
┌──────────────────── Settings ────────────────────┐
│  ┌───────────────┐  Getting Started                │
│  │      1        │    POP Account:                  │
│  │ Getting Started│   ┌──────────────────────────┐  │
│  │   ┌──┐        │    └──────────────────────────┘  │
│  │   │JDoe│      │    Real Name:                    │
│  │Personal Information│ ┌────────────────────────┐  │
│  │    ⚡         │    └──────────────────────────┘  │
│  │   Hosts       │    Connection Method:            │
│  │   ┌──┐        │      ● MacTCP                    │
│  │   │204│       │      ○ Communications Toolbox    │
│  │ Checking Mail │      □ Offline (no connections)  │
│  └───────────────┘                                  │
│  ┌──┐                          ┌────────┐ ┌──────┐ │
│  │  │                          │ Cancel │ │  OK  │ │
│  └──┘                          └────────┘ └──────┘ │
└───────────────────────────────────────────────────┘
```

As you can see, there are icons in the left column of this dialog box. Each of these icons is a group of settings, and if you use the down arrow, you'll find more of them. Clicking an icon lets you change the settings associated with it.

 Some settings, such as POP Account, are in a couple of different dialog boxes. You only need to enter those settings in one place and Eudora copies it to the others.

Personalizing Eudora

First, there are some things you need to do so Eudora knows the basics to get and send your mail, as well as some of the basics of how you want it to work.

How do I tell Eudora who I am?

Eudora needs to know who you are. After all, it can't send and pick up your mail if it doesn't know whose it is. By default, when the Settings dialog box first opens, the Getting Started settings are displayed. If they aren't, select Getting Started in the left side of the dialog box.

In the box under the label "POP account," enter your e-mail address. For example, **writer@first.book.com**.

{Note} **POP** stands for Post Office Protocol. POP servers function just like a real post office. They look at the address on the mail that comes to them and send it off in the direction it needs to go.

In the box under "Real Name" enter either your real name or the nickname you want to use. For example, **Book Writer**.

This will show up in the e-mail you send out next to your e-mail address. For example,

```
From: writer@first.book.com (Book Writer)
```

How do I tell Eudora where and how to send my mail?

Now Eudora knows who you are but not where to get your mail. You also need an **SMTP** (Simple Mail Transfer Protocol) server. Without an SMTP server, POP can receive mail, but not send it at all. Your POP server may not even be a computer you have an account on, but it could be the computer you've got your POP account on.

1 Open the Settings dialog box and choose the Getting Started option.

2 To use Eudora with MacTCP (a SLIP/PPP connection or a network), select MacTCP.

To use Eudora to dial up a shell account, select Communications Toolbox.

To make no connections, click the circle box to Offline.

3 Choose the Hosts option from the menu on the left. The dialog box changes to one like figure 5.2.

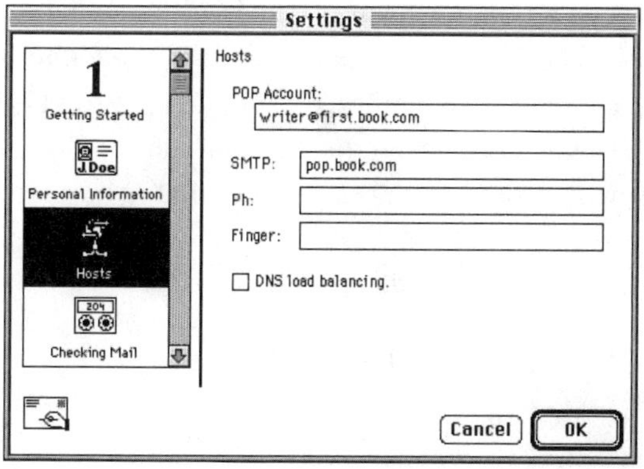

Fig. 5.2
The Settings dialog box, Hosts option.

4 Enter the SMTP server's name in the box next to SMTP Server. Otherwise, put the name of the computer that will be your SMTP server here. If you're not sure what computer your SMTP server will be, ask your service provider. (In the case of our example, the SMTP server is a different computer, so we typed **pop.book.com**.)

How do I get replies to my mail sent to a different address than I'm sending out from?

Sometimes the arrangement you have with your service provider means that you tell the POP server your full e-mail address to send mail out, but people writing to you only need part of that address. For example, in our case people can send us e-mail by typing just **username@renaissoft.com** instead of typing in the entire e-mail address. In the POP Account field, we have to fill in **username@davinci.renaissoft.com**, or **username@catherine.renaissoft.com** depending on which computer we'll be working from. The difference is that davinci and catherine are the names of specific computers, while renaissoft.com is the name of our site.

Say, for example, we have a few computers networked together: **elgreco.renaissoft.com**, **davinci.renaissoft.com**, and **michaelangelo.renaissoft.com**. If someone writes to us at **renaissoft.com**, we'll see that mail no matter which one of those computers we're using.

However, if someone sends e-mail specifically to **elgreco.renaissoft.com**, it would only show up on that computer. If we checked our mail on davinci or michaelangelo, we wouldn't see it. Choose the Personal Information option— the ID Card icon—from the left menu in the Settings dialog box. The Personal Information options in the Settings dialog box are shown in figure 5.3.

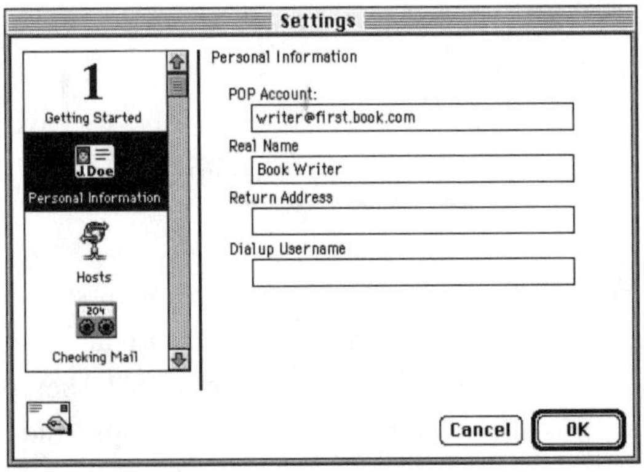

Fig. 5.3

The Settings dialog box, Personal Information option.

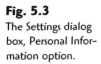

In the box next to Return Address, put the e-mail address you want your mail sent to if it's not your POP account. In the case of our example, Book Writer's specific computer is named "first," but you can write to her using just book.com, so that's what we will fill in the Return Address box.

①(Tip) _____ | Make sure that your Dialup Username box contains your userid without the host extension (for example, writer).

Fine-tuning Eudora for your needs

Now that you've set everything you need to, it's time to play with some other options. There are a lot of options you can set to let Eudora know how you want it to handle everything from when to send your mail to what kinds of fonts you want to use. If you want to go ahead to chapter 7 and try out your connection, go for it. There are default settings already, and you'll probably want to keep a lot of them.

How do I tell Eudora where to look for people?

Eudora has two ways of looking people up. The first method uses something called **Finger**, and the second method uses **Ph servers**. Finger talks to the computer where the person you're looking up has their account, while Ph uses a database of Internet users.

First you have to tell Eudora what servers to use to get the information. To set this up, do the following:

1 Go to the Special menu and select the Settings option.

2 Select the Hosts option in the Settings menu. (This option was shown earlier in figure 5.2.)

3 You'll need a Ph server to use Ph. Enter this server's name in the box next to Ph.

4 You'll need a Finger server to use Finger. Enter this server's name in the box next to Finger.

 **{Note}** If your site has a Ph server, use that one. Otherwise, there are some others out there, such as **ns.uiuc.edu**. As far as Finger servers go, your site probably has one. Ask your sysadmin.

Fig. 5.4
The Ph window.

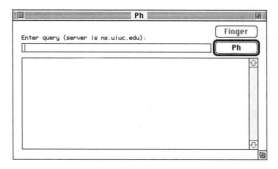

Finger

Finger is a program many people on the Internet have access to. Using it shows you the last time the person you're Fingering logged in and if she has unread mail. Not all service providers allow people to Finger their users, but most do.

Fill in the e-mail address of the person you are looking for in the box under Enter query, and then click the Finger button.

 **{Note}** If you know the specific computer the person you're looking for uses, include that in the e-mail address. For example, you may write to someone at **writer@book.com**, but that e-mail address is for a network of computers. Writer usually uses the computer named first, so you'd enter **writer@first.book.com**.

 (Tip) If you only enter the person's userid into the Command box—for example, dee—Finger uses what's in the Server box—for example, **davinci.renaissoft.com**—as the domain of the userid. This saves a little typing.

Figure 5.5 shows you what the output from Finger can look like.

Fig. 5.5
Example results
from Finger.

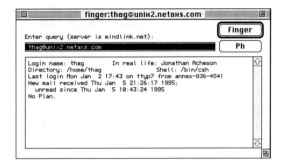

Ph

Ph is basically an electronic phonebook. Using it gets you general information on the person you're looking for, such as name, e-mail address, and perhaps office location. Just as with Finger, not all sites allow their information to be accessed for a Ph search.

Fill in the box under Enter query with the name of the person you're looking for, and then click the Ph button.

Fig. 5.6
Example results
from Ph.

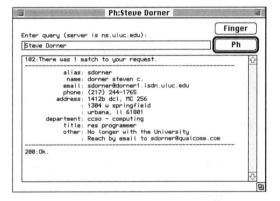

 You can type any Ph command in the Command box except for commands you have to login to use.

How do I tell Eudora to check my mail once an hour?

You don't have to be around to make sure Eudora checks your mail. You can tell the program how often to dial in. Just leave it running and leave your computer on, and it will take care of fetching your new mail.

In the Settings dialog box, choose the Checking Mail option from the menu on the left. Figure 5.7 shows what the dialog box will look like after choosing this.

❶(Tip)

Most people just leave the timed dial-in alone and have Eudora check their mail once when they start up the program, and then again when they send mail out.

✖<Caution>

If you're using a modem, make sure to check that Eudora hung up after dialing in. If your service provider doesn't time out your connection after Eudora logs out of your account, the program doesn't know to hang up the phone line.

The advantages of off-line readers

When you have to pay for the amount of time you're connected to your service provider—and most people do—you end up feeling pressured to get in, read your mail, send a few quick replies, and get out. However, using an off-line reader like Eudora lets you relax. You just let Eudora dial in and grab your mail, take your time reading and replying to it on your own computer, and then have Eudora dial in and send that mail out. It's an amazing cost difference to not have to read and compose your mail on-line.

Fig. 5.7
The Settings dialog box, Checking Mail option in the commercial version.

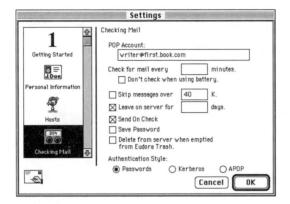

{Note}

The "Don't check when using battery" option is only available in the commercial version. If you are using a PowerBook and don't want Eudora to automatically check your mail while you are using the battery (and presumably not connected to your modem or network), check this option.

There's a box with Check for Mail Every on the left and Minute(s) on the right. If you want Eudora to check your mail once an hour, type **60** in the box.

If you want it more or less often, just type in that number.

SLIP/PPP connections

If you're using a SLIP/PPP connection that isn't permanent (for example, you're not always hooked up to a network), it's best to do your SLIP/PPP connection first and then have Eudora check your mail. Especially if dial-in lines are limited.

This way, you can also double-check and make sure that your SLIP/PPP connection is closed when your mail check is over.

Telling Eudora what to do with the mail on your server

There are a few more things you can configure to make Eudora's dial-ins more automated. Open the Settings dialog box and choose the Checking Mail option. Because the commercial and freeware versions are different here, we'll look at them separately.

Commercial version 2.1

The first thing you should look at is the box with "Leave Mail on Server for" on the left and "Days" on the right. Entering a number in this box means that Eudora will get your mail from the POP server, but not erase each piece until it has been there for the number of days you put in the box.

If you leave this number blank, the mail never gets erased, which isn't a good idea. However, you can select "Delete from server when emptied" from Eudora Trash. This will make sure that any message you don't want anymore won't remain on the POP server.

You can also choose to Skip messages that are larger than a particular size, or K (number of Kilobytes). This option is good if you have a slow connection or modem. Select this option and fill in a number, and Eudora will only grab the first few lines of large text messages, letting you decide if you want to download them or not later.

Leaving too much mail on your server

Be careful when using the "leave mail on server" option. If you leave too much mail behind, you can use up the disk space you're allowed by your service provider. Some service providers will just charge you more for the extra disk space, some won't accept any new mail for you, and some will just delete any old mail you have sitting around.

 **{Note}** Eudora considers a large text message in the default length to be 40K or larger. If you want to use a higher or lower number of K, just enter that in the box.

 Eudora does need some help from your POP server to do this. Eudora expects the POP server to add a "Status:" header after it's downloaded the first few lines of the message so it knows when to stop. If your POP server doesn't provide it, then this option won't work and you'll just download everything, regardless of size. If you're not sure what your POP server offers, ask your service provider if it does this.

Free Eudora 1.5.1

You have essentially the same options here as with the commercial version, just not as much flexibility in applying them. You can select Leave Mail on Server. This isn't generally something you want to select, because Eudora will dial in, get your mail, but not delete it from the POP server. Unlike the commercial version, you can't determine how many days to leave it on and you can choose to delete it from the server when you trash the message.

The Skip Big Messages options works the same way as in the commercial version except you can't change the size that Eudora considers "big." This is set to 40K and can't be changed.

How to skip over entering your password

You can also teach Eudora your password so you don't have to type it in all of the time. Open the Settings dialog box and choose the Checking Mail option. Select Save Password to activate this option.

 If other people can use your Macintosh, using the Save Password option also means they can read your mail and send stuff out through your account. This is very, very bad. Only use this if your Mac is in a place where other people can't use it.

Deciding when to send your mail

Eudora gives you much flexibility in choosing when to send your messages. Open the Settings dialog box and choose Sending Mail.

If you choose Immediate Send, Eudora will send the message whenever you choose Message, Send Message Now, or click the Send button. Figure 5.8 shows what you'll find.

Fig. 5.8
The Settings dialog box, Sending Mail option.

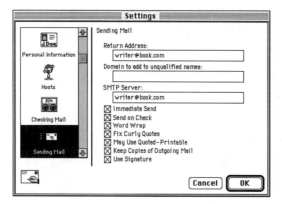

❓Q&A

When should I send my messages?

If you are connected to the Internet through a network and leave Eudora running all the time, you will probably want to send all of your messages immediately.

If you have a SLIP/PPP account, use Eudora to dial up to a shell account, or use UUCP, you probably won't want Eudora sending each message as you finish it. It will be more efficient to write several messages, queue them, then send them all at once. Especially since with these kinds of accounts you're usually charged for the time you spend online, and it adds up to less if you check your mail, reply to it and queue it up as you finish each message, and then just send it all out at once.

Also, if you don't always use Eudora from the same place, mail queuing is a wonderful feature. You can get your mail, save it to a floppy disk, take it somewhere else, reply to it, and send it off.

If you aren't sending your messages immediately, your messages will be queued. When you finish a message, you'll choose Message, Queue Message, or click the Queue button. (Yes, the menu options and the button change depending on whether or not Immediate Send is selected!) This puts them in line to be sent the next time you send the queue. If you choose Send on Check, Eudora will send any waiting mail out when it checks for new mail.

How do I tell Eudora how I want to write my mail?

There are several word processing features you can choose to use.

Open the Settings dialog and choose Sending Mail.

One option that's useful to select is May use Quoted-Printable. Quoted Printable encoding only applies to attachments. It's useful if you've got a text document with really long lines or special characters (such as international characters).

Another nice option to select is Word Wrap. This makes sure Eudora acts like a word processor instead of a typewriter. When you're in the middle of a word and get to the end of a line, that word goes down to the next line and stays in one piece. This option is on by default, and is very handy.

How do I keep copies of the mail I send out?

It's a great idea to keep copies of e-mail you send to other people. It's awful to have to ask someone what you told them before.

Open the Settings dialog box and choose the Sending Mail option. Select Keep Copies of Outgoing Mail. Copies of all of the mail you send out will go to the Out mailbox. If you turn it off, all copies of outgoing mail will go to the Trash.

How do I tell Eudora to always add my signature to my mail?

It's tedious to have to keep adding your signature manually. You can set Eudora to always add it. Keep in mind, though, that you don't always want to send your signature if you have personal information in it. Open the Settings dialog box and choose Sending Mail. Select Use Signature.

How do I make sure most people can read my attachments?

If you're not careful, a lot of people will get your attachments but not be able to do anything with them.

Open the Settings dialog box and choose Sending Mail. You can select Fix curly quotes to turn this option on. If you tend to write mostly to MIME users, it's not necessary, but if you write to people who read your attachments in ways other than using MIME, it's a good option to select.

How do I tell Eudora to always use the same encoding method?

Open the Settings dialog box and choose Attachments. Figure 5.9 shows what you'll find.

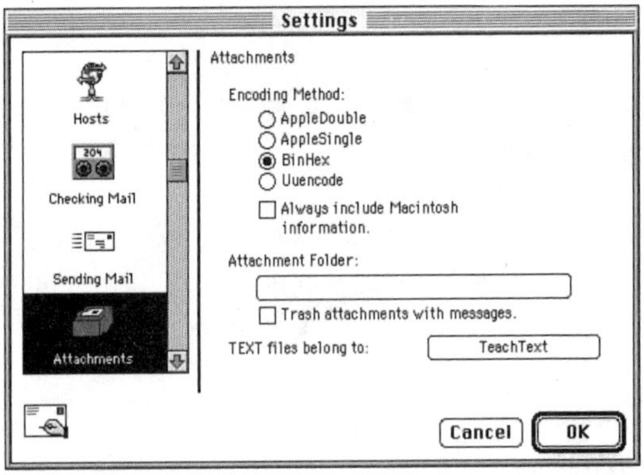

Fig. 5.9
The Settings dialog box, Attachments option.

Table 5.4 explains what choices are best for what situations.

Table 5.4   Encoding Methods and Uses

Encoding method	Best to use when sending to
AppleDouble	MIME users
AppleSingle	MIME users who use Macintosh computers
BinHex	Macintosh users
Uuencode	(Commercial version only) Users of UNIX systems, or of systems with mailer programs that don't support MIME

If you send e-mail to mostly Macintosh users, selecting "Always include Macintosh information" will make sure their Macs know what kinds of files your attachments are. If you send to a lot of non-Mac users, don't use this option. It will only confuse their e-mail programs.

How do I edit my saved mail using a different program?

Sometimes it's nice to save a piece of mail to add to or edit before you send it out. When it's time to work with it, it's really nice to be able to just double-click on that mail and use your word processing program.

1 Open the Settings dialog box and select Attachments.

2 Click in the "TEXT files belong to" button. Eudora pulls up a dialog box that allows you to select which program you want to use to edit your text files.

 **<Caution>** If you assign text files to Microsoft Word and then receive binaries (for example, Microsoft Word format files instead of text files) as attachments, you can run into problems.

How do I automatically save attachments?

It's possible to have the attachments that come in with your e-mail automatically saved to a folder of your choosing. This means you don't have to deal with them right when they come in.

- Open the Settings dialog box and choose Attachments. Click the button under Attachment Folder. A dialog box appears that allows you to select which folder you want to use to save your attachments in. When you have that folder open, click the Use Folder button.

**<Caution>** This feature doesn't allow you to create a new folder, so if you want a special folder for your attachments, you'll need to create it before you do this.

How do I change the size of my message window?

You're not stuck with the window sizes Eudora is set with. If you want to change them to better fit your screen, go for it!

1 Open the Settings dialog box.

2 Scroll down the left menu to the Fonts & Display icon and select it. Figure 5.10 shows you what you'll see.

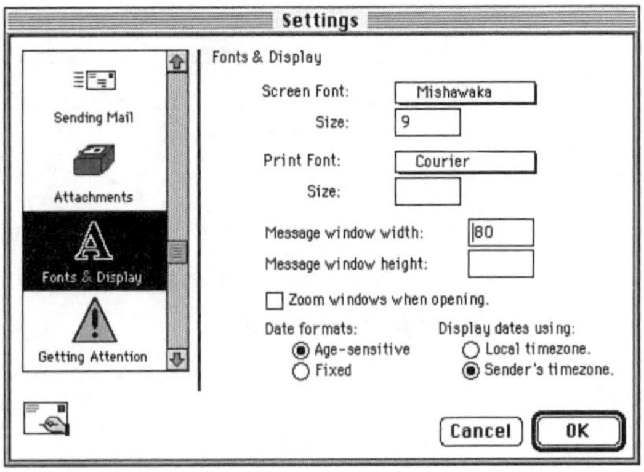

Fig. 5.10
The Settings dialog box, Fonts & Display option.

3 To change the width of your message window, go to the box next to Message Window Width. The default is 80 characters, which is pretty standard across the Internet.

4 To change the height of your message window, go to the box next to Message Window Height. The default is 20 lines. There's no real standard on the Internet for this, but it's often around 24 or 25 lines. Just choose a height that's comfortable for your screen.

How do I change the fonts?

You're also not stuck with the default fonts or font sizes Eudora uses.

1 Open the Settings dialog box.

2 Scroll the left menu down a bit to choose Fonts & Display.

3 To change the font you'll see on the screen, click on the Font box to open the list, then drag to select the font you want. Figure 5.11 shows you what the dialog box looks like with the font list open.

Fig. 5.11
The Fonts & Display window with Font List open.

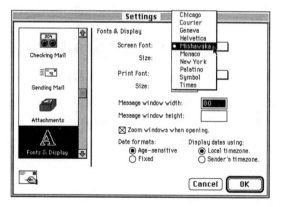

4 To change the size of the font on your screen, click in the box next to Size and enter the size you want. This size is in points. You may need to experiment to find a size you're comfortable with.

5 To change the font you'll print out your mail in, click the mouse button in the box next to Print Font and drag to select the font you want. Just like when you changed your screen font, the font list will appear.

6 To change the size of the font your printer will use, click in the box next to Size and enter the size you want. This size is also in points.

How do I manage my mail windows?

When you get a bunch of windows opened up at once, it gets a bit confusing to try to sort through them.

Open Settings dialog box and choose Fonts & Display. Selecting Zoom Windows when opening means that new mailbox and message windows open to their zoomed sizes.

 **{Note}**

The "zoomed size" for the following types of windows are:

- **Mailbox window**—just as wide as it needs to be to show the widest summary, and just long enough to show all of the summaries.

- **Message window**—as wide as it's set in the Configuration dialog, and just long enough to display the entire message.

- **Composition window**—just as wide and high as it's set to be in the Configuration dialog.

A zoomed window will never be longer than the actual screen.

How do I get Eudora to alert me about new mail or problems?

Eudora needs to know how to get your attention when it needs help or wants to give you news about what's going on.

1 Open the Settings dialog box and choose Getting Attention. Figure 5.12 shows you what you'll find.

2 If you want Eudora to use alerts to notify you of new mail, select Use an alert.

3 If you want alerts to include flashing icons in your menu bar, select Flash an icon in the menu bar.

4 If you want Eudora to make noise when it needs you, select Play a sound.

5 To change which sound is for new mail, click the New mail sound box and choose the sound you want.

6 To change which sound is for attention, click the Attention sound box and choose the sound you want.

Fig. 5.12
The Settings dialog box, Getting Attention option.

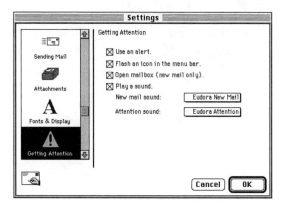

 **{Note}** In the free version, you don't get to choose the sounds played.

How do I tell Eudora to automatically open my "In" mailbox after I receive new mail?

Eudora automatically puts your new mail in your In mailbox. You can also get Eudora to open your In mailbox for you when you've got new mail, which is important if you zoom windows or closed your mailbox before you finished last time you used Eudora.

This option is on by default and is a nice one, so there's usually no reason to shut it off. Usually you'd want it shut off for privacy issues, so people walking by your computer couldn't see your In mailbox.

Open the Settings dialog box and choose Getting Attention. If you want your mail to get saved to the In mailbox as it comes in, select Open mailbox (new mail only). Eudora will then let you go to the first new message and start reading from there.

How do I tell Eudora who I want to reply to with group mail?

There are a few ways to handle replies to group mail. You can reply to only the person who sent the mail to the group, you can reply to all of the group except for yourself, or you can reply to all of the group including yourself.

1 Open the Settings dialog box and select Replying. Figure 5.13 shows you what you'll find there.

Fig. 5.13
The Settings dialog box, Replying option.

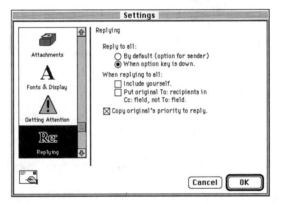

2 To tell Eudora to always reply to everyone included in a piece of group mail you received, select By default (option for sender).

3 To tell Eudora to usually reply to only the person who sent you a piece of group mail instead of to everyone listed, select When option key is down. If you want to reply to everyone for a specific note, you only need to hold the option key down when you click the reply button.

4 To be included in the list of people when replying to a group piece of e-mail, select Include yourself.

5 To reply directly to a person who sent you e-mail as part of a note to a group, but Cc the rest of the people in the list, select Put original To: recipients in the Cc: field, not the To: field.

6 To copy the priority of the messages you receive into the messages you're sending back, select Copy original's priority to reply.

Making it easier to delete messages

If you don't like to be prompted to confirm your decision every time you delete a message, you can configure Eudora to delete messages without asking for confirmation. Open the Settings Dialog box and choose the Miscellaneous option, which is shown in figure 5.14. By default, Require confirmation for deletes is selected. Turning this option off means that Eudora won't ask you if you really want to delete something. Don't turn this off unless you rarely make mistakes when you're deleting mail.

Fig. 5.14
The Settings dialog box, Miscellaneous option.

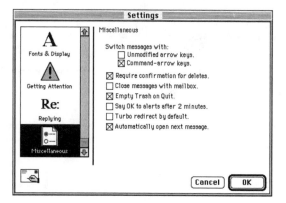

How do I set up what arrow keys I want to use?

It's great to be able to move around with your arrow keys if you don't have room on your desk for your mouse or don't want to take your hands off the keyboard.

Open the Settings dialog box and choose the Miscellaneous option.

You can choose what your arrow keys will do in this dialog box. If you select Unmodified arrow keys and have a message window open, you can use the arrow keys on the Macintosh keyboard to close the current message and open the next or previous. Table 5.5 lists what each arrow key does. If this option is off, you can use the arrow keys to move the insertion point in messages.

Table 5.5 Arrow Keys and Their Functions

Key	Function
up	opens previous message
down	opens next message
right	opens next message
left	opens previous message

 The arrow keys won't switch messages if you have a message composition window at the top of your screen. This is true even if you're using this option.

If you select ⌘+Arrows, you can use the arrow keys to switch messages only when holding the Apple/⌘ key down. The keys and functions are the same as in table 5.2. This allows you to use the arrow keys normally to move the insertion point in your message.

 You can use the ⌘+Arrow keys even when composition windows are open on the screen.

How do I close all messages from a single mailbox at once?

It's nice when you've been mucking about with mail for a while to be able to just close an entire mailbox. Otherwise, it takes a while to close each and every message, one by one.

If the Close messages with mailbox option in the Miscellaneous section in the Settings dialog box is selected, closing a mailbox window closes every open message from that mailbox.

How do I tell Eudora to empty the Trash as I quit the program?

It's nice to be able to not deal with mail anymore when you're done with Eudora. This includes having to go empty the Trash when you've finally finished.

If the Empty Trash on Quit option in the Settings dialog box Miscellaneous section is selected, Eudora empties the Trash mailbox when you quit the program. If it isn't selected, the Trash only gets emptied when you choose Special, Empty Trash.

 (Tip)

> You can delete some of the messages. Highlight the summaries you want to delete and then choose Message, Delete. A quicker way is selecting the summary you want to delete and pressing ⌘+d.

How do I tell Eudora to open the next message when I'm done with the current one?

If the "Automatically open next message" option in the Miscellaneous section of the Settings dialog box is selected, deleting or transferring the current message opens the next unread message in your mailbox.

Installing Eudora on Windows

In this chapter:

- Where to download the latest release of the free version of Eudora

- Install the free or commercial versions of Eudora

- Set up Eudora to know your e-mail account

- Configure Eudora for the way you work

Something to be aware of is that, while Windows is pretty good at keeping things simple for you, it can't do everything for you.

Now that you are convinced how wonderful electronic mail is, you're probably ready to install Eudora. This chapter covers the installation and configuration for both the free and commercial versions of Windows. In spots where the instructions are different for the freeware and commercial versions, this chapter tells you how to do both.

Getting the free version of Eudora

If you are just starting with Eudora and are planning to use the free version for a while before purchasing the retail version, you'll need to download this from the Internet before you can proceed. (If you purchased the retail version, you can skip over this section and go right to the "Installing Eudora" section.)

Downloading free Eudora

If you are just starting with Eudora and are planning to use the free version for a while before purchasing the retail version (or instead of purchasing it), you'll need to download this from the Internet before you can proceed. If you purchased the retail version—which you can do by calling 1-800-2-EUDORA or sending e-mail to **eudora-rep@qualcomm.com**— you can skip over this section and go to the section "Installing Eudora."

The best place to get the current freeware version (1.4) of Eudora is on Qualcomm's own FTP site. The information you need to get the program is:

FTP Site:	**ftp.qualcomm.com**
Directory:	/quest/windows/eudora/1.4
File:	eudor144.exe

To get the manual for the current freeware version you will use:

FTP Site:	**ftp.qualcomm.com**
Directory:	/quest/windows/eudora/documentation
File:	14manual.exe

⊛ {Note} While the freeware version of Eudora doesn't have a dialup connection feature, the commercial version does. While the commercial version comes with a selection of dialup scripts, there may be other available by FTP from Qualcomm's site, **ftp.qualcomm.com** in the directory /quest/windows/ eudora/dialup.

Installing Eudora

Now it's time to get down to business and install Eudora. The commercial version comes with an installation and setup program. The freeware version is so easy to install, you don't need a special program to do it.

Installing the freeware version

Installing the freeware version of Eudora involves just a few steps, and then you're ready to get started! First, you need to move and uncompress eudor144.exe. Choose or create a directory to put Eudora in. We'll use c:\eudora. Now, move eudor144.exe to this directory.

The file eudor144.exe is a **self-extracting archive**, meaning that all you have to do is run it and it uncompresses itself. To uncompress Eudora, do the following:

1 With the Windows Program Manager open, select File, Run.

2 Enter **c:\eudora\eudor144.exe** in the dialog box, substituting the path you chose for c:\eudora.

3 Select OK.

Next, you need to go to your autoexec.bat file and make sure it contains the following:

```
set temp=
```

Installing WinSock

In order to use Eudora with a SLIP/PPP service provider or on a network connected to the Internet, you will need WinSock. (If you'll be using a dialup (shell) account, you don't need to install it.) Several books that get you started on the Internet, such as Que's *Special Edition Using the Internet, Second Edition* and *Using the Internet* include WinSock software on disk.

If you don't have WinSock set up and intend to use it, you need to do this before going any further with Eudora. The best way to do this is to buy one of the books mentioned previously

and follow the directions for installing and configuring the software. Another option would be to purchase commercial Internet connection software, such as NetManage's Chameleon. This software is a bit more expensive than the books listed, but it does include automatic configuration and some free online time with several major Internet service providers. A version of this software without the free connect time is also included with *Special Edition Using the Internet, Second Edition* along with several freeware and shareware WinSock programs.

The directory name after this is important in that DOS and Windows use this directory to store all temporary files. If you don't have that line in your autoexec.bat, you'll need to add it. Create a directory to be your temporary directory—common ones are c:\tmp or c:\temp—then add **set temp=c:\tmp** to your autoexec bat, substituting the name you've chosen for your temporary directory for c:\tmp.

Now to set things up in Windows so you can run Eudora with just a double-click of the mouse.

You can either add Eudora to an existing program group or create a new one for it. If you wish to create a new group, open the Program Manager and select File, New. In the Description box, enter the name of the group (this is the name that will appear underneath the group's icon in the File Manager). Leave the Group File box blank. When finished, select OK.

The final step is actually adding Eudora to the program group. To do this, do the following:

1 Open the program group you're adding Eudora to.

2 Go to the File Manager and select File, New.

3 Select the Program Item button and then OK.

4 In the Description box, enter the label you want to have underneath Eudora's icon.

5 In the Command Line box, enter **c:\eudora\eudor144.exe**, substituting the path you chose for c:\eudora.

6 In the Working Directory box, enter the name of the directory you stored Eudora in, for example c:\eudora.

7 Select Change Icon.

8 If you want to use the default icon, select OK, and select OK again in the Program Item Properties box. If you want to use another icon, scroll through the list and select the one you want, and then select OK, and OK again.

Installing the commercial Eudora

The commercial version comes with a program to do the work for you. To install commercial Eudora, do the following:

1 Open Windows.

2 Take note of where the Eudora files are located. If they're on a floppy disk, insert that disk into the appropriate drive. If they're on your hard drive, take note of the path name.

3 Go to the Program Manager.

4 Open the File menu and choose Run. The Run dialog box appears.

5 Type **a:setup.exe**. If you don't have the file on your a: drive, use the appropriate path.

 *{Note}*

If you aren't using a floppy in drive a: to install Eudora, substitute whatever drive letter and path is appropriate.

6 When you're done, choose OK.

First, you'll see a dialog box stating that the installation program is initializing. Just wait while it does its work. Once that is complete, you'll get the setup screen shown in figure 6.1. If you're ready to begin installing Eudora, choose Continue. If you're not, choose Exit.

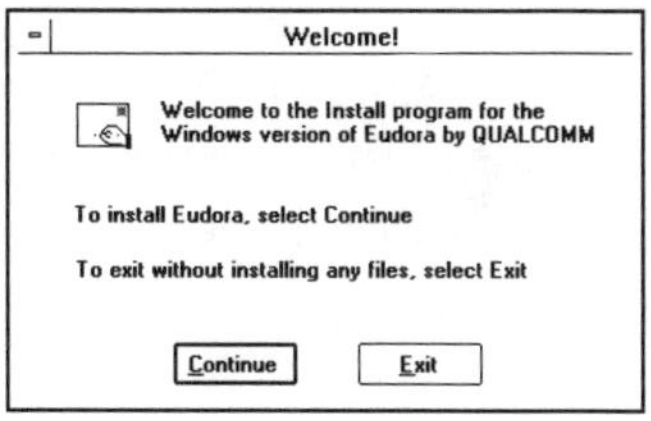

Fig. 6.1
Initial Installation
dialog box.

```
=|              Welcome!
   ┌──┐   Welcome to the Install program for the
   │  │   Windows version of Eudora by QUALCOMM
   └──┘
   To install Eudora, select Continue

   To exit without installing any files, select Exit

        ┌──────────┐    ┌──────────┐
        │ Continue │    │   Exit   │
        └──────────┘    └──────────┘
```

(Tip)

If you want to start your installation, but aren't sure of everything you need to know, go ahead and choose Continue. You can minimize the window if you need to look at something else and come back to the installation later.

At any time during the installation process when the Exit button is shown, choose Exit and the installation program saves where it left off. You can then go back to it later without having to start all over.

The next dialog box, in which you tell the Installation program what directory to put Eudora's files in, is shown in figure 6.2.

Fig. 6.2
Directory Name
Installation Setup
dialog box.

⊛ **{Note}**

If you've installed Eudora before and are now installing a new version, use the same directory you used for the old version.

 (Tip)

If you want the installation program to go ahead and create a program group and icon for Eudora then leave the Create Program Groups/Icon option selected. This will create a program group called "Eudora by Qualcomm" and an icon called "Eudora" automatically. If you want to do it yourself so you can do something different, unselect this option.

Enter the name of the directory to use and choose Install. You'll have to wait a bit while the installation program copies files, but it's just a "fetch a drink" wait, not a "walk around the block" wait.

If you will be using WinSock then you don't need to configure Eudora for dialup use, so you're finished with the installation (answer NO to configuring Eudora for dialup use) and can skip the dialup configuration section. If you will be using Eudora via dialup instead of WinSock, answer YES to configuring Eudora for dialup use and continue to the next section.

Configuring for dialup use with a shell account

There are a few extra things you have to set up in the Eudora installation program if you're dialing into a shell account.

 (Tip)

> If you're installing a newer version of Eudora over an older one and already had the dialup information configured, you don't need to do it again.

If you decide to configure Eudora's dialup features, you'll see the dialog box shown in figure 6.3.

Fig. 6.3
Dialup Installation
Setup dialog box.

```
┌─────────────────────────── Configuration ───────────────────────────┐
│ ┌─ Network Configuration ──────────────────────────────────────────┐ │
│ │  POP Account:       [                                          ]  │ │
│ │  Real Name:         [                                          ]  │ │
│ │  SMTP Server:       [                                          ]  │ │
│ │  Return Address:    [                                          ]  │ │
│ │  Check For Mail Every  [0  ]   Minute(s)                          │ │
│ │  Ph Server:         [                                          ]  │ │
│ └──────────────────────────────────────────────────────────────────┘ │
│ ┌─ Message Configuration ──────────────────────────────────────────┐ │
│ │  Message Width: [80]   Message Lines: [20]   Tab Stop: [8]        │ │
│ │  Screen Font:  [Courier New      ±]   Size: [9 ]                  │ │
│ │  Printer Font: [Courier New      ±]   Size: [12]                  │ │
│ │  ☐ Auto Receive Attachment Directory: [                    ]      │ │
│ └──────────────────────────────────────────────────────────────────┘ │
│ [≡≡]                                        [ Cancel ]  [  OK  ]       │
└──────────────────────────────────────────────────────────────────────┘
```

Alter the information in this dialog box until it's correct. If your service provider and/or modem brand aren't included in the listings, use the default settings. Most of the other information is most likely correct except for modem speed and com port. Be sure to change the baud rate and com port to whatever is appropriate for your setup.

Select the box on the left of Modem and/or Internet Service Provider if you want these values to be changed from what they were originally.

After you finish, you'll get a dialog box telling you the setup was successful. Just click OK and you're done!

Configuring Eudora

Now that you have Eudora installed, it's time to tell it how to get and send your mail and personalize it for your use. If yours is a SLIP/PPP account or permanently linked to a network, all of the instructions in this chapter apply. If yours is a shell account or uses UUCP, see chapter 7, "Connecting with Eudora," for additional instructions.

All of the configuration options are accessed by choosing Special, Configuration. This will open the dialog boxes shown in figures 6.4 (for the freeware version) and 6.5 (for the commercial version).

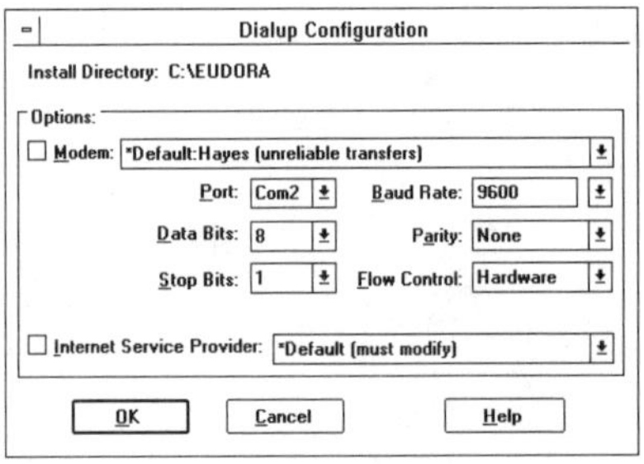

Fig. 6.4

This is the main Eudora configuration dialog box in the Windows freeware version.

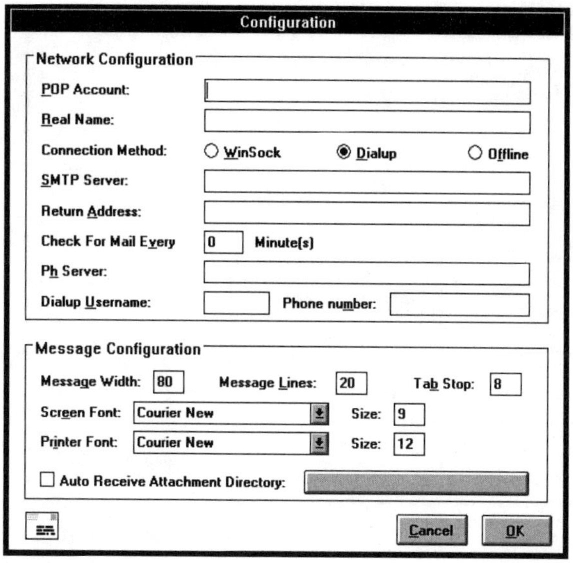

Fig. 6.5
This is the main Eudora configuration dialog box in the Windows commercial version.

The second set of options (called switches in Eudora) are accessed by choosing Special, Switches. This will open the dialog boxes shown in figures 6.6 (for the freeware version) and 6.7 (for the commercial version).

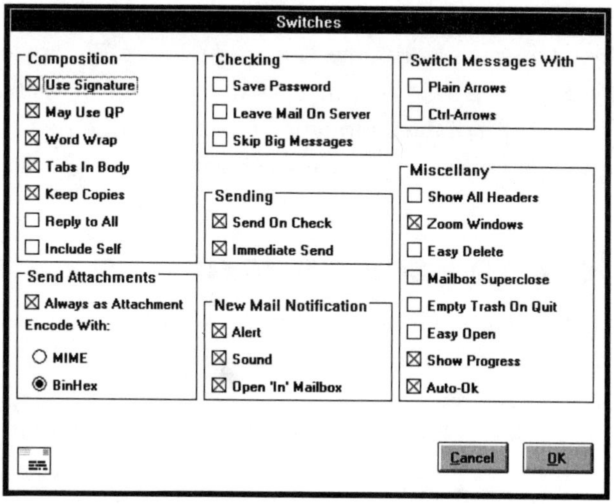

Fig. 6.6
This is the Eudora Switches dialog box in the Windows freeware version.

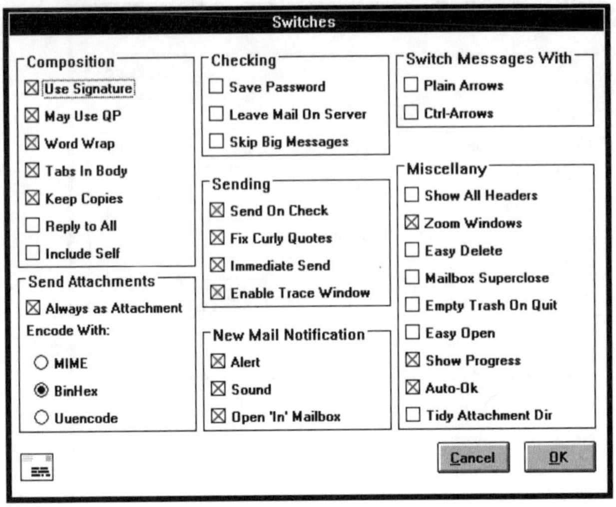

Fig. 6.7
This is the Eudora
Switches dialog box
in the Windows
commercial version.

At this point, you're ready to jump in and configure Eudora to work the way you need it to.

Personalizing Eudora

First, there are some things you need to do so Eudora knows the basics of how to get and send your mail, as well as some of the basics of how you want it to work. All of the information needed in these sections will be entered in the Configuration dialog box, so choose Special, Configuration.

How do I tell Eudora who I am?

Eudora needs to know who you are. After all, it can't send and pick up your mail if it doesn't know whose mail it is.

In the POP account text box, enter your e-mail address. For example:

writer@first.book.com

In the box next to Real Name, enter either your real name or the nickname you want to use. For example:

Book Writer

This will show up in the e-mail you send out next to your e-mail address. For example:

```
From: writer@first.book.com (Book Writer)
```

How do I tell Eudora where and how to send my mail?

Now, Eudora knows who you are but not where to get your mail.

You need an SMTP (Simple Mail Transfer Protocol) server. Without an SMTP server, POP can receive mail, but not send it. Your POP server may not even be a computer you have an account on, but it could be the computer you've got your POP account on. Put the SMTP server's name in the box next to SMTP Server. Otherwise, put the name of the computer that will be your SMTP server here. If you're not sure what computer your SMTP server will be, ask your service provider. In the case of our example, the SMTP server is a different computer:

pop.book.com

How do I get replies to my mail sent somewhere else?

Sometimes the arrangement you have with your service provider means you tell the POP server your full e-mail address to send mail out, but people writing to you only need part of that address. For example, in our case people can send us e-mail by typing just **username@renaissoft.com** instead of typing in the entire e-mail address. In the POP Account field, we have to fill in **username@davinci.renaissoft.com** or **username@catherine.renaissoft.com**, depending on which computer we'll be working from. The difference is that davinci and catherine are the names of specific computers, while renaissoft.com is the name of our site.

Say for example we have a few computers networked together: elgreco.renaissoft.com, davinci.renaissoft.com, and catherine.renaissoft.com. If someone writes to us at renaissoft.com, we'll see that mail no matter which one of those computers we're using.

However, if someone sends e-mail specifically to elgreco.renaissoft.com, it would only show up on that computer. If we checked our mail on davinci or catherine, we wouldn't see it.

Fine tuning Eudora to work best for you

The last few sections showed you the essential information you need to tell Eudora for it to run. With that information entered, you can now use Eudora.

But, you may find that as it comes out of the box, Eudora doesn't work the way you want it to. Maybe you want to have Eudora automatically check your mail for you at a preset interval, like once an hour. Or maybe you don't like the default font. Whatever the case is, chances are you can customize it; the remainder of this section will show you how.

❶ (Tip)

> You don't *have* to read anything in the rest of this chapter. Eudora will work fine without changing any of these settings. In fact, you may find that the best thing to do *is* to go on to another chapter, like chapter 9, "Sending E-mail," and get started using Eudora. When you find something you want to change, you can always refer back to this chapter to find out how.

How do I tell Eudora to check my mail once an hour?

You don't have to be around to make sure Eudora checks your mail. You can tell the program how often to dial in. Just leave it running and leave your computer on, and it'll take care of fetching your new mail.

Make this change in the Configuration dialog box. There's a box with Check for Mail Every on the left and Minute(s) on the right. If you want Eudora to check your mail once an hour, type **60** in the box. If you want it more or less often, just change that number.

How do I tell Eudora where to look for people?

Eudora has two ways of looking people up. The first method uses something called **Finger**, and the second method uses **Ph** servers. Finger talks to the computer where the person you're looking up has his account, while Ph uses a database of Internet users.

Both of these commands are available by going to the Window menu and selecting the Ph option. Figure 6.8 shows you what the Ph window looks like.

Fig. 6.8
The Ph Window.

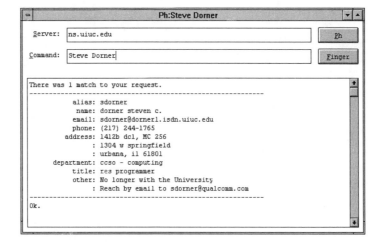

Finger

Finger is a program many people on the Internet have access to. Using it shows you the last time the person you're Fingering logged in and if they have unread mail. Not all service providers allow people to Finger their users, but most do.

To use Finger, fill in the person's service provider in the Server box, for example, **davinci.renaissoft.com**. Also fill in the person's userid in the Command box, such as **dee@davinci.renaissoft.com**. Eudora then connects to your service provider and executes the Finger command.

**{Note}**_____ | If you know the specific computer the person you're looking for uses, include that in the Server address. Finger usually only contacts one specific computer.

(Tip)_____ | If you only enter the person's userid into the Command box (for example, dee), Finger uses what's in the Server box (for example, davinci.renaissoft.com) as the domain of the userid. This saves a little typing.

Figure 6.9 shows you what the output from Finger can look like.

Fig. 6.9
Example results
from Finger.

```
┌─────────────────────────────────────────────────────────┐
│  ─          Finger:thag@unix1.netaxs.com          ▼ ▲    │
│  Server:  mindlink.net                          [  Ph  ] │
│                                                          │
│  Command: thag@unix1.netaxs.com                 [Finger] │
│  ──────────────────────────────────────────────────── ▲ │
│  Login name: thag              In real life: Jonathan Acheson│
│  Directory: /home/thag         Shell: /bin/csh          │
│  Last login Thu Jan 12 09:38 on ttyp2 from annex-836-4355│
│  Mail last read Sat Jan 14 13:13:08 1995                │
│  No Plan.                                               │
│                                                       ▼ │
└─────────────────────────────────────────────────────────┘
```

How do I change the size of my message window?

You're not stuck with Eudora's default window size. If you want to change them to better fit your screen, go for it!

This setting is in the Configuration dialog box. There are two settings that you can play with, window width and window height.

To change the width of your message window, go to the box next to Message Width. The default is 80 characters, which is pretty standard across the Internet. In this example, leave the screen width at the default.

To change the height of your message window, go to the box next to Message Lines. The default is 20 lines. There's no real standard on the Internet for this, but it's often around 24 or 25 lines. Just choose a height that's comfortable for your screen. In this example, change the window height to 24 lines by typing **24** in the box next to Message Lines.

To change the size of the tabs, go to the box labeled Tab Stops. The default is 8 characters. For this example, change that to **5**.

How do I change the fonts?

You're also not stuck with fonts or font sizes that Eudora uses by default.

Again, these options are in the Configuration dialog box.

To change the font you'll see on the screen, select the box next to Screen Font. A small dialog box appears. Select the font you want, or leave it alone. In this example, leave the font as is.

Figure 6.10 shows the commercial version's Configuration dialog box with the font list open.

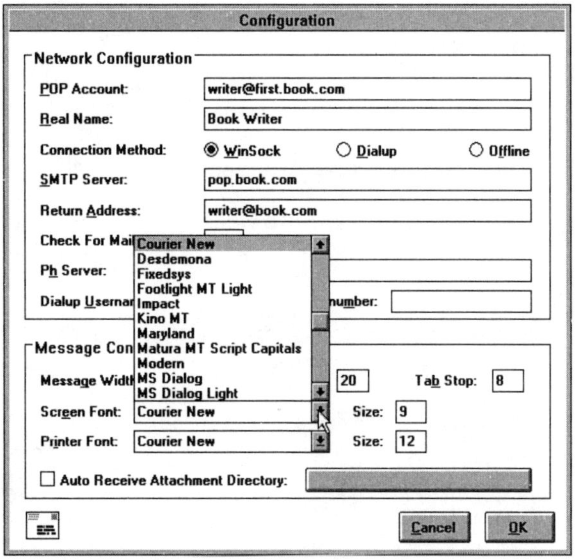

Fig. 6.10
Font List dialog box in Configuration dialog box.

To change the size of the font on your screen, click the box next to Size and enter the size you want, or use the combo box to select a number. This size is in points. You may need to experiment to find a size you're comfortable with. In this example, leave the font size as is.

To change the font you'll print out your mail in, click the box next to Printer Font. Just like when you changed your screen font, a combo box appears. Choose your new font, or leave it alone. In this example, leave the font as is.

To change the size of the font your printer will use, click the box next to Size and enter the size you want, or use the combo box to select a new number. This size is also in points. In this example, leave the font size as is.

How do I automatically save attachments?

It's possible to have the attachments that come with your e-mail automatically saved to a folder of your choosing. This means that you don't have to deal with them as soon as you receive them.

To do this, do the following:

1 Select Special, Configuration.

2 Select Auto Receive Attachment Directory.

3 Select the bar next Auto Receive Attachment Directory. Figure 6.11 shows an example of the dialog box that will appear.

Fig. 6.11
The Select Auto
Receive Directory
dialog box.

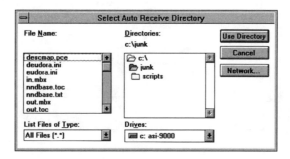

4 Scroll through the directories, choose the directory to which you want to save attachments.

5 With the directory you chose open, select Use Directory. In this example, we chose c:\eudora.

How do I tell Eudora how I want to write my mail?

There are several word processing features you can turn on or off. These are in the Switches dialog box.

①(Tip)

Remember, you open the Switches dialog box by choosing Special, Switches.

One option that's useful to select is May use QP.

❷Q&A

What is QP and how is it used?

QP means Quoted Printable encoding. QP only applies to attachments. It's useful if you have a text document with really long lines or special characters (say, international characters).

Another nice option to select is Word Wrap. This makes sure Eudora acts like a word processor instead of a typewriter. When you're in the middle of a word and get to the end of a line, that word goes down to the next line and stays in one piece.

Finally, another option you can use is Tabs in Body. This means that you can use the Tab key to indent lines. It's a great option, and it's a good idea to leave this one selected, as it is by default. After all, it also determines what Eudora will do with the tabs that come in the mail you receive.

How do I keep copies of the mail I send out?

It's a great idea to keep copies of e-mail you send to other people. It's awful to have to ask someone what you told them before.

In the Switches dialog box, select Keep Copies. Copies of all of the mail you send out will go to the Out mailbox. If you turn it off, all copies of outgoing mail will go to the Trash.

How do I tell Eudora to always add my signature to my mail?

It's tedious to have to keep adding your .sig manually. You can set Eudora to always add it. Keep in mind, though, that you don't always want to send your .sig if you have personal information in it.

In the Switches dialog box, select Use Signature if you want to always attach your .sig.

How do I tell Eudora who I want to reply to with group mail?

There are several ways to handle replies to group mail. You can reply to just the person who sent the mail to the group, you can reply to all of the group except for yourself, or you can reply to the entire group including yourself.

If you want to reply to everyone in the group except for yourself, select Reply to All.

(Tip)

> If you want to shut this option off or turn it on for just one note here and there, just hold down the Option key while you click Reply for that note. If you do this, for just that note Eudora will act like you've either turned the option on or shut it off, whatever's the opposite of what you've got in your settings.

Another item that you can select is Include Self. If it's selected and you reply to a group, you're also replying to yourself because you're in that group. If it's off, Eudora ignores the fact that you're in the group and only replies to the rest of the group.

How do I tell Eudora to always send my text attachments as attachments instead of putting them inside my e-mail?

If you try to use a text file as an attachment, Eudora will add it inside the body of your e-mail. If you select Always as Attachments, Eudora will treat the text file as an attachment, encoding and sending it as a separate document just like it does with all other attachments.

How do I tell Eudora to always assume the same kind of encoding for my attachments?

On the Internet, Uuencoding is the most popular form of encoding, so you may simply want to select Uuencode. If you write to a lot of MIME users, selecting MIME is a good idea. If you send to a lot of Mac users, select BinHex.

If you would rather be able to decide on the encoding process with each attachment you send, make sure none of these three options (MIME, BinHex, or Uuencode) are selected.

You also can teach Eudora your password so that you don't have to type it in all of the time; this is done in the Save Password box.

> If other people can use your PC, using the Save Password option also means they can read your mail and send messages out using your account. This is very, very bad. Only use this if your computer is in a place where other people can't use it.

Another option you can set in the Switches window is Easy Delete. Selecting this option stops Eudora from asking you if you really want to delete something. Don't select this unless you rarely make mistakes when you're deleting mail.

Telling Eudora what to do with the mail on your server

There are a few more things you can configure to make Eudora's mail checks more automated.

In the Switches dialog box, the first thing you should look at is Leave Mail on Server. This isn't generally something you want to select; if selected, Eudora will dial in and get your mail, but will not delete it from the POP server.

⊛ {Note}_____ Be careful when using the Leave Mail on Server option. If you leave too much mail behind, you can use up the disk space you're allowed by your service provider. Some service providers will just charge you more for the extra disk space, some won't accept any new mail for you, and some will just delete any old mail you have sitting around.

Skip Big Messages is another option you can consider. If you have a slow connection or modem, select this option and Eudora will only grab the first few lines of large text messages, letting you decide whether you want to download them later.

⊛ {Note}_____ Eudora considers a large text message to be 40K or larger.

⊗ <Caution>___ Eudora does need some help from your POP server to do this. Eudora expects the POP server to add a Status: header after it has downloaded the first few lines of the message so that it knows when to stop. If your POP server doesn't provide it, then this option won't work and you'll just download everything, regardless of size. If you're not sure what your POP server offers, ask your service provider.

Deciding when to send your mail

Eudora gives you much flexibility in choosing when to send your messages.

One choice is the Send on Check option. This tells Eudora to go ahead and send any waiting mail while it's dialed in to check for new mail. This is a useful option to select. If this option is selected, the button in the upper-right of your composition window will say Queue instead of Send.

If you select Immediate Send, Eudora will dial in whenever you click the Send button. If this option is selected, the button in the upper right of your composition window will say Send instead of Queue.

Remember to select only one of these two options.

How do I make sure most people can read my attachments? (commercial version only)

If you're not careful, a lot of people will get your attachments but not be able to do anything with them.

In the Switches dialog box, click the Fix Curly Quotes box to select this option. If you tend to write mostly to MIME users, it's not necessary, but if you write to people who read your attachments using something other than MIME, it's a good option to select.

How do I get Eudora to alert me about new mail or problems?

Eudora needs to know how to get your attention when it needs help or wants to give you news about what's going on.

If you select the Alert check box, Eudora uses an alert to tell you that you have new mail.

If you select the Sound option, Eudora makes one noise when it wants to tell you that you have new mail, and a different noise when it wants your attention for something else.

How do I tell Eudora to automatically put my new mail in the In mailbox?

Eudora needs to know where you want your new mail. Eudora will ask you what to do with it every time, unless you tell it where you always want it placed.

In the Switches dialog box, select the Open In Mailbox option if you want your new mail to just go into your In mailbox. Eudora will then let you go to the first new message and start reading from there.

How do I set up what arrow keys I want to use?

It's great to be able to just move around with your arrow keys if you don't have room on your desk for your mouse.

Go to the Switches dialog box. If you turn the Plain Arrows option on and have a message window open, you can use the arrow keys on the IBM (or IBM compatible) keyboard to close the current message and open the next or previous one. Table 6.1 lists what each arrow key does. If this option is off, you can use the arrow keys to move the insertion point in messages.

Table 6.1 Arrow Key Functions

Key	Function
up	opens previous message
down	opens next message
right	opens next message
left	opens previous message

 The arrow keys won't switch messages if you have a message composition window at the top of your screen. This is true even if you're using the Plain Arrows option.

If you select the Ctrl+Arrows option, you can use the arrow keys to switch messages only when holding down the Ctrl key. The keys and functions are the same as in table 6.1. This allows you to use the arrow keys normally to move the insertion point in your message.

 You can use the Ctrl+Arrow keys option even when composition windows are open on the screen.

How do I make sure Eudora always shows me full headers?

If you're curious about the routes e-mail takes as it zips through the Internet, you can find out by looking at the full mail headers. Go to the Switches dialog box and select the Show All Headers option. When this option is selected, Eudora will show the full header, including routing information, each time it opens a message.

How do I manage my mail windows?

If you have a bunch of windows opened up at once, it gets a bit confusing trying to sort through them.

In the Switches dialog box, selecting the Zoom Windows option means that new mailboxes and message windows open to their zoomed sizes.

{Note}

> The **zoomed size** for a mailbox window is just as wide as it needs to be to show the widest summary, and just long enough to show all of the summaries.
>
> The zoomed size for a message window is as wide as it's set to be in the Configuration dialog box, and just long enough to display the entire message.
>
> The zoomed size for a composition window is just as wide and high as it's set to be in the Configuration dialog box.
>
> A zoomed window will never be longer than the actual screen.

How do I close all messages from a single mailbox at once?

When you've been mucking about with mail for a while, it takes a while to close each and every message, one by one.

If the Mailbox Superclose option in the Switches dialog box is selected, closing a mailbox window closes every open message from that mailbox.

How do I tell Eudora to empty the Trash as I quit the program?

It's nice to be able to just not deal with mail anymore when you're done with Eudora. This includes having to go empty the Trash when you've finally finished.

If the Empty Trash on Quit option in the Switches dialog box is selected, Eudora empties the Trash mailbox when you quit the program.

(Tip)

> You can just delete some of the messages. Highlight the summaries you want to delete and then open the Message menu and choose Delete.

How do I tell Eudora to open the next message when I'm done with the current one?

If the Easy Open option in the Switches dialog box is selected, deleting or transferring the current message opens the next unread message in your mailbox.

How do I tell Eudora to show me what's happening while it's connecting?

It's a good idea to be able to watch what's going on while Eudora is dialing in and sending/receiving mail.

If the Show Progress option in the Switches dialog box is selected, Eudora displays a Progress window at the top of your screen. This window advises you of the progress it's making while it makes its network connection, transfers mail, or does some other process that takes a while.

Connecting with Eudora

If you have access to
MacTCP (Macintosh) or a
Winsock client (Windows)
and a SLIP or PPP
account, using Eudora
becomes virtually painless.

In this chapter:

- How to connect to a network
- Using Eudora for a dial-up connection
- Should I upgrade from a shell account to SLIP or PPP?
- Using a UUCP connection
- Testing your setup

Now that you've got Eudora installed and configured, you're probably just itching to take her for a test drive on the Information Superhighway. All you need to know now is where to find yourself an "on-ramp"—a connection to the Internet.

Connecting with SLIP/PPP or to a network

If you have access to MacTCP (Macintosh) or a Winsock client (Windows) and a SLIP or PPP account with a local service provider, you're in luck—Eudora was designed for just such a connection. If you have installed MacTCP or Winsock on your machine and configured it for use with your service provider (as described in chapters 5 and 6), using Eudora becomes virtually painless. Likewise, if you're lucky enough to have a dedicated line connecting your computer to the Internet (as part of your company's network, for example), you can use Eudora without any fuss at all.

In any of these cases, all Eudora needs from you are the particulars for accessing your service provider's POP3 and SMTP servers. By setting these within the Configuration dialog box, you should be all set. See "Configuring Eudora" in chapter 5, "Installing Eudora on a Macintosh," or chapter 6, "Installing Eudora on Windows," for more on the Configuration dialog.

If your account is all set up, you are ready to connect by following these steps:

1 Connect to your service provider by using your Winsock or MacTCP.

2 After the connection is made and you are logged in to your account, start Eudora.

3 If you have Eudora configured to automatically check for mail at regular intervals, it will prompt you for your password when you start. If you want to check your mail, enter your password. Otherwise choose Cancel. See "How do I tell Eudora to check my mail once an hour?" in chapter 5 (Macintosh) or 6 (Windows) for more details about this setting.

Eudora is now running and ready for your command.

Dialing in

Perhaps the most inexpensive way to use Eudora on the Internet is to use your modem to dial into a shell account on a UNIX or VMS system. Shell accounts are generally the least expensive form of Internet access, and while Eudora prefers to have better access than this, some provisions have been made to help those who can't afford or obtain a SLIP/PPP connection.

 **{Note}** The dial-up features of Eudora are not present in the Windows freeware (1.4) version.

If your Eudora distribution did not come with the files "Direct UNIX Navs" and "srialpop.shar", you can obtain these files from Qualcomm's FTP site, **ftp.qualcomm.com** in the directory /mac/eudora/dialup. You'll also find navigation files there for popular service providers such as Netcom, the Well, and so on.

A dial-up connection to your service provider has to give Eudora access to a POP3 server (from which it can get your incoming mail) and an SMTP server (to which it can send your outgoing mail). Since this is awkward to do from the shell prompt, Eudora tries to use the shell's Telnet command to reach these servers more directly.

Unfortunately, to use this dial-up type of connection on the Mac, you have to use ResEdit to properly configure Eudora. On the Windows side, you'll need to understand some fairly complex scripting (programming) commands to get the configuration right.

So, we recommend that you get a SLIP/PPP account and use Eudora that way. It's easier to configure MacTCP or Winsock to work with your provider and you'll find the service to be a much better value. If you absolutely must use a shell account, the versions of Eudora that support this feature cover this setup in their documentation.

Upgrading from a shell account to SLIP or PPP

If you have a shell account through a service provider, you should consider upgrading to a SLIP or PPP account. Having direct SLIP/PPP service will allow you better access to other parts of the Internet, such as the World Wide Web, Gopher, and FTP, which are much easier to use in a SLIP/PPP setting.

Fierce competition among service providers has driven down the price of a SLIP/PPP account to the point where, in most major cities in the U.S., SLIP/PPP accounts cost only a few dollars a month more than a shell account does. For example, in Indianapolis, where Que is located, a shell account costs $10/month and a SLIP/PPP account is only $15/month, both with a generous number of hours included and a low hourly cost after that.

Using a UUCP connection

Another popular way to connect to the Internet is via **UUCP**, a system in which your computer dials up your service provider at regular intervals to pick up any new incoming mail and send out any outgoing mail. Eudora can be made to work via UUCP with a few minor adjustments.

Whether you use a Macintosh or Windows system, the place to start is the Settings dialog box (see figs. 7.1 and 7.2).

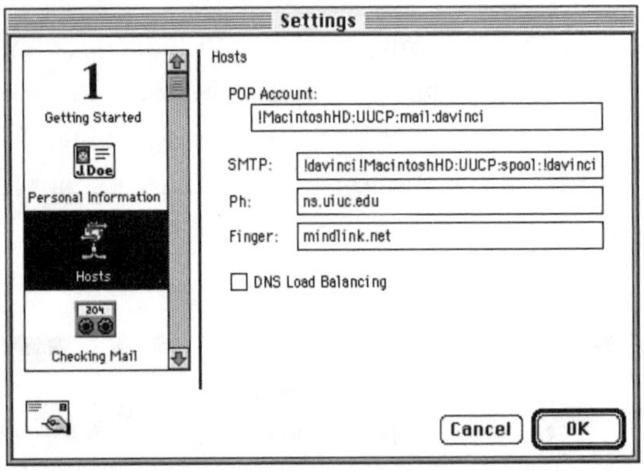

Fig. 7.1

Configuring Eudora for UUCP on Macintosh systems.

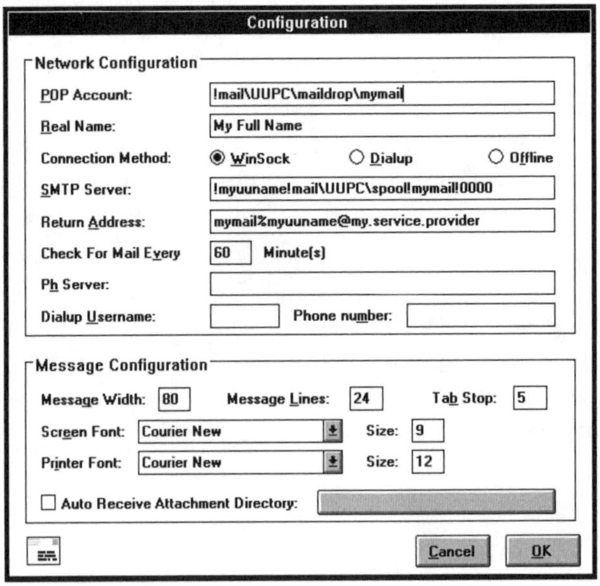

Fig. 7.2

Configuring Eudora for UUCP on Windows systems.

In place of your POP Account, you'll want to enter the full path to your UUCP mail drop, which is simply the file where your UUCP program stores your incoming mail. You have to start the path name with an exclamation point (!) to show Eudora that this isn't an ordinary POP account.

The Connection Method field only matters if you still want to use SMTP and/or POP to transfer mail. If you intend to rely solely on UUCP to move your mail for you, you can ignore this setting.

The SMTP Server field is a little more complicated if you want to send outgoing mail by UUCP. The format must adhere to the following:

!<UUCP name>!<UUCP dir>!<user name>!0000

The <UUCP name> is the UUCP name by which your computer is known to the outside world.

The <UUCP dir> is the full path to the spool directory where the UUCP program stores its outgoing mail.

The <user name> is your name, as you're known to your computer. If you have a UUCP system set up, your computer can be home to many different users, each of which can receive personal mail.

The Return Address field must contain your complete UUCP mail address if you want to receive mail by UUCP.

Last, it should be noted that the Leave Mail on Server option doesn't work under UUCP, so you might as well turn it off (though leaving it on is harmless, but potentially confusing).

Testing, testing,...1,2,3...

One of the most frustrating aspects of setting up a new e-mail connection can be trying to figure out what the problem is when nothing works at all. If you made some mistakes during the installation and configuration steps, you might not get any feedback at all when you try to connect to your service provider—not even a trite error message. This can make it extremely difficult to fix the problem or get help from others.

Fortunately, there are some simple tests you can perform to make sure your system is set up properly, and to try to isolate the source of the problems you might be having.

Write yourself a letter

Most people don't realize they can send themselves e-mail, just as they can send themselves postal mail. If you address the e-mail to yourself and send it out, you'll be performing a pretty good test of your Eudora setup. To send the mail out, Eudora has to use your service provider's SMTP server, which should deposit the mail in your server's mailbox to be picked up the next time you check your mail. This tests Eudora's ability to talk to your POP3 server. In short, if you get your own piece of mail back, you can be pretty confident that Eudora's working the way it should.

If, on the other hand, your mail gets returned to you with some sort of mailer error message attached to it, this suggests a problem with the SMTP (outgoing) portion of your configuration. The POP3 (incoming) portion is working fine, because the error message was properly delivered to you. Take a look at your SMTP server information in the Settings dialog box and make sure it's correct.

If you receive no message at all, chances are you've got a problem with your POP3 (incoming) configuration. In truth, you could also be experiencing problems with your SMTP (outgoing) configuration, but that's a moot point if you can't receive any mail! Deal with the problems one step at a time and make sure your POP3 configuration is set properly before you mess with the SMTP stuff.

If you're having trouble getting the SMTP or POP3 service to work, your best resort is to contact your service provider and ask what addresses you should be using to access their services. You'll find that the initial hassle of getting things configured is well worth it in the long run, when you don't have to do anything more than press a button to send and receive mail.

Start up a conversation

If you know someone else who has an Internet e-mail address, you can use him as a "sounding board" for your mail problems. Send him some short notes asking him to quote the entire letter back to you in his reply. That way the letter you get back from him will show you exactly what he received.

If your problems are serious and you're not even sure the mail reached him, exchange phone numbers and give each other a call whenever you send out a piece of e-mail, letting the other party know that something's on its way. If nothing arrives within a few hours (at the latest!), you can be pretty sure your mail is orbiting Saturn.

Now if you discover that you can *receive* mail but not send mail, your problem lies with your SMTP server configuration, so check the Configuration dialog box.

Examine your mail headers

Once you've got mail working, you might still want to have a look at the full mail headers you find on incoming mail, particularly in letters that are replies to your own mail. In particular, take note of the return addresses in the headers and make sure they're accurate. If they've been altered by mail programs along the way (such as, your e-mail address shows up differently in the replies than it was in your original note), you should point this out to your service provider, who should be "interested" in this phenomenon.

8 Staying Informed

Qualcomm has several ways for you to keep up with the new versions of their software.

Qualcomm has several ways for you to keep up with what they're doing. After all, they'll be making new versions of their software and they want you to know about them.

Why subscribing to announcement mailing lists is a good idea

Announcement mailing lists don't send you a lot of e-mail, but what they do send is something you probably wanted to know. In the case of announcement mailing lists dedicated to software products, it's a great way to keep up with what the current versions of the program are. Why use an old version of a program when newer versions generally have new features?

Subscribing to the product announcements mailing lists

Due to the vast increase in Eudora use, both commercial and freeware, Qualcomm will no longer be able to offer technical support to freeware users via e-mail. They are not abandoning the users of the freeware versions, though, and instead have created mailing lists for freeware users to join and discuss problems among themselves. We speak from experience when we say that this is an effective way to solve technical problems.

Qualcomm offers a mailing list for commercial product announcements as well, and will most likely offer other lists in the future.

To get up-to-date information on where to write to join the various mailing lists available through Qualcomm, write to **eudora-info@qualcomm.com** as discussed in the section, "General info."

Questions

There are also ways to get general information on Eudora and ask questions through e-mail.

General info

A useful thing to get is the general information file available from Qualcomm. This file will give you the latest information on how to get help, how to order the commercial version, and how to order the spelling checker.

To get this information, send e-mail to

eudora-info@qualcomm.com

The subject and body of the e-mail aren't important.

❷Q&A

How will I get the information I want without typing in a request?

When you send e-mail to Eudora-info, you're writing to a computer program that knows to send the information file to you. It just sees that you sent it mail and sends you back the information file, assuming that's what you wanted.

Sales

You can also get product literature from Qualcomm through e-mail.

To get this information, send e-mail to

majordomo@qualcomm.com

No subject is necessary for this note. In the body, put **index quest_marketing.**

What you will get back is a note containing a list of marketing packets in different file formats (for example, Postscript, Microsoft Word format). Once you've decided on the format you want, send another piece of e-mail to

majordomo@qualcomm.com

No subject is needed, as usual. In the body, type **get quest_marketing <name of file you want to retrieve with full path>.**

For example:

get quest_marketing mac/Eudora2Info-CG.sea.hqx

❋{Note}

This e-mail address is also a computer. Sending e-mail to this address tells the computer at the other end to send you a Eudora information packet.

❶(Tip)

To talk to a live sales representative at Qualcomm, you can send e-mail to **eudora-rep@qualcomm.com**.

Hotline

There are several ways to get help with problems you may have with Eudora. These are:

- This book. If you're having a problem with trying to do something in Eudora, find the section in the book dealing with what you want to do and make sure that you're following all of the steps correctly. Often, the problems most of us have with running computer programs turn out to be caused by omitting a period somewhere, or forgetting a step.

- Manuals. This book and the manuals that come with Eudora aren't identical. There may be something in the manuals that points you in the right direction for getting your problem solved.

- README files. README files sometimes contain information that isn't in the manuals because it was included at the last minute, or suggestions of how to deal with common problems.

- Other files available through Qualcomm's FTP site. This is discussed later in this section.

- The hotline. The cavalry is there to help you.

(Tip)

> If you do all of these things, in order, you're more likely to get your questions answered as fast as you want them to be. Also, if you've tried all of these things, the people at Qualcomm will be able to narrow down what's wrong. After all, you'll be able to give them a whole list of things that worked and didn't work.

To write to the hotline, send e-mail to

eudora-hotline@qualcomm.com

Once again, this e-mail will be read by a person.

Bugs

Software is rarely perfect. Qualcomm provides a way to report problems you think might be bugs in their programs. After all, if there's something wrong, they will want to fix it as soon as possible.

To report a bug, send e-mail to the hotline. You should write down these things before calling to get faster answers:

- What you were doing when you encountered the bug

- What happened when the bug occurred

- Which version of Eudora you are using

- What the error messages were, especially the numbers in the brackets, for example {5}

- What kind of computer you have

- What version of the system software you use (for example, System 7.1 for the Mac? Windows 3.1 for the IBM?)

- Anything else that might help Qualcomm understand what happened

Getting files from Qualcomm's FTP site

Eudora also allows you to FTP to their site and download files of various kinds. Qualcomm's FTP site is

ftp.qualcomm.com

If you use a Macintosh system, go to the /quest/mac directory. If you use a Microsoft Windows system, go to the /quest/windows directory.

From there you've got lots of options. The directory you're in has information files you can fetch.

The Eudora directory (/quest/mac/eudora or /quest/windows/eudora) contains freeware versions of Eudora as well as the freeware manuals in various formats.

There are also items at this FTP site that can help you set up servers, set up for dialup access (such as Trumpet Winsock for Windows), customize Eudora even more than before, and much more. As these directories change on a regular basis, the best thing to do is to take some time and go through them.

Qualcomm's World Wide Web site

Qualcomm also has a WWW site. You can find it at

http://www.qualcomm.com/quest/QuestMail.html

This site contains product information and newsletters from Qualcomm.

Part III:

Using Eudora

9

Sending E-mail

Once you're done composing your message, are you ready to send it?

Now that you're all set up, we'll show you how to actually use Eudora. When there are differences among the various versions, we'll give you screen shots of all of them (Mac freeware, Mac commercial, Windows freeware, and Windows commercial).

Composing the message

Before you can send a message out, of course, you have to write it. And before the message can get where it's going, you have to address it.

The Composition Window

You'll write your message in the Composition Window. These figures show you what the Composition Window will look like in the Macintosh and Windows versions of Eudora.

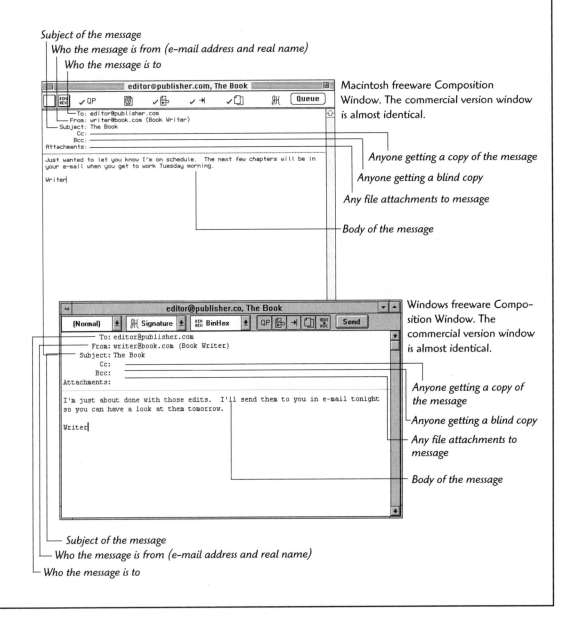

Subject of the message
  Who the message is from (e-mail address and real name)
    Who the message is to

Macintosh freeware Composition Window. The commercial version window is almost identical.

Anyone getting a copy of the message

Anyone getting a blind copy

Any file attachments to message

Body of the message

Windows freeware Composition Window. The commercial version window is almost identical.

Anyone getting a copy of the message

Anyone getting a blind copy

Any file attachments to message

Body of the message

Subject of the message
Who the message is from (e-mail address and real name)
Who the message is to

! *(Tip)* _____ | If your e-mail address doesn't show up in the From: line of your mail, check over your configuration settings again.

To open this windows choose <u>M</u>essage, <u>N</u>ew Message.

* *{Note}* _____ | The underlined letters in the commands in the previous paragraph are shortcuts for Windows users. Mac users don't have these. Throughout the book, we'll be using this convention to show this.

See the tearout card for quick key shortcuts.

The cursor in the composition window will be in the To: field. Type the e-mail address of the person you're writing to here. If you want to send your note to more than one person, you can put more than one address here. Each e-mail address has to be separated by a comma and then a space, for example **editor@book.com, publisher@book.com**.

X *<Caution>* _____ | You must use both a comma and a space between e-mail addresses. Otherwise, you'll get errors.

After entering the address, use the mouse or the Tab key to move to another field.

* *{Note}* _____ | You can't just press Return to add another e-mail address to your list in the Composition Window.

The next field you need to fill in is the Subject: field. Type the subject of your note here. The person who gets your note will see your e-mail ID and the subject of the note before he actually reads it, so it's up to you whether to put something meaningful, silly, or completely unrelated to your note. Also, if you don't put any subject in, he won't have any idea what the note's about. It all depends on what your note is about and who it's to. It's good to keep the subject pretty short because different mail programs allow different subject lengths to be read. If your subject is long, the person you send it to may only be able to see half of it.

The next field is the Cc: field. If you want to send a carbon copy to someone, this is where you put that person's e-mail address. You don't have to put anything in this field. If you want to put more than one e-mail address here, type it the same way you would type multiple addresses in the To: field. The person you wrote to originally can see who the mail was copied to.

The next field is the Bcc: field. (Bcc stands for Blind Carbon Copy.) If you want to send a carbon copy to someone but don't want the original recipient to know you did it, put the address(es) you want to copy to here. You can use more than one here as well.

The next field is the actual body of the letter. Here's where you type your actual message. If Word Wrap is on, you don't need to press Return at the end of every line. (You can tell if Word Wrap is on by looking at the icon shown in figure 9.1. In the Mac version, "on" is indicated by a checkmark. In Windows, the button will be pressed in for "on.")

Fig. 9.1
This shows Word Wrap on in the Mac version.

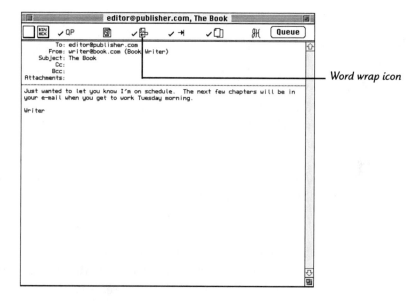

Word wrap icon

Once you're done typing in your message, the mail is ready and you can send it. You can also go back and edit it, add file attachments (which are discussed later in this chapter), change the recipients, the subject, or anything else.

Sending it out

Now you have the message typed and you are ready to send it. There are a few different ways you can send your messages out.

Sending immediately

If you want to send your message immediately, be sure the Immediate Send option is selected and then choose <u>M</u>essage, Send Immediately or click the Send button. The Immediate Send option is covered in chapter 5 (Macintosh) and chapter 6 (Windows).

 **{Note}** If you didn't select the Immediate Send option, Queue for Delivery appears in the <u>M</u>essage menu instead of Send Immediately.

Queueing messages

You can also queue a group of messages to send out later. To do this, the Immediate Send option must be off. If this is so, then every time you finish with a message and select Queue or Queue for Delivery, the message is queued up and waiting to actually be sent. If you're done writing your e-mail and want to send it all out, just select Send Queued Messages from the File menu.

If you want to set Eudora to send queued messages when it dials in to check mail, select the Send on Check option in the Switches dialog.

Timed messages

Instead of sending the messages yourself, you can just leave them in the Queue and have Eudora dial in at specific times. This feature is useful especially if your service provider charges different amounts for different times of day, or if you have to pay toll/long distance charges to connect to your service provider. Using timed messages could allow you to only automatically check messages at the times when the connect rates/phone rates are lowest.

You can set a time for a specific message to be sent by either opening the message or selecting its summary in the Out mailbox, and then selecting "Change Queueing" from the Message menu. The dialog box is shown in figures 9.2 and 9.3.

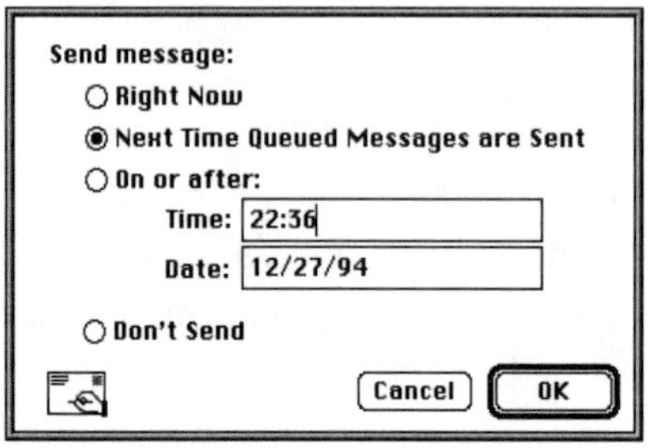

Fig. 9.2
The Macintosh Change Queueing dialog box.

Send message:
- ○ Right Now
- ◉ Next Time Queued Messages are Sent
- ○ On or after:
  - Time: 22:36
  - Date: 12/27/94
- ○ Don't Send

[Cancel] [OK]

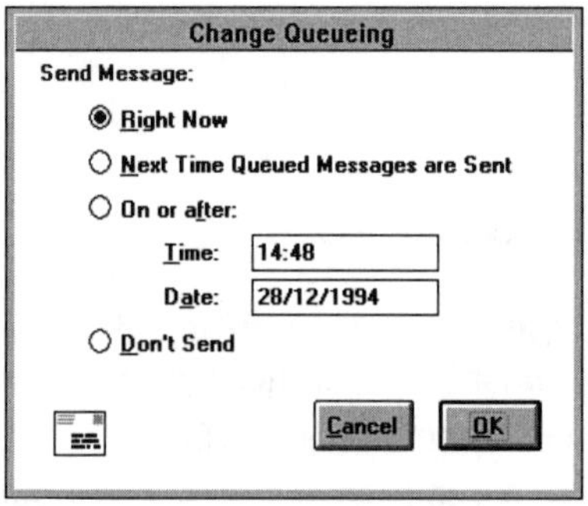

Fig. 9.3
The Windows Change Queueing dialog box.

Change Queueing

Send Message:
- ◉ Right Now
- ○ Next Time Queued Messages are Sent
- ○ On or after:
  - Time: 14:48
  - Date: 28/12/1994
- ○ Don't Send

[Cancel] [OK]

If you want to send your message immediately, select Right Now. If you want it to go with the other queued messages, select Next Time Queued Messages are Sent. If you want to select the exact time and date it goes out, select "On or after" and fill in the Time and Date boxes. Or, you can cancel the message by selecting Don't Send.

 **{Note}**

Cancelling a message doesn't erase it. Instead, it saves it in your Out mailbox so you can try to send it again later. It's just like using the Save As option.

Selecting message priority

You can also set the priority of your messages.

Why a priority message?

A priority message doesn't go out any faster than any other message. However, it's marked so the person you sent it to knows how urgent or not urgent it is. That way, if she has a lot of mail, she knows to read your message quickly or that it can wait if she has something important to tend to.

 {Note}  | Message priorities are only useful when writing to other Eudora users. People who don't use Eudora won't see the priorities.

Setting priority

At the top left of the Composition Window is the Priority Pop-Up Menu icon. When you click this icon and hold the mouse button down, you get the Priority Pop-up Menu. This menu is shown in figures 9.4 and 9.5.

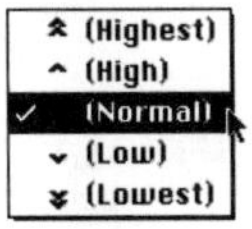

Fig. 9.4
The Macintosh Priority
Pop-up Menu.

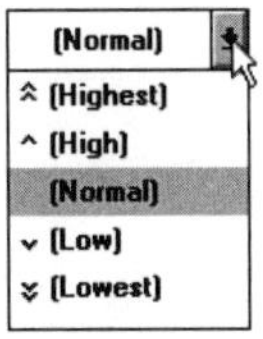

Fig. 9.5
The Windows Priority
Pop-up Menu.

Now, all you do is drag the mouse to the priority level you want to assign.

Editing a mail message

You're finished composing your message, but do you want to send it? If you don't, you can save it for now and edit and send it later. To do this, go to the Save menu and select File. Now, you can close the Composition Window by selecting Close from the File menu or by double-clicking in the little white box in the upper-left corner of the window. When you want to go back to the note later, it will be waiting in the Out mailbox to be sent or deleted.

The following editing features in Eudora are all in the Edit menu.

Turning off Word Wrap

If you want Eudora to work more like your shell text editor than a word processing program, click on the Word Wrap icon as shown in figure 9.3.

Moving text around

If you want to move a letter, word, or group of words around, use Cut and Paste.

1 Select the text you want to cut.

2 Select the Cut command.

3 Put the cursor where you want to move the text.

4 Select the Paste command.

 (Tip)

If you want to just get rid of something, only complete steps 1 and 2, but don't Paste it back in.

Copying blocks of text from one place to another

If you want to copy a block of text from one spot to another, you can do that too by using Copy and Paste.

1 Select the text you want to copy.

2 Select the Copy command.

3 Put the cursor where you want the text to go.

4 Select the Paste command.

Undoing a mistake

If you goof up when you're editing, and want to "take it back," select the Undo command.

Selecting all of the text

If you want to delete all of the body of your note, or perhaps copy all of it to the clipboard to paste into your word processing program, you can do this by selecting the Select All command.

Finding that cursor

Sometimes you need to jump around in the body of the current piece of e-mail but don't want to lose your place. If you leave your cursor where it is and go through the note, you can get back to your cursor by selecting the Show Insertion Point command.

Finding something in your note

Sometimes you're looking at a long, long note and just know that, somewhere in the body a particular item (for example, a meeting date) was mentioned that you want to see again. To do this:

1 Select the Find command.

2 Enter the piece of text you want to look for (for example, you know the meeting date was in October, so you enter **10**).

3 If the piece of text appears more than once, you can select Find Again from the Find submenu.

The Find command is covered in more detail in chapter 15, "Working with Mail."

Sending a message again

There are a few reasons you might want to send a message out that you've already sent out before.

Sending a message similar to the previous one

If you want to send out a note that's very similar to one you've sent already, do the following:

1 Select the message you want to use.

2 Go to the Message menu and select the Send Again command.

3 Edit the To: header and the body of the note and make any changes you want to make.

4 Select Send.

Sent the message before but never got an answer

E-mail does get lost out there occasionally. If you sent out something that you need an answer to, and never got one, you can resend it by doing the following:

1 Select the message you want to resend.

2 Go to the <u>M</u>essage menu and select the Send Again command.

3 Select Send.

 **{Note}** You could also open the message you want to resend, select Send, and close the note.

Resending a bounced message

Sometimes you get e-mail bounced back to you because you mistyped part of the address. To try it again, do the following:

1 Select the message you want to resend.

2 Go to the <u>M</u>essage menu and select the Send Again command.

3 Edit the e-mail address.

4 Select Send.

Nicknames

E-mail addresses can get long and complicated. Even seasoned users of e-mail and the Internet use nicknames. Nickname files are the electronic version of the little black address book.

What is a nickname?

A **nickname** is just a name you assign to an e-mail address so you don't have to type the whole thing out over and over, or memorize it. It's easy to think that you'll forget your friend's address pretty quickly if it's **dl9x8yy7@turquoise.east.widget.com**. However, if you assign the nickname **dawn** to it, there's no need to try to remember that mess. Even better, you don't have to worry about mistyping it!

❶ (Tip)

It's a good idea to keep a printed copy of your nickname list around that has each nickname and e-mail address in it. That way, if something happens to your nickname file, you don't have to worry about remembering the e-mail addresses of everyone you write to!

The Nicknames Window

To open the Nicknames Window, go to the Special menu in the Mac Freeware version, or the Windows menu in the Mac Commercial version, and select Nicknames.

Figures 9.6 and 9.7 show you what the Nicknames Window looks like in the different versions of Eudora.

Fig. 9.6
The Macintosh freeware and commercial version Nickname Window.

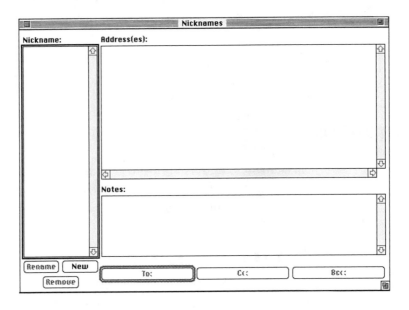

Fig. 9.7
The Windows freeware
and commercial version
Nickname Window.

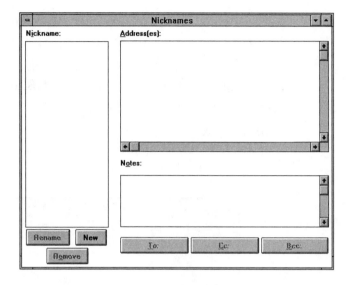

Adding new nicknames

1 To add a new nickname, first click the New box. The dialog box shown in figures 9.8 and 9.9 will appear.

Fig. 9.8
The Macintosh
Nickname Assignment
window.

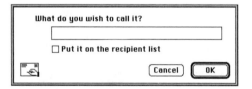

Fig. 9.9
The Windows Nick-
name Assignment
window.

2 In the box under "What do you wish to call it?," type the nickname you want to use.

3 If you want this nickname added to the Recipient List (which is discussed in the next section), put an X in the box next to "Put it on the recipient list." Otherwise, leave the box blank.

4 Press Return. The nickname is now highlighted and the cursor moves into the Address(es) box. Type the e-mail address the nickname belongs to here.

5 Pressing Tab will take you to the Notes box. Here you can add any notes about the person whose nickname you've just assigned.

6 To add more nicknames, click the New box and follow the same instructions again. Figure 9.10 shows you what a nickname list with a few entries in it looks like.

Fig. 9.10
A nickname list with some entries.

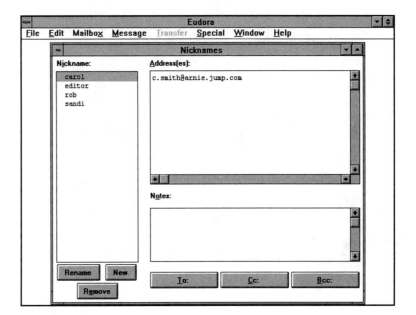

7 Once you're finished adding your nicknames, you can close the window to exit by clicking the small white box at the top left of the Nicknames Window. Figures 9.11 and 9.12 show you what you'll see as you exit.

Fig. 9.11
The Macintosh Nickname Save Changes window.

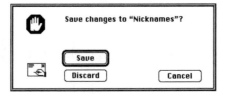

Fig. 9.12
The Windows Nickname Save Changes window.

Editing nicknames

1 Open the Nickname Window, click the nickname you want to change, and click the Rename box. You'll get the same window from figure 9.13 or 9.14, depending on whether you're using a Macintosh or Windows system.

2 Type the new nickname you want to use for that person.

3 If you want to edit the e-mail address for that nickname, highlight the nickname and use Tab, or use the mouse, and either replace or change the e-mail address you've got there.

4 If you want to edit the note for that nickname, use Tab or the mouse to select the note and then replace or edit it.

(Tip)

You can also select a nickname by using something called Type-to-Select. We'll demonstrate this method by giving you an example.

Let's say that you have a nickname list consisting of: Jack, Jill, Fred, and Barney. You want to write a note to Jill. Instead of clicking "Jill," you can type the letter J, which will select Jack because it comes before Jill alphabetically. Then, you type the letter I, which selects Jill, because it's the only nickname starting with JI.

Deleting nicknames

Open the Nickname Window and click the nickname you want to delete. Then, click the box labeled Remove. This deletes the nickname you selected.

Group nicknames

If you want to have one nickname belonging to a list of people, you can do that too. Instead of just stopping after typing the first e-mail address in the Address(es) window, put a comma after it (or press Return) and type the next, and continue until you're done.

Group nicknames are useful as very small mailing lists. When someone replies to a note you've sent out to the group, he can reply just to you or to the entire list of people.

Sending mail messages using nicknames

You can send mail using nicknames by just opening the Nicknames Window, selecting the nickname you want to write to, and clicking the To: box. The Nicknames Window will remain open behind the Composition Window. If you want to Cc or Bcc the note to someone, select the Nicknames Window again, select the person you want to Cc or Bcc to, and click the Cc: or Bcc: box. When you're done selecting, click the Composition Window.

You can do this in the reverse order too. If you've got a Message Window open, you can open the Nicknames Window and add a recipient to the message by selecting To:, Cc:, or Bcc:. This feature is nice if you forget at first that you need to copy the note you're working on to Phil and not just send it to Jane.

Making a nickname

When you add a nickname, you type everything into the Nicknames Window. When you make a nickname, though, you select things that already exist.

There are two different ways to make a nickname. First, you can make a nickname out of the e-mail address in a message you've received or sent before.

1 Open the mailbox the message is in.

2 Select the message.

3 Use the Make Nickname command.

4 The Nickname Assignment box will open so you can give the e-mail address the nickname you want it to have. If the message you're using is just something you received, the address from the From: header is assigned to the nickname. If it's something you sent, the addresses from the From:, Cc:, and Bcc: headers are used.

You can also make a group nickname this way by selecting several messages from several different people.

You can also use the Make Nickname command to make group nicknames without a lot of typing.

1 Open the Nicknames Window.

2 Hold down the Command key for Mac systems and click the nicknames you want to include in the new group nickname.

3 Then, go to the Special menu and select the command Make Nickname. The Nickname Assignment Window will open.

4 Enter the nickname for the group and click OK.

The Quick Recipient List

It's possible to avoid having to go to the Nicknames Window every time you want to send a message to someone you have a nickname for. This is especially useful for people you send a lot of e-mail to.

Using the Quick Recipient List

To use the Quick Recipient List, go to the Message menu and drag the mouse down to the New Message To command. A small box will appear with the nicknames you've got in your Quick Recipient List. Drag the mouse, still holding down the mouse button, to the nickname you want to send e-mail to. This will take you directly to the Composition Window with the To blank filled in.

Adding Quick Recipients

There are several easy ways to add someone to your Quick Recipient list. The easiest way is to open your Nicknames Window and double-click on the nickname you want to add. The bullet next to the nickname means that it has been added to the list.

You can also add an e-mail address from your Nicknames list instead of a nickname. All you have to do is open the Nicknames Window and select the e-mail address of the person you want to add. Then go up to the Special menu and select the Add as Recipient command.

If you have a piece of e-mail from someone but don't have a nickname for him, you can add him anyway. Open the note from the person you want to add, select the e-mail address from the note, and use the Add as Recipient command.

Deleting Quick Recipients

To remove someone from your Quick Recipient list, go to the Special menu and select the Remove Recipient command. Drag the mouse to the person you want to delete, and let go of the mouse button when that name or address is highlighted.

Attaching files to your messages

Now you're in the Attachments: field. If you want to attach something, such as a picture or a word processing document, do the following:

1 Go to the Message menu and select the Attach Document option.

2 A dialog box appears that lets you move through your folders until you locate the one containing the file you want to attach.

3 Select the file you want.

4 Choose OK.

If you create a folder for the documents you'll want to attach to your e-mail, you don't have to do so much searching through the folders on your hard drive.

Be aware that not all e-mail programs support attachments, so you may want to check with people before you send them to make sure they'll be able to use them. You can attach multiple files by just going back through the steps. If you don't want to attach anything, leave this field blank.

You got a brief introduction to the kinds of encoding necessary to send the kinds of files mentioned previously in chapter 5 (for Macintosh systems) or chapter 6 (for Windows systems). Chapter 12, "Accessing FTP and Gopher through E-mail," is devoted to dealing with these kinds of files, and you'll probably find it helpful to read through it before you try to use attachments.

Detaching attachments

If you want to remove an attachment from a piece of e-mail before you're finished with it, just click anywhere inside the attachment name in the Attachment: field and press Delete or use the Clear command in the Edit menu.

Receiving attachments

You can receive your attachments two different ways, manually and automatically.

Manually receiving attachments

If you didn't choose "Automatically save attachments to" in the Configuration dialog, you'll have to tell Eudora where to save each attachment that comes in. When an attachment arrives you'll be asked where you want to save it. Then, you can open that file outside of Eudora and look at it.

Automatically saving attachments

If you chose "Automatically save attachments to" in the Configuration dialog, Eudora will save every attachment you get to the folder you told it to use. How to configure this option is explained in chapter 7.

Signatures

In chapters 5 and 6, we covered how to automatically add your signature to your mail. To create a signature, go to the <u>W</u>indow menu and select Signature. It's best to follow the guidelines outlined in chapter 4.

❋{Note}_____ | If you configured Eudora to sign your mail automatically, you don't need to do anything. If you configured Eudora not to sign automatically, clicking the Signature icon signs the note for you.

10

Receiving E-mail

You may not have any mail waiting for you yet, but you will soon.

If sending your first piece of electronic mail makes you feel like you've joined the '90s, receiving your first piece of e-mail makes you feel like you've joined the ranks of the "connected." It's sort of like buying an answering machine and waiting expectantly to come home to that first message. However, with answering machines, people can forget to leave their phone numbers, their names, or just read them off too fast. With electronic mail, all of the information you need is right in front of you.

Checking for and retrieving mail

You may not have any mail waiting for you yet, but you will soon. Especially if you sent off for the files we recommended.

Passwords

If you turned on the Save Password option when you configured Eudora, it will only ask you for your password the very first time you use Eudora to check for mail. If the Save Password option is off, Eudora asks you for your password the first time you check for mail after shutting off the program and starting it up again. If you don't want Eudora to remember your password between mail checks at all, open the Special menu and choose Forget Password.

> If your computer is in a place where people can easily get to it, you may want to use the Forget Password option, which means that if you want the computer to check for mail automatically, you'll have to be there every time it does to give it your password. Of course, you could also be tricky and lock down or disconnect your keyboard or use another security program so people can't get your password from Eudora but you don't have to enter it every time.

Figures 10.1 and 10.2 show the Enter Password dialog boxes for Macintosh and Windows systems.

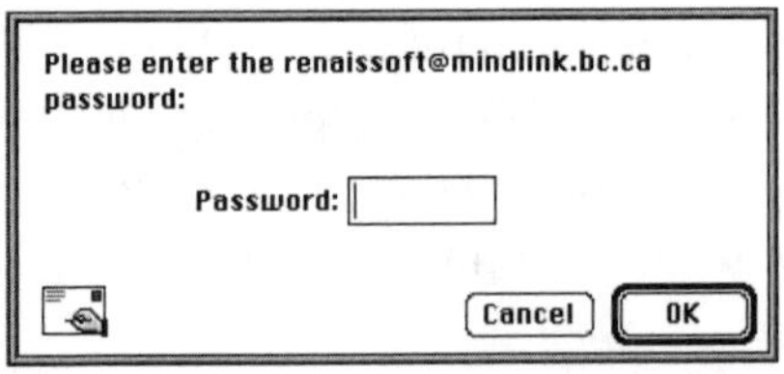

Fig. 10.1
The Macintosh Enter Password dialog box.

Please enter the renaissoft@mindlink.bc.ca password:

Password: [   ]

[Cancel]   [OK]

Fig. 10.2
The Windows Enter
Password dialog box.

Checking mail manually

You can check your mail two different ways with Eudora, manually or automatically. Even if Eudora's configured to check mail automatically, you can check manually when you feel like it.

**<Caution>** Eudora doesn't count that manual mail check as one of its automatic checks, so it will still dial-in at the next scheduled time. This happens even if you check manually only five minutes before the automatic check was scheduled.

To check your mail manually, simply open the File menu and choose Check Mail (or use Ctrl+M). If Eudora needs your password, you'll get the Password dialog box. After that, you'll get a series of Progress windows that let you know how your connection is progressing.

If there's no mail waiting for you, you'll get the No New Mail dialog box. Figures 10.3 and 10.4 show the No New Mail dialog box for Macintosh and Windows systems.

Fig. 10.3
The Macintosh No
New Mail dialog box.

Fig. 10.4
The Windows No New
Mail dialog box.

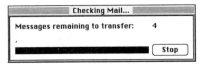{Note}_____ If you selected the Open 'In' Mailbox switch in the Windows versions of
Eudora, you won't get the No New Mail dialog box. Instead, the In mailbox
simply won't open.

If you do have mail, the Progress Window will show you how much mail you
have, what piece it's on, and how far it is into that piece (see figs. 10.5 and
10.6).

Fig. 10.5
The Macintosh Progress
Status window.

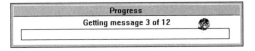

Fig. 10.6
The Windows Progress
Status window.

When Eudora's finished downloading your mail, you'll get the New Mail
dialog box. Figures 10.7 and 10.8 show you what that looks like.

Fig. 10.7
The Macintosh New
Mail dialog box.

Fig. 10.8
The Windows New
Mail dialog box.

Checking mail automatically

You've already configured Eudora to check mail automatically if you wanted it to. You've also configured Eudora so that it knows how to tell you if you've got new mail. That's all you need to do to check mail for now.

If you skipped past most of chapter 5 (Macintosh setup) or 6 (Windows setup), you may want to go back at some point and configure the options you haven't looked at yet.

One of the options available in these chapters is setting Eudora to check mail automatically.

Leaving mail on the server

Normally, Eudora gets your mail from the POP server, saves it on your computer, and then deletes your mail from the POP server. However, if you want to read your mail from a secondary computer, it's a good idea to configure Eudora to leave mail on the server. That way, if you read a message on your primary computer but want to respond to it later from the secondary computer, you can still get to it.

Leaving mail on the server is especially useful if you use both Macintosh and Windows systems and people send you attachments from both. That way, if you use a Mac to check your mail and find a Windows attachment, you can check your mail from a Windows system later and get that attachment again.

Skipping large messages

If you activate the Skip Large Messages option, Eudora won't download messages larger than 40K (or whatever you define large to be) until you turn it off. Remember, though, Eudora needs help from the POP server and this option doesn't always work.

Aborting a mail check

If you're in the middle of a mail check and want to stop, it's easy:

- If you're using a Macintosh setup, press ⌘+. (period).
- If you're using a Windows setup, press the Esc key.

Reading mail

Okay, you've got your mail on your computer. That's the first step. Now, how do you read it?

Opening a mailbox

Open the Mailbox menu and choose the mailbox you want to open. New mail will be in the In mailbox. Figures 10.9 and 10.10 show you what the mailbox looks like in both the Macintosh and Windows versions of Eudora.

Eudora and portability

Using the Save As command, you can choose to save to a floppy disk instead of your hard drive if you want to take mail with you. You can do this with mail you received or haven't sent out yet.

This is especially useful if you received an attachment but don't have the software to read/look at it on the computer you received your mail on. Also, it allows you to take your mail home and work on it with a text editor so it's ready to go out the next time you use Eudora, or even send it off from home if you've got Eudora on your home computer.

 **{Note}**_____ Chapter 14 discusses how to use and manage mailboxes in more detail.

Fig. 10.9
The Macintosh In
mailbox.

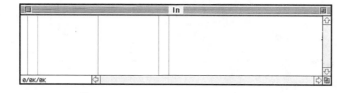

Fig. 10.10
The Windows In
mailbox.

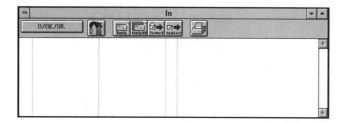

Message section

Now that you've got the mailbox open, all that's left to do is read your new mail.

Each line in your mailbox has a Message Summary in it containing information like who sent the message and the message subject. Notice the markings on the left side of each message summary. These show the status of your message, for example, whether you've read it or not, forwarded it, and so on. Tables 11.1 and 11.2 list the status markings in the In (which includes any mailbox you save messages you've received from other people) and Out mailboxes and what each stands for.

You also may find a message priority in this section. Message priorities are discussed in chapter 9.

Table 10.1 Message Status Characters for In Mailbox(es)

Character	Meaning
•	You haven't read this message yet.
<blank>	You read the message already.
R	You chose to reply to the message.
F	You chose to forward the message.
D	You chose to redirect the message.
-	The message was taken out of the Out mailbox before being sent, so it never got sent.

Table 10.2 Message Status Characters for Out Mailbox

Character	Meaning
•	This message is ready to go but isn't queued yet.
R	You chose to reply to the message.
F	You chose to forward the message.
D	You chose to redirect the message.
S	The message was sent.

Opening a message

To open a message, double-click anywhere on the line containing the summary of the message you want. Or, you can use your arrow keys to move through your mailbox and press Return on the message you want to read. That's it!

You'll find yourself in the Message window. Figures 10.11 through 10.14 show you what you'll find in each of the versions of Eudora.

Fig. 10.11
The Macintosh
freeware Message
window.

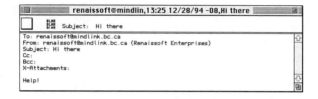

Fig. 10.12
The Macintosh
commercial Message
window.

Fig. 10.13
The Windows
freeware Message
window.

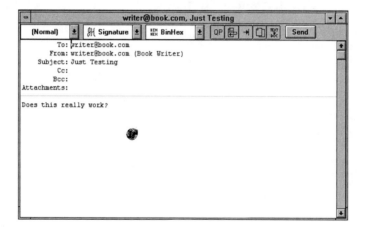

Fig. 10.14

The Windows commercial Message window.

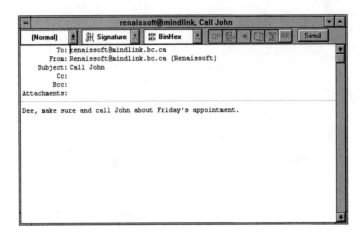

Next, in chapter 11, we'll go into the different things you can do when you're ready to forward, redirect, or reply to the volumes of e-mail you've gotten and will get in the future.

11

Answering E-mail

Because you're respond-
ing to a message instead
of starting from scratch,
half of your work's done
for you already!

You've already learned how to send mail and read mail, as well as how to reply, forward, and redirect mail in chapter 9. All that's left to give you the complete electronic mail experience is learning how to reply to mail.

Writing back

Since you're writing back to a message instead of starting from scratch, half of your work's done for you already! Replying to an e-mail message copies the userid of the person who wrote to you into the new To: field, and copies the subject into the Subject: field with the letters "Re:" in front of it so it's obvious that it's a reply. Also, the entire text of the note you're replying to is quoted on the inside of your new mail message, with a **>** character in front of each line to show what the old text is.

All you need to do now is edit the message and send it back out.

Replying

1 Open up the message you want to reply to.

2 Open the Message menu and choose Reply.

3 Write your new message.

4 Send the message.

You can also reply to messages in a couple of other ways.

1 Select the message in the mailbox window and choose Message, Reply. When you do this, you reply without opening the original message too, and if you have more than one message in the window selected, Eudora opens a reply window for each one of them.

2 Select the message in the mailbox window and press Ctrl+R for a Windows system or ⌘+R for a Macintosh system.

A new message window will open and the person's address that you're replying to will be in the To: line. Everything from the original message is in the new message, with a > in front of every line that's being quoted. You can insert lines wherever you want to add your own comments, or you can reply after the original message. Of course, you can also delete lines that aren't necessary.

Figures 11.1 through 11.4 show you examples of what you'll get when you reply to a message in the Macintosh and Windows, freeware and commercial versions of Eudora.

Fig. 11.1
Replying in Macintosh
freeware.

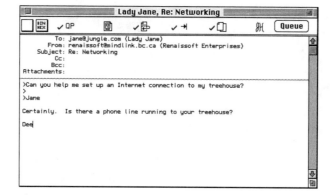

Fig. 11.2
Replying in Macintosh
commercial.

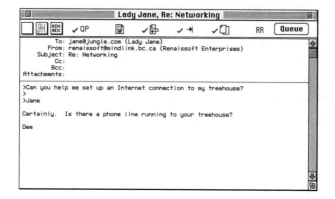

Fig. 11.3
Replying in Windows
freeware.

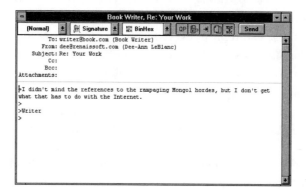

Fig. 11.4
Replying in Windows
commercial.

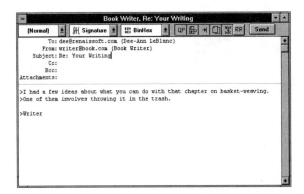

You can see that these are replies right away by noticing the "Re:" in the subject line. Also, the > character in front of each line is a good tipoff, but people won't always quote anything from the message they're replying to.

Options

There are a few different ways to reply to a message, depending on how it was sent to you in the first place.

Reply to All

Let's say that you didn't turn on the Reply to All switch when you configured Eudora. If a message you received was sent to a group of people and not just to you, you can reply to everyone in the group by holding down the Option key for Macintosh systems, or the Shift key for Windows systems, while you open the Message menu and choose Reply. A "normal" reply to a group message just goes to the person who sent the message. If you're confused about who will get a message you're sending, check out the To: line. You can even edit the To: line if you don't want someone included for some reason.

If you did turn on the Reply to All option when you configured Eudora, you'll reply to everyone by default. In this case, holding down the Option/Shift key while opening the Message menu and choosing Reply turns Reply to All off only for that note. That means you'll only reply to the note's sender, but next time you reply to a group note the reply will go to the whole group.

Include Self

Let's say you turned on the Include Self option when you configured Eudora. When you're using the Reply to All option, Eudora will take the word "All" literally and send you a copy of the note as well, since you're on the list of people the first note was written to.

 **{Note}**

> If you don't save a copy of every message you send out, this can actually come in handy. It's a way to make sure you don't lose track of what you said to the group. However, if you do save copies of all messages you send out, this option is redundant.

If you didn't turn the Include Self option on, Eudora knows that by "All," you mean "everyone else."

Quote selection only (for Macintosh versions only)

Sometimes you're responding to a very large note, but you only want to talk about one paragraph of it. Because Eudora automatically includes the entire note you're responding to when you open the <u>M</u>essage menu and choose <u>R</u>eply, you're in for a lot of deleting.

There's another way, though, if you're using a Macintosh system. If you only want to quote part of a mail message, use your mouse to highlight the section you want to quote, hold down the Shift key, and open the Message menu and choose Reply. Only the text you selected will be quoted, which means that you don't have to spend extra time getting rid of what you don't want.

 (Tip)

> You can also reply to messages by quoting only part of the original text in a couple of other ways.
>
> **1** Select the message in the mailbox window, hold down the Shift key and choose <u>M</u>essage, <u>R</u>eply. When you do this, you reply without opening the original message too, and if you have more than one message in the window selected Eudora opens a reply window for each one of them.
>
> **2** Select the message in the mailbox window and press Shift+Ctrl+R for a Windows system or Shift+⌘+R for a Macintosh system.

Forwarding mail

Sometimes you get a piece of mail that should really go to someone else. Instead of writing back and telling the person who to write to—though that's certainly an option—you can **forward** the e-mail.

What mail forwarding does

When you forward a piece of electronic mail to someone, Eudora copies the entire note—headers and all—into a new note that comes from you. You can also insert comments into messages you're forwarding just like when you're replying. The From: line is your e-mail address, which means that replies to that mail will come back to you. Sometimes you want that, though.

It's best to write a note at the beginning of the forwarded message telling the person that you want the reply sent to the original sender or to you to look over.

Why use mail forwarding?

Mail forwarding is a very useful feature. If someone sends you a question, for example, and you're really not sure how to answer it, you can forward the message to someone who you're pretty sure does know the answer. Because you can add comments as well as pass the message along, you can give the person you're forwarding the message to some background so they have all the information they need to deal with the question.

Of course, mail forwarding is also nice if you just want to pass something along to someone else with or without comments.

How to use mail forwarding

1 Select the message you want to forward.

2 All you have to do now is go to the <u>M</u>essage menu and select Fo<u>r</u>ward. The header of the message you're forwarding and the message itself will have a > in front of it just like in a Reply message.

3 Fill in the To: line.

4 If you want to, edit the forwarded message, add to it, or just leave it the way it is. Figures 11.5 and 11.6 show you what forwarding a message looks like in Eudora for Macintosh and Windows, freeware and commercial versions.

5 Send or queue the message.

Fig. 11.5
Forwarding in
Macintosh.

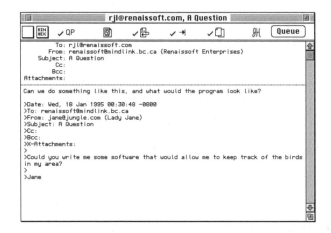

```
rjl@renaissoft.com, A Question
        BIN
        HEX    ✓ QP         ✓ ⊞    ✓ ⇥    ✓ ◻    ⌘H   [ Queue ]
              To: rjl@renaissoft.com
            From: renaissoft@mindlink.bc.ca (Renaissoft Enterprises)
         Subject: A Question
              Cc:
             Bcc:
     Attachments:
    ─────────────────────────────────────────────────────────────
    Can we do something like this, and what would the program look like?

    >Date: Wed, 18 Jan 1995 00:30:48 -0800
    >To: renaissoft@mindlink.bc.ca
    >From: jane@jungle.com (Lady Jane)
    >Subject: A Question
    >Cc:
    >Bcc:
    >X-Attachments:
    >
    >Could you write me some software that would allow me to keep track of the birds
    >in my area?
    >
    >Jane
```

The convenience of forwarding...

For example, our good friend Max works for a company that designs, manufactures, and markets widgets. He's in charge of the company's generic e-mail address, **info@widget.com**.

Max, through the "info" account, talks back and forth with Amy about what working for Widget, Inc., is like. One day she wrote asking what kinds of jobs were open. He forwarded her note to Irene, the Human Resources Manager, with some background information at the beginning to let Irene know how interested Amy was in working for them. Then, Irene replied to the note and sent it back to Max. Max then edited everything out of her reply except for the section where she listed the job openings, and sent it to Amy. Forwarding mail doesn't have to go through that many steps, of course, but we wanted to point out how useful mail forwarding is for passing questions around to the correct people without giving out those people's e-mail addresses.

Fig. 11.6
Forwarding in
Windows.

You can glance at these messages and tell they were forwarded because the entire message header is included in the text of the new message, with >'s in front of each line.

⊛ {Note}_____ If you forward a mail message, your .sig is appended to it if you are using a .sig.

Redirecting mail

You can also redirect mail instead of forwarding it.

What mail redirection does

Mail redirection, often referred to as "bouncing a message," is similar to mail forwarding. However, when you redirect a message, the person you send it to sees the original sender's e-mail address in the From: line with a note saying the e-mail came "by way of" you. This means that replying to a redirected message is replying to the person who originally sent it, not to the person who redirected it.

Another difference is that a redirected message doesn't have symbols in front of the text from the original note. You can still add things, but make sure to mark them somehow so that the person you redirect it to knows which comments are yours and which comments are from the original sender.

Why use mail redirection?

The reasons for using mail redirection are similar to those for mail forwarding. Often, mail redirection is used when you don't have any comments to make and don't want or need to look over the answer before it goes back to the original sender.

How to use mail redirection

Redirecting a message is simple.

1 Open the message you want to redirect, open the Message menu, and choose Redirect.

2 Fill in the To: line and can add comments (remember to mark them clearly) if you want. Figures 11.7 and 11.8 show you what a redirected message looks like in Eudora for Macintosh and Windows, freeware and commercial versions.

3 Send or queue the message.

Fig. 11.7
Redirecting in
Macintosh.

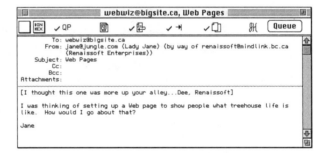

Mail redirection in action...

Back to Max. This time, an employee sent her timesheet to the "info" e-mail address because she couldn't remember the Human Resources e-mail address. Max just redirected the timesheet to the proper address.

Fig. 11.8
Redirecting in
Windows.

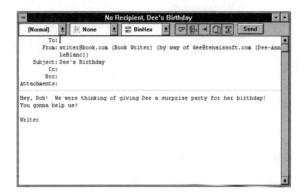

* **{Note}**_____| When you redirect a file, your signature is not appended to it.

You can tell at a glance that this message was redirected because of the
(By the way of...) line in the From: header.

"Canned" messages

Sometimes you just get in a rut. People keep asking the same, or similar,
questions and you're getting tired of typing in the same answers over and
over and over. You can type up a "form letter" answer if you want and store
it to send out when more of those questions come in.

1 Open up a brand new message.

2 Type it exactly like you want it, filling in every field except the To: field.

3 Save the message.

4 If you want to, you can use the <u>T</u>ransfer menu to move it from the Out
mailbox to a new one, for example, one named Canned Messages.

Canned messages...

This time, Max is checking info's mail and found
a request for a list of products that Widgets, Inc.,
sells. He has a canned message for that one
already set up, so he can open it, fill in the To:
line, and send it out.

Now, every time you get that same old question, you just open your canned message, open the <u>M</u>essages menu, and choose Red<u>i</u>rect. Fill in the To: field, and send it off.

Canned messages don't just save you from a lot of unnecessary typing. They also save you from mistyping something at some point and accidentally sending out incorrect information. Plus, keeping information like that in a central place means you can go in and change it when you need to.

If you've made up form letter stationery of some kind in your word processing program, you can copy and paste it into Eudora to make a canned message out of it!

12 Accessing FTP and Gopher through E-mail

You'll often run across people who'll tell you, "FTP to this site; they have some great stuff!" The problem is, how do you do it through e-mail?

In this chapter:

- Finding lists of mailing lists
- What FTP is and how to use FTP through e-mail
- What Gopher is and how to use Gopher through e-mail
- Reading and participating in UseNet through Gophermail
- What Archie is and how to use Archie through e-mail

As we've mentioned many times before, you can do much more with e-mail than send letters. The Internet is a wealth of information and e-mail is just one way of getting to it.

⊛ {Note} If you have access to an account that offers such features as FTP and Gopher directly (that is, direct connection to the Internet, SLIP/PPP, and even most shell accounts), you can do both directly from there. Otherwise, as you'll see in this chapter, it's possible to do these things through e-mail, so nobody's left out of the most famous strength of the Internet: the ability to gather information.

FTP by e-mail

You'll often run across people who'll tell you, "FTP to this site; they have some great stuff!" The problem is, how do you do it if you want to or have to use e-mail?

①(Tip) | Even if you have access to an account that allows you to FTP directly, it's recommended that you use e-mail if you have the time to wait (it can take a day or two to process an FTP by e-mail request). If you use e-mail, you don't have to deal with the problem of your FTP session taking far longer than it should because of overworked FTP servers.

What is FTP?

FTP is a file transfer protocol that allows you to connect to other computers on the Internet and get or add files. FTP has the advantage that you often don't need an account on the machine you're fetching files from or adding files to, allowing you to go in anonymously and access the areas considered to be "public."

How to get files with e-mail

There are several sites that allow FTP through e-mail. Table 12.1 lists them. The "decwrl" site is very popular so it's not recommended that you use that one. Popular equals slow on the Internet.

Table 12.1 FTP by E-Mail Sites

Site	Location
bitftp@pucc.princeton.edu	USA/NJ
bitftp@vm.gmd.de	Europe
ftpmail@cs.uow.edu.au	Australia
ftpmail@decwrl.dec.com	USA/NJ
ftpmail@doc.ic.ac.uk	UK

Site	Location
ftpmail@ftp.uu.net	USA
ftpmail@sunsite.unc.edu	USA/NC

The first piece of e-mail you should send to the server you've chosen is something with no subject and just one word in the body, such as "help."

Table 12.2 lists the commands and command descriptions you'll probably get back through the help file. You may find some differences between the servers.

Table 12.2 FTP Server Commands

Command	What It Tells the Computer
reply-to <e-mail address>	Sends the files requested to the e-mail address listed here. If you're not sure your headers will come out right, or want to send the files to a different account, use this option. The default is your e-mail address.
help	Sends a file containing the commands available to you.
open [site [user [pass]]]	Tells the FTP server what computer you want to FTP to. Site is the name of the FTP site you want to access, user is probably anonymous, and pass is probably your full e-mail address (these user and pass settings are fairly common). The default is sunsite.unc.edu, anonymous, and your reply-to address.
cd pathname	Tells the server to change to the directory listed in pathname. If you didn't give it a site, it assumes you want something on the FTP server. If you told it a site, it changes to that directory on that site.
ls [pathname]	Gets a short list of the files in the directory you chose. The default is the current directory.
dir [pathname]	Gets a long list of what's in the directory you chose. The default is the current directory.
get [pathname]	Gets the file listed and sends it back. You can list the entire file including directories, or use the cd command to go to the directories and then type just the file name with the get command.

continues

Table 12.2 Continued

Command	What It Tells the Computer
compress	Compresses the files or directory listings you request before sending them back.
uuencode	Uuencodes the requested files before sending them back.
mime	Sends message as Mime Version 1.0 message.
no [compress|uuencode|mime]	Shuts off compression/encoding.
size num[K|M]	Sets the maximum size a file can be before it gets split up in either kilobytes or megabytes.
mode binary|ascii	Tells the computer what kind of files you're going to get. Binary files are files that aren't text (programs, pictures, sounds, and so on) Ascii files are text files. The default is binary.
quit	You're done.

✱ {Note}

A word between the [] is optional. For example, if you wanted a listing of the files in the directory you're already in, you could just type **ls**.

However, if you had a particular directory you wanted the computer to give you a file listing for, you would type (for example) **ls /gifs/animation**.

Words with a | (pipe symbol) in between them are options. For example, when you see binary|ascii, you can select either of those options and only either of them.

It's a good idea to always type a **/** (backslash) in front of the directory name when you're jumping around from directory to directory. That makes sure the computer knows it needs to back up to the main directory and start from there. Otherwise, things can get confused.

The files you'll find in the index will be in all sorts of cases. Some will be partially upper- and lowercase; some will be all lower, and some will be all upper. It's important when typing anything that fills in a [path] or [filename] blank that you type it just as it looks. For anything else, it doesn't matter what case you use.

①(Tip)___

The first time you FTP to a particular FTPMail server, you should get the help file. Also, you should do an ls to get a feel for what kinds of files are there (this goes for any FTP session).

Now, let's go through an example. We'll use **ftpmail@cs.uow.edu.au** as our FTP server. First, we'll send e-mail to find out what files are in the main directory of **cs.uow.edu.au**. Figure 12.1 shows the e-mail we're sending. Note that the subject is blank because it's unnecessary.

Fig. 12.1
Initial request to FTPMail site.

Figure 12.2 shows the initial e-mail we get back from FTPMail site telling us it's received our request and where it is in its queue of jobs.

Fig. 12.2
FTPMail site's Queuing Notice.

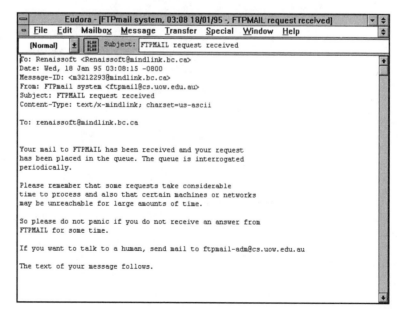

{Note}_____ It can take one hour to get the results of your request back, or it can take three days. It depends on the server's workload.

Now, we'll choose a file, say README, to fetch. Figure 12.3 shows the e-mail we're sending this time.

Fig. 12.3
Second request to
FTPMail site.

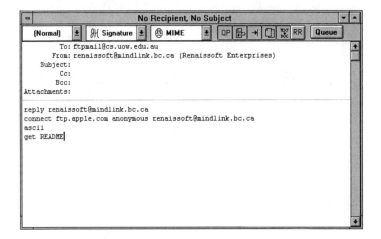

We'll get a queuing notice again, and then we'll get the file we requested.

Archie by e-mail

Often, people will say, "Hey, you should get this great program off of the Internet!" They're kind enough to tell you the program's name and where to find it. Then, you get home and remember the name (or most of it) and have completely forgotten the site. Archie is the solution to this problem.

What is Archie?

Archie is actually a collection of servers around the world that contain databases, or large lists, of the files you can get using FTP. When you use Archie, you list the filename you think the program has, or parts of the name, and the server tells you where the file is if it can find it.

How to use Archie with e-mail

Archie actually can take a long time to run if you're doing it directly, so using it through e-mail is a good idea. Table 12.3 lists Archie servers you can use.

Table 12.3 Archie Servers that Accept E-Mail Commands

Address	Location
archie@archie.rutgers.edu	USA/NJ
archie@archie.sura.net	USA/MD
archie@archie.unl.edu	USA/NE
archie@archie.doc.ic.ac.uk	UK
archie@archie.luth.se	Sweden
archie@archie.kuis.kyoto-u.ac.jp	Japan

First, as usual, it's a good idea to send e-mail to one of these servers with a blank subject and one word inside, for example, "help."

When you're ready to do your search, you have a few options.

If you know the exact name of the file you want, you can send the Archie server e-mail with a blank subject and a body containing "find <file>".

 **{Note}** Replace the word <file> with the exact name of the file you're looking for. If the Archie server doesn't find that exact filename anywhere, it will tell you it found 0 matches.

If you want to just tell Archie to look for files whose names contain things you're interested in, you can do that too. You'll send e-mail to the Archie server with a blank subject and in the body.

find <search criteria>

mail <your e-mail address>

quit

Figure 12.4 shows an example of a note requesting an Archie search for "eudo," since in this case we want to look for Eudora but often the full name won't appear in the filename.

Fig. 12.4

Archie search request.

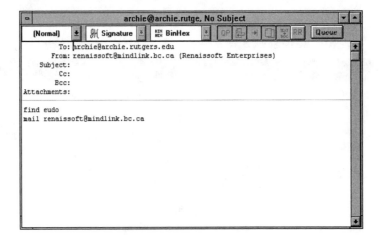

Figure 12.5 shows part of the result of the search. This file is actually several screens long, listing dozens of sites that have files containing eudo in their names, as well as the location of the file on each site.

Fig. 12.5

Archie search results.

You'll replace <search criteria> with the word or part of a word you want to find in the names of the files Archie will look through. You may need to try this a few times trying different parts of the word or words that mean similar things.

Table 12.4 lists some commands you might want to put in your note.

Table 12.4 Useful Gopher Commands

Command	What It Tells the Computer
set maxhits 20	You only want up to 20 locations for the file listed. The default number is 100.
set match_domain usa	You only want the Archie server to look at sites in the USA.
set output_format terse	You only want a condensed reply from Archie, not the full reply.

The commands previously listed go after the "set search sub" command and right before the "find <file>" or "find <search criteria>" command.

Mailing lists

As we discussed in chapter 2, there are plenty of mailing lists out there covering topics you're interested in, and topics you didn't think people would care about. The problem is, how do you find any of them?

Lists of lists

There are several "lists of mailing lists" available through e-mail on the Internet. These lists take some time to wade through, but it's worth it. By the time you're done with them, you should have found at least one list you're interested in—probably more.

(Tip) If you have access to UseNet, look in the group news.lists. A list of mailing lists is posted there on the 19th of every month.

Where and how

The "lists of mailing lists" are maintained by people on the Internet and stored at a site called **InterNIC**. InterNIC is where all service providers have to register to get their domain number and name, and is generally a wealth of information.

We recommend getting the following files at first from the directory /using-internet/basic-services/email/mailing-lists/:

> interest-groups
>
> mailing-lists-part1
>
> mailing-lists-part2
>
> (continued for 3 through 13)
>
> mailing-lists-part14

{Note}

The "interest-groups" file is an alphabetical listing of mailing lists registered with the person who maintains this list. Information on what subjects the mailing list covers is given, plus what e-mail address to write to so you can subscribe and the e-mail address you can write to so you can ask the list maintainer any questions you may have before you subscribe.

The "mailing-lists" files, all 14 of them, are another alphabetical listing of mailing lists. It's worth getting these files too because some of the lists are probably registered only with the interest-groups list or the mailing-lists lists instead of being in both.

In order to get these files, you have to write to InterNIC's automated mailserver. The e-mail address you will use is

mailserv@is.internic.net

You can just leave the subject line blank. Then, in the body of the message, you can do as many things as you want as long as you use the correct commands.

Figure 12.6 shows the mail you'd send to InterNIC to get the files we recommended previously.

Fig. 12.6

Lists of lists request to InterNIC.

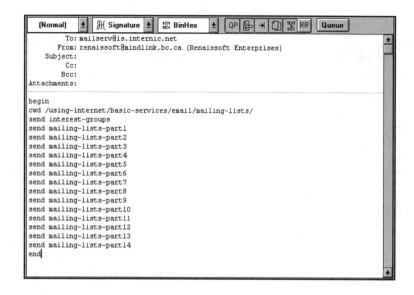

```
              To: mailserv@is.internic.net
            From: renaissoft@mindlink.bc.ca (Renaissoft Enterprises)
         Subject:
              Cc:
             Bcc:
Attachments:

begin
cwd /using-internet/basic-services/email/mailing-lists/
send interest-groups
send mailing-lists-part1
send mailing-lists-part2
send mailing-lists-part3
send mailing-lists-part4
send mailing-lists-part5
send mailing-lists-part6
send mailing-lists-part7
send mailing-lists-part8
send mailing-lists-part9
send mailing-lists-part10
send mailing-lists-part11
send mailing-lists-part12
send mailing-lists-part13
send mailing-lists-part14
end
```

Table 12.5 lists the commands InterNIC's mailserver understands and what each command means.

{Note} A lot of the files you're requesting are large, so they'll probably each arrive in your mailbox in several pieces. You should have quite a lot of mail coming your way after sending the list of lists request out!

Table 12.5 InterNIC Mailserver Commands

Command	What It Tells the Computer
begin	Ignore everything that shows up before you typed **begin**.
send help	You want a help file. It will send it.
reply <e-mail address>	Ignore the e-mail address in the header of your note, and send the files you requested to the e-mail address you gave here. Use this if you're not sure your e-mail address comes out right in your headers.
mail <address>	Send the files to the address you gave here. Use this if you want the files to go to another account you have.
limit <number>	Don't send any more than <number> kilobytes in a file at a time. Default is 64K. This limit applies to every request AFTER you typed this command.

continues

Table 12.5 Continued

Command	What It Tells the Computer
[encoding] {UUENCODE}	Encode the files requested after this command. The files won't be encoded at all if you don't include this command. If you only type "encoding," the files will be Uuencoded. If you you want to use another form of encoding (for example, BinHex), type it after the word "encoding."
cwd [<path>]	Change to the directory (or path) here.
dir [<path>]	Send a list of files and directories in the directory (or path) listed here.
index [<item>...]	Look through the archives and find files with the item(s) listed in them. If you don't list any items, it looks for the word "index". Typing **send index** gets you a list of all of the files available on the InterNIC server.
search [<item>...]	<item> Look up the items listed and send back a list of the files they were found in.
send [<item>...]	<item> Send the file(s) listed according to the rules you set previously (for example, encoding, and so on). If you didn't list any special rules, the files will just be sent as a normal e-mail message, or a group of them if the file you requested is longer than 64K.
resend <item> [<part>...]	<part> Resend the part of the item you requested. The encoding and limit must be the same as in your original request. This command is used when something went wrong with one or more of the files you requested.
pack {tar|zoo|zip|off}	Take the entire directories requested after this command, compress and send them using the indicated method. Before moving on to request individual files after this, remember to type **pack off**.
end	Ignore everything after this word. The request is done.

⊛{Note}

A word between the symbols <> is something that you need to substitute a value for. For example, to limit the size of each piece of e-mail sent to you from InterNIC to 32K intead of 64K, you would type **limit 32**.

A word between the [] is optional. For example, if you wanted the computer to change directories to the main directory, you would only type **cwd**.

However, if you had a particular directory you wanted the computer to change to so you can fetch a file from it, to have it change /about/internet-history you would type **cwd /about/internet-history**.

It's a good idea to always type a **/** in front of the directory name when you're jumping around from directory to directory. That makes sure the computer knows it needs to back up to the main directory and start from there. Other-wise, the computer may get confused and think that the first directory name, "about" in our case, is inside the directory it's currently in.

A word or words between {} are some of the options available to you. For example, when requesting a directory, you would type **pack zip**.

The files you'll find in the index will be in various cases. Some will be partially upper- and lowercase; some will be all lower, and some will be all upper. It's important when typing anything that fills in a <path> or <item> blank that you type it just as it looks. For anything else, it doesn't matter what case you use.

❶(Tip)

The InterNIC server has all sorts of interesting information available on it. If you send e-mail with the command "send index," it will send you a list of all of the files it has available. You could add "send index" in the note you send requesting the lists of mailing lists, or send it separately.

⊛{Note}

Just as with the other FTP servers, InterNIC may take a day or two to get back to you. It also might just take an hour. It depends on its current workload.

Word of mouth

An important way most people find out about mailing lists is word of mouth. Hang out on the Internet long enough and people will let you know about mailing lists they've heard about that discuss the subjects you're inter-ested in.

Of course, until you meet people on the Internet who have that kind of information, your best option is to check the lists of lists. And, remember, these do change over time. You may want to get new copies of them in a few months if you're looking for another mailing list to join.

Subscribing to a mailing list

Now that you've got these lists of lists, you'll have to take some time to wade through them and pick some you're interested in. You're certain to find at least one.

Each list description has a Subscription Address. That's the e-mail address you'll use to add yourself to the list. Most of the lists contain instructions on what to include in the mail, but not all of them do. Sending e-mail to the Subscription Address with "help" in the subject should get you back some instructions. If you have problems subscribing to the list, write to the List Owner, whose e-mail address is also included. Figure 12.7 shows the list description for the list we'll use in our example.

Fig. 12.7
Description of the
Inet-Marketing mailing
list.

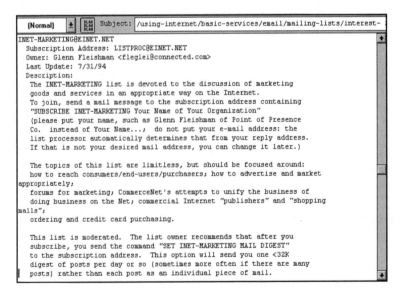

Note that the Subscription Address is **listproc@einet.net**. Note also that the description contains instructions on how to subscribe. Figure 12.8 shows what the e-mail we would send to join this list would look like.

Fig. 12.8
Subscription note
to Inet-Marketing
mailing list.

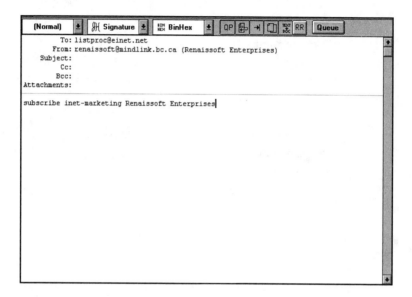

When the list software receives your mail, it will subscribe you and will send you back a piece of e-mail with list rules, instructions for how to un-subscribe, and how to post to the list (as a general rule). It's important that you keep this mail, otherwise if you want to unsubscribe at a later date you'll be at a loss as to how to do it.

In the case of the example list, there are even fancy options you can set. You can choose to get posts to the list as they come, or in a digest format occasionally, depending on whether you want lots of small e-mail or one occasional piece of larger e-mail. Once you're subscribed, the message you get back gives you even more options you can set. However, not all lists have the software behind them to give you such options.

Being on a mailing list

There are a few things to keep in mind once you're on a mailing list.

For one, there's no hard and fast rule to tell you how much e-mail lists get. Some only get a few posts a week, some get 20 a day. The best thing to do is subscribe for two weeks or so and see what the list averages out to. You may find out the traffic is just too much for you in the beginning, but suddenly levels off to a reasonable amount in a few days.

Another thing to remember is that the list and the list software are two different things. If you want to unsubscribe, or access archives (if the list has archives available), do so through the list's Subscription Address. If you want to post, do so through the address given to you in the mail you receive when you join.

Also, keep in mind that some lists are set up so that using Reply sends mail to only the person whose post you're replying to, and some are set up so that using Reply sends mail directly to the list. Some are even set up so that you can only see the list's e-mail address and can't see the poster's.

Gopher by e-mail

Gopher is an incredible source of information. Sites all over the world maintain Gopher servers in one huge Gopher network, allowing people from other sites to access them and browse. Through Gopher one can find information on graduate studies at a university on the other side of the world, find out what the weather's like where your friends are vacationing, or use it to do a bit of research.

What is Gopher?

Gopher is a menu-based system that lets you give it a keyword, or a few keywords, and then looks around the Internet for you to find items that contain the keyword(s). Once again, there are Gopher servers that allow you to use e-mail to do your searches. This time, at least, there aren't many commands to learn!

 **{Note}** A **keyword** is a word, or even part of a word, used to tell a computer program the subjects you're interested in.

E-mail isn't exactly the best way to use Gopher, since you have to do it one menu at a time, but it's a powerful enough tool that it's worth it if e-mail is the only option you have. Keep in mind that it can take several days if you're doing a deep Gopher search (going through a lot of levels of menus).

How to use Gopher with e-mail

Table 12.6 gives a list of Gopher servers that accept commands through e-mail.

Table 12.6   E-Mail Gopher Servers

Server	Location
gomail@ncc.go.jp	Japan
gopher@dsv.su.se	Sweden
gopher@earn.net	USA
gophermail@calvin.edu	USA
gophermail@mercury.forestry.umn.edu	USA
gophermail@pip.shsu.edu	USA
gophermail@ucmp1.berkeley.edu	USA

 **<Caution>** Gopher sites tend to change. Don't be surprised if the first one you try doesn't work.

The first thing you'll want to do, once again, is send a piece of e-mail with no subject, and in the body type the word **help**.

All you have to do now is follow the menus, putting an **x** next to the menu item you want each time. Figure 12.9 shows an example of a Gophermail help request.

Fig. 12.9
Gophermail help
request.

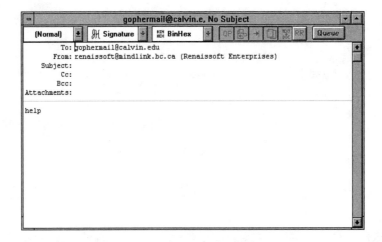

Figure 12.10 shows most of the response you'll get back after sending your
mail for help.

Fig. 12.10
Gophermail help
response.

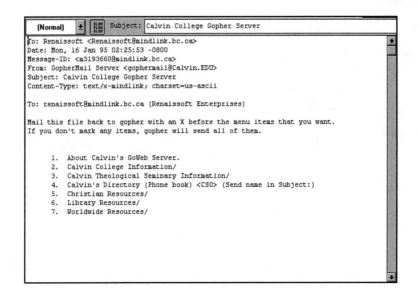

✱{Note}___

The "^L" translates to pressing the ⌘ key plus the letter L.

If you want the messages to be split more or less than 64K per message, then you'll want to change the number next to "Split=". If you don't want any split files at all, put a 0 there.

If you want more or less than 100 items listed in a menu the Gophermail server will send you in one message, then you'll want to change the number next to "Menu=". If you want all of your menu options in one note, then just put a 0 there.

If you wanted information on, say, User Services Documentation, you would just reply to the note, putting an **x** next to that option on the menu, and mail the entire note back. You just keep doing this, with the Gophermail server sending you menus and you sending back an "x" next to the option you want until you finally get a file instead of a menu option. Figure 12.11 shows an example of sending a menu back having selected a couple of options.

Fig. 12.11
Sending Gopher a
menu selection.

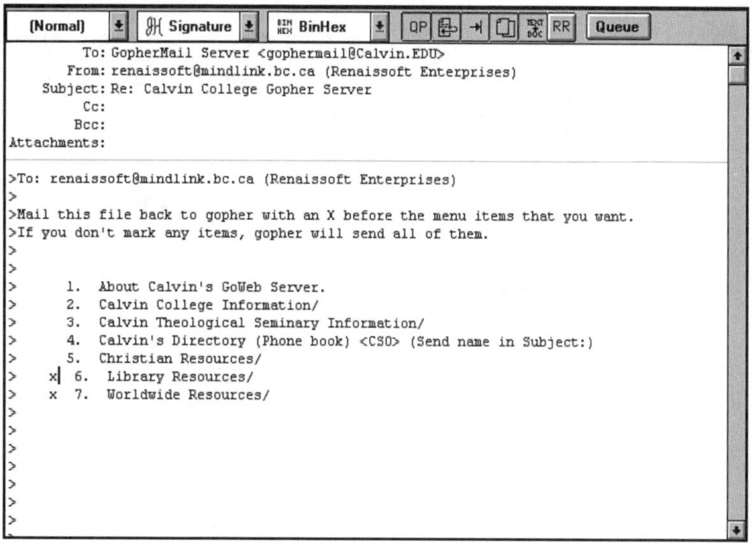

```
[Normal]  ⬍  ⑆ Signature ⬍  BIN BinHex ⬍  QP ⬆ ➔ ⬜ TXT RR  Queue

         To: GopherMail Server <gophermail@Calvin.EDU>
       From: renaissoft@mindlink.bc.ca (Renaissoft Enterprises)
    Subject: Re: Calvin College Gopher Server
         Cc:
        Bcc:
Attachments:

>To: renaissoft@mindlink.bc.ca (Renaissoft Enterprises)
>
>Mail this file back to gopher with an X before the menu items that you want.
>If you don't mark any items, gopher will send all of them.
>
>
>     1.  About Calvin's GoWeb Server.
>     2.  Calvin College Information/
>     3.  Calvin Theological Seminary Information/
>     4.  Calvin's Directory (Phone book) <CSO> (Send name in Subject:)
>     5.  Christian Resources/
>   x  6.  Library Resources/
>   x  7.  Worldwide Resources/
>
>
>
>
>
>
>
```

❶(Tip)___

You can select more than one menu item. If you don't select any, Gopher will assume you wanted all of them.

UseNet by e-mail

Generally, you would read the articles in UseNet using a "newsreader," or a program that helps you navigate through the heirarchies and read only the groups you're interested in. If you don't have access to an account that lets you do that, there are ways to read and even participate in UseNet through e-mail.

Mailing lists

Some UseNet groups are **echoed** to a mailing list. This means that everything that's sent to the newsgroup is sent to the list, and everything that's sent to the list is sent to the newsgroup.

The mailing lists that echo UseNet groups are listed in the "lists of lists" files you've already gotten in your search for other mailing lists, so all you have to do is look through the descriptions of each mailing list and find them.

 **{Note}**

> You probably don't want to subscribe to a group in this manner unless you don't have access to UseNet through any other way, or you really want a group that's not normally available through your site but is available through a list. Be aware that many groups get hundreds of posts per day!

Gophermail

You can also read and participate in UseNet groups through Gophermail.

First, you'll want to send e-mail to **mail-server@rtfm.mit.edu**. with no subject, and in the body, type

send usenet/news.answers/news-newusers-intro

send usenet-by-group/index

The first file, news-newusers-intro, isn't necessary to actually access UseNet, but this file will give you a lot of useful information on things like UseNet etiquette. Requesting the second file will give you a complete listing of group names to chose from. The list is pretty big, so it will probably come in two parts.

Now that you've got your list of groups, you can go through it and pick out the ones you want to read. For our examples on how to fetch previous postings to a group, we'll use the group **news.announce.newusers**, because that group contains a lot of information you should read through if you'll be participating on UseNet. You can't post to this group, however. Its function is to provide new members of UseNet with information that will help orient them.

 **{Note}** Not all of the groups in the list will be available through Gophermail.

First, you'll want to get a list of recent postings to the newsgroup. You'll send your e-mail to the same Gopher server you sent e-mail to before (one of the addresses listed in table 12.4). Instead of making you go through a bunch of menus, which can take a while by e-mail because you can pick only one menu at a time, figure 12.12 shows an example.

Fig. 12.12
Request for list of recent postings to **news.announce.newusers.**

For menus and query responses

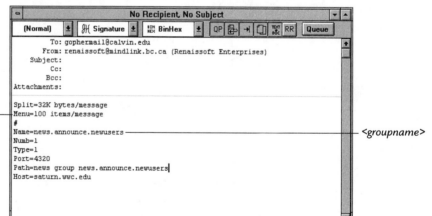

<groupname>

**{Note}**_____ Instead of <groupname> you'll put the name of a group you're inter-
ested in. For example, if you want to read articles from the group
news.newusers.questions, you type that instead of <groupname>.

Also, you can change the size of the individual notes you'll get, and the
number of menu options you'll get in a single note, by changing the numbers next to "Split=" and "Menu=" as you did before.

The host **saturn.wwc.edu** is where Gopher will look for the information
you've requested.

The Gopher server will send back to you a menu listing a bunch of recent
postings to the newsgroup. Part of the result of our sample query is shown
in figure 12.13. The full piece of e-mail is several screens long.

Fig. 12.13

List of recent posts in
news.announce.newusers.

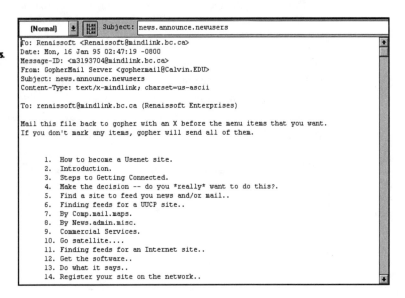

Just put an **x** next to each article you want and the server will send those
articles to you, or leave it blank and it will send you all of the articles. Keep
in mind that some groups get more than 100 postings per day. In the end, how
many articles you request depends on just how much you want to read.

Now, posting to a group is pretty easy compared to getting the articles. You just send e-mail to either

<newsgroup name>.usenet@decwrl.dec.com

or

<newsgroup name>@news.demon.co.uk.

This time, you'll actually use the subject line. Just put something in it that lets people know what your post is about. In the body of the post, ask your question. Also, make sure to put your name (or the nickname you're using) and your e-mail address in your post so people can write back to you to answer your question!

Figure 12.14 shows an example of a post going to **news.newusers.questions**.

Fig. 12.14

Posting to a group through e-mail.

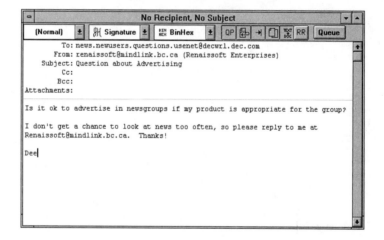

13
Sending and Receiving Files

If you want to send files by e-mail, you have to somehow convert them into ASCII text format, and make sure that the receiver can convert them back to the original binary format.

Electronic mail can be a very useful tool for sending letters back and forth, but things get a little more complicated when your e-mail pen pal writes to you asking, "Can you send me that neat program you mentioned in your last letter?" You *know* there has to be a way to do it, but every time you try mailing anything that isn't simple text you end up with useless garbage. Why does this happen, and what can be done about it? That's the topic of this chapter.

Why is this a problem?

In the early 1970s, when the Internet was in its infancy, the mainframe computers it connected weren't as efficient as the machines we use today, and the data lines that connected them to one another were prone to line noise and other technical problems. In short, there were transmission errors everywhere. As a result, the network architects decided to add special error-checking information to the data being sent from one computer to another, which made perfect sense. Unfortunately, this meant using one of the eight bits in each byte for error control, leaving only seven for the data itself. Newer machines and better data transmission methods have made it safe to use all 8 bits for data. But because there are still a lot of older machines in use that can't handle 8 bits reliably (mostly old mainframes), play it safe and limit yourself to the 7-bit system that all machines can understand.

To put it another way, suppose you have an 8-person traveling band and you want to book reservations on a bus. Now let's be a little absurd and suppose that all buses are designed to carry at the most 8 passengers, but in older models one of those seats is reserved for a security guard. This leaves only seven seats for the passengers. Newer buses don't reserve any seats for guards (they can hold the full complement of 8 passengers), but there are still some older buses that do. Because you can't know which kind of bus is going to be picking you up, you have to play it safe by planning for a group of seven, not eight—thus the problem.

The upshot is that the Simple Mail Transfer Protocol (SMTP) the Internet's architects developed does not allow you to send an 8-bit binary file because it expects the 8th bit to be an error-control bit, and not part of the data. If you want to send binary files by e-mail, you have to somehow convert it into 7-bit (ASCII text) format, and make sure the receiver can convert it back to its original 8-bit (binary) format.

?Q&A

What's a binary file?

A **binary file** is just about anything that isn't made up of simple ASCII text characters. This includes things like executable programs, data files, sound files, graphics, and so on. Be careful with word-processor documents—more than likely they're not stored as plain text because of all the formatting commands hidden within them. It's also worth noting that "simple ASCII text" refers to the symbols you can produce on a U.S. keyboard; international symbols with accents, umlauts, and other fancy additions are binary, not text.

Uuencoding: A way to mail binary files

One of the oldest and most widespread methods of converting binary files into text is called **Uuencoding** (pronounced "you-you-encoding"). You'll find that among most mainframes and UNIX machines this is still the method of choice, and it may well be the de-facto standard encoding method for use on the Internet.

Uuencoding is pretty simple to recognize when you see it in an e-mail message. Your first clue is the fact that all of the lines are the same length, and the motley assortment of characters looks like gibberish. If you look a little more closely however, you'll see there's some order to this chaos—the first character of almost every line is 'M', which is the signature of Uuencoding. You'll also notice that the first line in a Uuencoded file contains the name of the original file (see figs. 13.1 and 13.2).

Fig. 13.1
The beginning of a Uuencoded file.

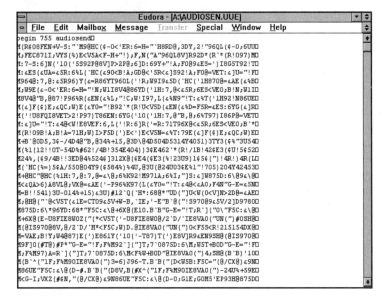

Fig. 13.2

The end of a
Uuencoded file.

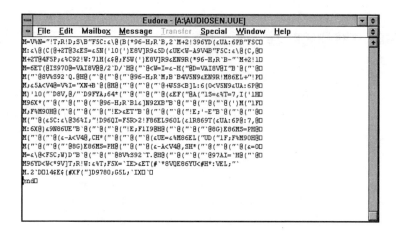

If you've got the commercial version of Eudora (versions 2.0 or higher),
sending a binary file with Uuencoding is almost as simple as sending a
normal text letter. After you've written your letter in the Composition
window, click on the Attachment Type selector on the icon bar (see
figs. 13.3 and 13.4).

Fig. 13.3

Locating the
Attachment Type
selector in the
Windows version.

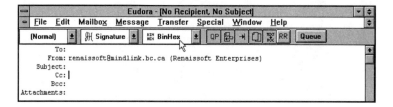

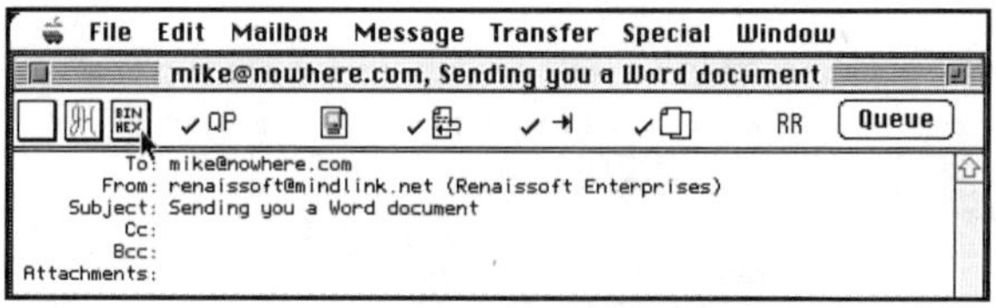

Fig. 13.4

Locating the
Attachment Type
selector in the
Macintosh version.

In the Windows version, the Attachment Type selector is a combo box;
clicking on the button at the right of this selector drops down a list of attachment types. Select "Uuencode" from this menu of choices.

In the Macintosh version, the Attachment Type selector is a button that calls
up a popup that lists the supported attachment types. Select "Uuencode Data
Fork" from this menu of choices.

Attach the binary file by opening the Message menu (see figs. 13.5 and 13.6) and choosing Attach Document. Then navigate through your files to find the file you want to send (see figs. 13.7 and 13.8). You're done! You should see the filename of the file you selected in the Attachments: header of your letter (see figs. 13.9 and 13.10).

Fig. 13.5
Attaching a binary file to an outgoing letter (Windows).

Fig. 13.6
Attaching a binary file to an outgoing letter (Macintosh).

Fig. 13.7
Locating the binary file to attach (Windows).

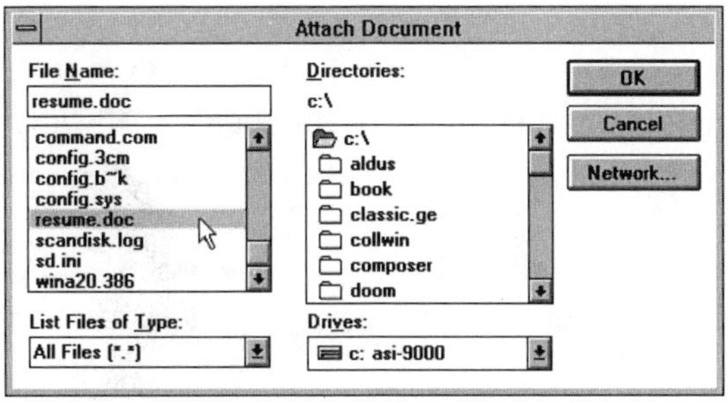

Fig. 13.8

Locating the binary file to attach (Macintosh).

Fig. 13.9

The outgoing letter, complete with attachment (Windows).

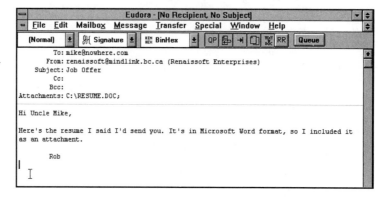

Fig. 13.10

The outgoing letter, complete with attachment (Macintosh).

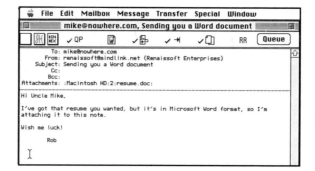

Receiving a file with a Uuencoded attachment is not a problem for Eudora; the program is smart enough to figure out how the attachment is encoded and can do you the service of converting it automatically.

Specifically, you can have Eudora do one of the following three things with a Uuencoded attachment (or any kind of attachment, for that matter):

- Save the attachment in a directory of your choice

- Save the attachment in a pre-arranged directory

- Incorporate the attachment into the incoming letter

Saving the attachment in a directory of your choice

To manually choose where the attachment should be saved when it is received, you have to ensure that auto-saving of attachments is turned off.

If you're using version 2.0 of Eudora for Windows, you can do this by opening up the Configuration dialog and making sure the check box next to Auto Receive Attachment Directory: option is blank (the text field itself can contain anything, but the check box on the left has to be blank). Now when you receive an attachment, Eudora will prompt you to tell it where you want to save it—or whether you want to save it at all.

If you're using version 2.1, you can do this from the Settings dialog, selecting Attachments. Select the Attachment Folder: box, which brings up a directory selector. At the top of this list you should see an entry called "Move&Rename". By selecting this entry instead of an actual directory, Eudora will prompt you when it receives an attachment, rather than automatically saving it somewhere.

Saving the attachment in a pre-arranged directory

By contrast, you may find it handy to create an "attachments" directory to store all incoming attachments. That way Eudora doesn't have to prompt you when it receives an attachment in your incoming mail, and you'll always know where it's been saved.

To do this with the 2.0 Windows version of Eudora, go to the Configuration dialog and fill in the text box next to Auto Receive Attachment Directory:, supplying the name and path of the directory where you want Eudora to save incoming attachments. Make sure the check box in front of this option is selected as well.

If you're using the 2.1 Macintosh version, go to the Settings dialog and select Attachments. Clicking on the Attachment Folder: box calls up a directory selector that lets you browse through your directories to find the one you want Eudora to store incoming attachments.

Incorporating the attachment into the incoming letter

If you're prompted by Eudora to tell it where to save an attachment (for example, auto-saving of attachments has been disabled), you don't necessarily have to save it at all. By clicking the Cancel button in the directory selector, you're effectively telling Eudora to insert the attachment into the letter itself, without decoding it. If you want to decode the attachment later, you'll have to save the letter to a file and extract the attachment to decode it manually.

You can run into a tricky situation, however, if the sender included the Uuencoded file as part of the *body* of the message, rather than as an attachment, where Eudora looks for such things. If this happens to you (as it might if you were sent a Uuencoded file from someone who doesn't use a mailer that supports attachments), one way around this is to select the Uuencoded portion of the message and save it as a file of its own, which can then be Uudecoded later using a separate Uudecode utility; shareware and freeware versions are widely available for Macintosh and Windows systems. It's recommended you find one that meets your needs, since Uuencoded files are widely used on the Internet. If you don't know of any Uudecoders that work with your system, a listing at the end of this chapter can get you started.

!)(Tip)

If the sender's message is relatively short and the rest of the letter contains just the Uuencoded file, it's often easier just to delete the sender's text and save what's left (that is, the Uuencoded portion) to a file. This saves you the trouble of selecting and extracting the Uuencoded portion, and it can be a lot less work to get rid of a paragraph or two at the beginning of the letter.

Some Uudecoding programs such as WinCode are smart enough to ignore any lines of text before the "begin" line (where the Uuencoded portion begins), which means you don't have to do any editing or extraction at all on your mail. Just save it to a file and process it with your smart Uudecoder.

In any case, you don't have to worry about text that follows the "end" line (the end of the Uuencoded portion); all Uudecoders stop processing when they see this line, so anything that follows (such as, a signature) will be safely ignored.

BinHex: A Macintosh alternative to Uuencoding

Just as Uuencoding converts binary files to ASCII text in the UNIX world, **BinHex** is the method of choice for Macintosh users. It's worth noting that Macintosh binaries contain two "forks"—a data fork and a resource fork, both of which must be kept together; Uuencoding fails to do this properly, so Mac users should use BinHex instead. Windows users can certainly use BinHex as well, but it's far more essential to Macintosh users, whose binary files will not remain intact without it.

To include and BinHex an attachment to an outgoing letter, select BinHex from the Attachment Type selector in the Composition Window, as we discussed previously for Uuencoding, and then attach the file as usual.

If you'd like to make BinHex the default encoding method for outgoing attachments, you can do this through the Settings or Switches dialogs.

If you're using the 2.0 version for Windows, or any of the freeware versions, go to the Switches dialog and have a look at the Send Attachments options. Select BinHex, and now whenever you enter the Composition Window you should see BinHex listed as the default attachment type.

If you're using the 2.1 version for Macintosh, go to the Settings dialog, and select Attachments. Choose BinHex from the Encoding Method options, and now whenever you enter the Composition Window you should see BinHex listed as the default attachment type.

A BinHexed file looks like garbage (see fig. 13.11), even to the well-trained eye; it lacks the tidy formatting that Uuencoding has. But you can rest assured that it's plain ASCII text that you can send by e-mail.

Fig. 13.11
A BinHexed file can
look like a random
mess of characters.

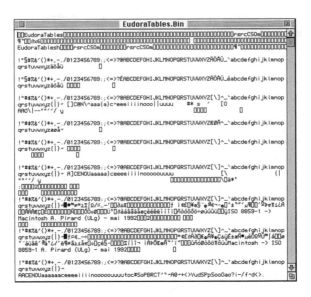

Fig. 13.11
A BinHexed file can
look like a random
mess of characters.

As with all encoded files sent by other Eudora users, receiving and converting BinHexed file attachments is done for you automatically. On the other hand, if the BinHexed file is included in the body of the message instead of as an attachment, you'll have to select the BinHexed portion of the message and save it to a separate file to be decoded separately, as we discussed in the previous section on Uuencoding. For Macintosh and Windows users, there are several shareware and freeware utilities worth looking into if you find yourself sending and receiving a lot of BinHexed files. If you can't seem to find any of these utilities, a listing at the end of this chapter can get you started.

All the world loves a MIME

MIME stands for Multipurpose Internet Mail Extensions, and it was designed to do just that—extend the capabilities of Internet electronic mail. MIME uses its own special encoding techniques to convert binary files to ASCII text and it supports the concept of attachments the way Eudora does. MIME also is used to send those fancy international character symbols the US-ASCII character set doesn't support.

One of the nice things about MIME is that it enables you to send e-mail with attachments to people who don't use Eudora; they *do* have to have a mailer that supports MIME, of course, but MIME is becoming increasingly popular across the Internet.

The downside is that if you send MIME-encoded mail to someone who doesn't have a MIME-compatible mailer, he won't be able to read it. Even if he can, it isn't likely to come out the way you intended it to. Unlike Uuencoding and BinHex, you can't easily save the MIME-encoded portion to decode separately. For this reason, you should be sure to check with the people you write to to see whether their mail programs support MIME.

If they do, you're all set. MIME attachment types can include text, graphic images, sounds, animated video clips, or any combination of these things in one letter. Imagine being able to send an e-mail message to your brother on his birthday, with a photo of the inside and outside of a birthday card, and a short voice recording of you singing "Happy Birthday"—that's the power of MIME.

Of course, you can do all of these things with Uuencoding or BinHex as well. What distinguishes MIME is the fact that you can also include international characters in your outgoing mail, and translate them properly if someone should send you a non-English letter.

MIME also keeps track of the *content-type* of an attachment, which helps determine the application the attachment is associated with. For example, a Microsoft Word document that's been Uuencoded just looks like a binary file with a "*.doc" extension when it reaches the recipient; sending the same document MIME-encoded, the recipient knows the file was created by Microsoft Word.

Perhaps the best reason for using MIME is that for Internet users who don't use Eudora, MIME is the most popular way to send and receive attachments. If you've received attachments from non-Eudora users, chances are it was MIME-encoded.

Sending MIME-encoded mail is just as simple as sending any other kind of encoded e-mail. You start by writing the text message in the Composition window, and then clicking on the Attachment Type selector, as we did in the previous section on Uuencoding.

If you're using any of the Eudora versions for Macintosh, select AppleDouble from the menu that appears (AppleDouble is MIME-compatible).

If you're using the Windows versions of Eudora, select MIME from the menu that appears.

Open the Message menu and choose Attach Document, then browse to find the binary file you want to attach, as we described earlier in this chapter. The result will be readable by anyone who uses Eudora *and* anyone whose mailer supports MIME.

MIME tries to be a bit clever about naming the binary files it finds as attachments in the mail you receive. If you receive an image file, for instance, MIME tries to figure out what format the file is, and what extension to use in the filename when MIME extracts the file from the mail message. This process is called **mapping**, and it's done slightly differently on Macintosh and Windows systems.

Mapping on Macintosh systems

On Macintosh systems in particular, proper file-mapping can be essential. This is because a Mac file has a "creator" and a "type" attribute that have to be properly set if an application program is to recognize the file as one of its own. You might have a perfectly good Microsoft Word document, for example, but if its creator isn't set to "MSWD", Microsoft Word won't recognize it, and may refuse to load it.

This is less of a problem in more recent versions of Eudora (1.5+), where a good number of file types are recognized automatically, but the problem will always exist for those obscure applications Eudora doesn't know about. If you've got some custom applications whose files you figure you might want to send to people as attachments, you'll need to learn how to edit Eudora's mapping tables.

Eudora for the Macintosh uses two "resource tables"—one for mapping incoming data (EuIM) and one for mapping outgoing data (EuOM). These are resource files in the normal sense, and they're most easily viewed and edited with a program like ResEdit (see fig. 13.12). ResEdit can be a bit complicated to figure out unless you know what you're doing, so you might want to ask your local guru for some help if you've never used it before.

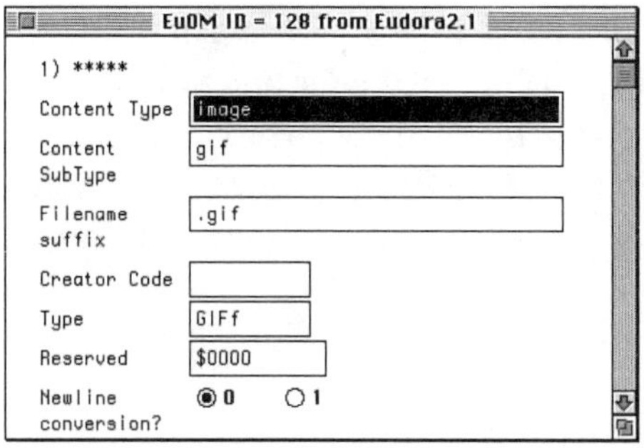

Fig. 13.12
Using ResEdit to edit the EuOM Outgoing mapping table.

The various fields, in order, are

- Content Type

- Content Subtype

- Filename Suffix

- Creator Code

- Type

- Newline Conversion flag

- May Suppress Resource flag

Content Type and Content Subtype are the MIME file type and subtype, which are generally found in the Content-Type header of your e-mail. Their purpose is to tell Eudora (and the receiver's mailer) what kind of information is stored in a message. Content Type is fairly general, such as text, image, video, audio, or application, while Content Subtype gets more specific. For example, if you were sending a GIF graphic image, its type would be image and its subtype would be GIF.

Filename Suffix is the filename extension that you want MIME to tack on to the end of the filename when you receive a file of this type, if it matches this mapping entry. In other words, if you receive a message that matches this resource entry in your EuIM file, MIME will automatically append this filename suffix to the filename when it saves the file to disk.

Creator Code and Creator Type are the Macintosh-specific codes that tell Eudora what program created the file and in what format it's stored. For instance, a file created by Microsoft Word might have a creator code of MSWD and a file type of WDBN. This is important information; many applications won't recognize text or data files that don't have the right Creator and Type Codes.

❓Q&A

What's a newline?

A **newline** is a carriage return followed by a linefeed (often called a CR/LF pair). The carriage return moves the cursor to the left margin, while the linefeed moves it down a line. This is what normally happens when you press the Enter key in your favorite word processor and other text applications.

The Newline Conversion flag determines whether a carriage return in your messages should be expanded to a carriage return and a linefeed (newline). For text messages, this should be set to 1. Binary files shouldn't be tampered with (set to 0).

The May Suppress Resource fork flag lets you determine whether the resource fork, including creator and file type data, is sent with the file, or whether only the data fork gets included. If you're using version 2.0 or the freeware version of Eudora, you can override this flag by selecting Always As Mac Documents from the Switches dialog; while this option is turned on, the May Suppress Resource Fork flag is ignored, and the resource fork will always be included. If you're using version 2.1, you can do this by going to the Settings dialog and selecting Attachments, then turning on the "Always include Macintosh information" box.

The main reason for including the resource fork is to keep the creator and type information with the file, so that other Macintosh programs can read them properly. You don't need to include the resource forks for binaries you send to non-Mac users (such as, graphics, sound files, and so on).

If you discover that some of the file types you use aren't recognized by Eudora, you can also add new entries to the EuOM and EuIM resources with a resource editor like ResEdit. Just remember that if you want a mapping to work for both incoming and outgoing files, you have to make matching entries in the EuOM and EuIM resources.

①(Tip)

While it's often sufficient to create a single mapping for a file type in the outgoing resource (EuOM), you'll likely find it useful to create several different mappings for incoming file types (EuIM). This is due to the fact that you'll be receiving files from all sorts of different mailers, and they won't all send much descriptive information for Eudora to use to identify the file type. By creating several slightly different mapping patterns for each file type, you make sure that even if the incoming mail isn't very descriptive, it's still enough for Eudora to map it to the right file type.

As an example, receiving a GIF type might involve setting several EuIM mappings. The complete mapping might look like this:

Content Type: image

Content Subtype: gif

Filename suffix: .gif

Creator Code: JVWR

Type: GIFf

However, in case the sender's mailer fails to include the proper Content Subtype information, you can include a second entry like this:

Content Type: image

Content Subtype:

Filename suffix: .gif

Creator Code: JVWR

Type: GIFf

This mapping entry will interpret all incoming files of MIME type image as GIF files, complete with .gif extension and the proper Macintosh creator and type codes. Note that this doesn't change the format of the file to a GIF, it simply makes the blind assumption that all image files will be GIFs; this might be useful if GIF is the only image format you can view, for instance.

When you have multiple mapping entries for an incoming file to match itself against, Eudora will try to find the most specific match (the entry that matches the most fields). If it ends up with a tie, the first of the tying matches is chosen.

Mapping on Windows systems

If you take the time to look through the EUDORA.INI file, you'll find a section that begins with the label Mappings. The lines that follow in that section are maps which tell Eudora all it needs to know about how to handle various types of files. By default, it contains entries such as:

```
[Mappings]
in=txt,,TEXT,text,plain
out=txt,ttxt,TEXT,text,plain
both=doc,MSWD,,application,msword
out=mcw,MSWD,WDBN,application,msword
in=xls,XCEL,,,
out=xls,XCEL,XLS4,,
both=xlc,XCEL,XLC3,,
both=wav,SCPL,WAVE,audio,microsoft-wave
both=wri,,,application,microsoft-write
both=zip,pZIP,pZIP,application,zip
```

The format of each entry is as follows:

```
Direction = PC Extension, Mac Creator, Mac Type, MIME type, MIME subtype
```

The Direction field can be "in" (use this map for incoming messages only), "out" (use this map for outgoing messages only), or "both" (use this map for incoming and outgoing messages).

PC Extension is the filename extension Eudora should use to save the attachment as, if it matches the rest of the fields that follow.

Mac Creator and Mac Type are fields which apply to Macintosh files, describing the program which created the file and the file's type. You'll find that these fields are useful if you intend to send files from a PC to a Macintosh or vice-versa. In the PC world, the file extender is usually a good indicator of the creator program and file type, but in the Macintosh world, programs expect this information to be stated explicitly; by keeping both PC and Macintosh values here, you can do things such as sending Microsoft Word for Windows documents from your PC to someone with a Macintosh, and he'll be able to load it directly into Microsoft Word for Macintosh without a fuss.

MIME Type describes the file type for MIME's benefit. Typically, it's one of text, image, audio, video, or application. This information is sent in the headers of your e-mail under Content-Type, so that the receiving mailer can use its own mapping tables to figure out what kind of extension and file ownership information to use when saving the file.

MIME Subtype allows you to be a little more specific about the basic MIME type. For example, an image file might be stored in GIF format, or perhaps as a JPEG file, PCX file, and so on.

Blank fields imply that any value will be considered a match, which is sort of a wild-card entry.

As an example, let's have a look at the entry:

```
both=gif,JVWR,GIFf,image,gif
```

This entry says that for both incoming and outgoing mail with a Content-type: image/gif header, the file attachment should be stored with a .gif extension on PC systems, and on Macintosh systems it should be saved with type GIFf and creator JVWR. That way, whether the image is being sent from a PC to a Macintosh or vice-versa, it'll be saved properly at the receiving end.

If you want to add more entries to the maps in the EUDORA.INI file, you can do so by editing the file with any text editor, such as the Windows Notepad.

Special utilities for files

As mentioned earlier, there are times when you may want or need to use another program to send or receive a file with Eudora. This section gives you a brief introduction to the best programs to use, both in Windows and on a Mac.

WinCode: The cream of the Windows crop

WinCode 2.6 is a helpful utility for Windows that allows you to Uuencode and Uudecode files. It's smart enough to ignore any text before the Uuencoded portions when it's decoding, so you can have it reconstruct binary files that are embedded in your mail without having to strip away the surrounding text of the message. Particularly helpful is a feature that can be used to incorporate WinCode's menus directly into programs like Eudora.

Like most of the files in this section, WinCode is widely available and is distributed as shareware. You can find it by FTP at **oak.oakland.edu** as /pub/win3/encode/wncod261.zip.

Stuffit for Mac

Perhaps the single most essential utility a Mac user should have is a tool to decode BinHexed files, because this format is used to transfer virtually all Mac binaries.

Stuffit Expander 3.52 is a useful tool for this purpose, and also uncompresses *.SIT files. Stuffit Lite 3.5 does the reverse, allowing you to BinHex and compress files before sending them. DropStuff 3.52 works with Stuffit Expander to let you do the decoding in the background. These programs are either freeware or shareware, and a commercial version (Stuffit Deluxe) exists for heavy-duty users.

You can find these files by FTP at **wcarchive.cdrom.com** in the directory /pub/mac/umich/util/compression as:

· dropstuff3.52.sea.hqx

stuffitexpander3.52.sea.hqx

stuffitlite3.5.sea.hqx

UUTool for Mac

Just as Windows users have WinCode to do their Uuencoding and Uudecoding for them, Mac users have UUTool 2.32. It's also a smart Uudecoder that can extract a binary file from the middle of a text message.

UUTool is shareware, and is available by FTP from **wcarchive.cdrom.com** in pub/mac/umich/util/compression as:

uutool2.32.hqx

File compression: Squeezing more data into less space

Chapter 3, "How Internet E-mail Works," explained that all mail programs are not created equal. Some will support mail messages of enormous length, while others are more frugal and happily exile long messages to the outermost rings of Saturn. You may never get anywhere near the magical size limits in your letters to Uncle Mike, but it's very easy to do so when you're sending binary files.

It's a good idea to compress your binary files before you encode them as attachments to your e-mail, whether that means using a program like PKZIP, LhArc, or Stuffit. These programs also will let you package a number of files together before compressing them, so you can keep related files together as one attachment.

Keep in mind, of course, that the receiver has to be able to uncompress the attachment once she gets it, so you should choose a compression tool she likely has access to. In the Windows world, PKZIP (*.ZIP) is a popular choice, while Stuffit (*.SIT) is in widespread use among Macintosh users. In addition, some of these utilities let you produce **self-extracting** files—compressed files that don't require the receiver to have any special programs to expand them. Essentially, the receiver just executes the file as though it were just an ordinary program, and it expands itself.

It's also worth keeping in mind that while programs like Stuffit are Mac-specific, and PKZIP is PC-specific, you can generally find ZIP utilities for the Mac and SIT utilities for the PC. This can be handy if you accidentally (or intentionally) end up with a file for the other platform, for instance.

WinZip for Windows

Windows users no longer have to exit to DOS to ZIP and UNZIP files. WinZip 5.5 lets you package files together ("archive" them) and compress them before sending them to others, and it can likewise take *.ZIP files apart when you receive them. It supports drag-and-drop as a means of adding files to archives, lets you view the contents of an archive, and even executes programs from within an archive.

WinZip is shareware, available from **oak.oakland.edu** in the directory /pub/ win3/archiver as:

winzip55.exe

Stuffit for Mac

Stuffit Lite 3.5 is the archiver and compression tool of choice for Mac users, producing the ubiquitous *.SIT files. Stuffit Expander 3.52 takes apart these archives, and also takes care of BinHexing for you. DropStuff 3.52 allows these tasks to take place in the background. These programs are shareware or freeware, and a commercial version (Stuffit Deluxe) is available for power users.

Among other places, you can get the various Stuffit packages by FTP from the site **wcarchive.cdrom.com** in the directory /pub/mac/umich/util/compression as:

dropstuff3.52.sea.hqx

stuffitexpander3.52.sea.hqx

stuffitlite3.5.sea.hqx

Part IV:

Maintenance

14

Mailboxes and Folders

You can create mailboxes of your own to better organize your mail. If you're a compulsive organizer, you'll love the way Eudora lets you file your mail.

Now that you've learned how to send and receive mail with Eudora, you've probably come across the terms "mailbox" and "folder" a few times and wondered what the distinction between them is. This chapter explains this often-confusing difference, and much more.

What is a mailbox, anyway?

Eudora uses the term **mailbox** to refer to a file where you can store mail messages. Certain mailboxes like In, Out, and Trash are standard, and fit pretty well with our post office concept—the In box is where incoming mail gets put, outgoing mail waits in the Out box, and you can think of the Trash box as the little round can in the corner.

In addition to the standard mailboxes, you can also create mailboxes of your own to better organize your mail. That way, you can keep all of your mail to and from Uncle Mike in its own mailbox, for instance. In fact, if you're a compulsive organizer, you'll love the way Eudora lets you file your mail.

You can keep all of your mail that's to and from a particular person in its own mailbox to help keep things straight. Store your correspondence with Uncle Mike in a mailbox called "Mike," for example, and the letters you exchange with your mother in a box called "Mom." You might keep mail to and from your boss in a mailbox called "Big Cheese," and make another mailbox called "Joe" for one of your coworkers.

As you can imagine, this can get out of hand pretty quickly if you write to a lot of different people. That's where **folders** come in. A folder is like a mailbox for mailboxes; it groups selected mailboxes together the way a file folder groups sheets of paper.

For instance, you might group together your mail to friends and family (your mother and Uncle Mike) in a folder called Personal, and keep your business mail (your boss and Joe) in a folder called Business.

The nice thing about folders is that they let you organize your mailboxes in a hierarchy, much the same way Windows and Macintosh systems let you organize files. Think of the mail system as a filing cabinet, where a folder corresponds to a drawer, a mailbox to a hanging folder, and an individual mail message is a piece of paper in the file.

Mailbox windows

In everyday use, you'll become intimately familiar with the mailbox window (see figs. 14.1 through 14.3). Let's take one apart and have a look at what all this information means.

 **{Note}**_____ It's easy to confuse the terms "mailbox window" and "Mailboxes Window," which refer to very different things. A **mailbox window** is a window in which you can view the contents of a mailbox. The **Mailboxes Window** is a special window that is really more of a dialog than a window, and lets you create and manipulate mailboxes and folders. In this chapter, we'll distinguish between them by using lowercase to refer to a mailbox window, and we'll capitalize references to the Mailboxes Window.

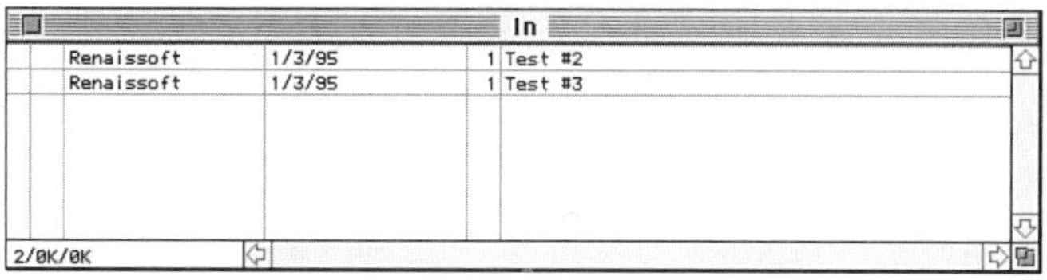

Fig. 14.1

The In mailbox is typical of what a mailbox window looks like (Macintosh freeware).

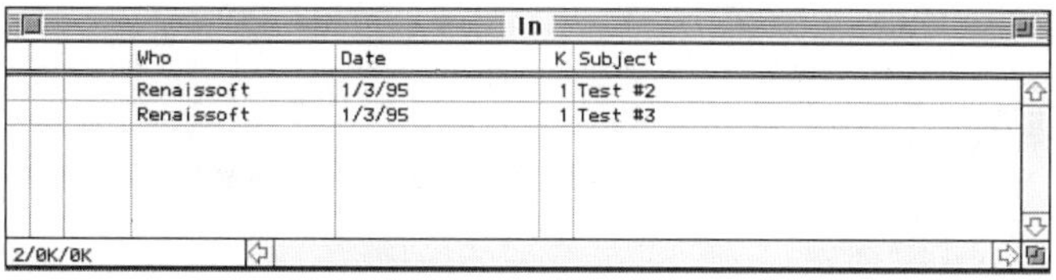

Fig. 14.2

The In mailbox is typical of what a mailbox window looks like (Macintosh commercial).

Fig. 14.3

A mailbox window in the eyes of a Windows user.

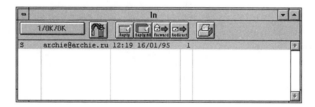

What makes up a mailbox window?

Sender/Recipient Column   Size Column   Subject Column

Macintosh freeware version

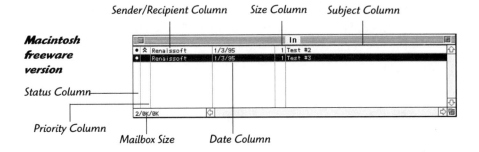

Status Column

Priority Column   Mailbox Size   Date Column

Label Column   Sender/Recipient Column   Size Column

Macintosh commercial version

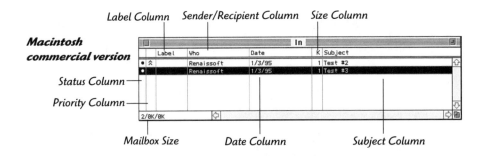

Status Column

Priority Column

Mailbox Size   Date Column   Subject Column

Mailbox Size   Reply   Forward   Print

Trash   Reply All   Redirect

Windows freeware and commercial versions

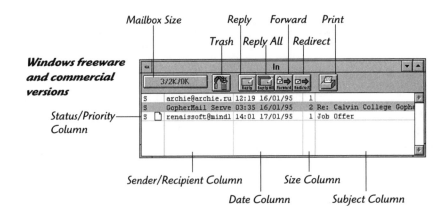

Status/Priority Column

Sender/Recipient Column   Size Column

Date Column   Subject Column

The title bar of a mailbox window tells you the name of the mailbox you're looking at.

For Windows users, there's also an icon bar directly below the title bar that contains some useful buttons and information. The next section describes these buttons, from left to right.

Buttons speed your way in Windows

The Mailbox Size button looks more like an information window than a button; it's the widest button on the bar and it contains three numbers separated by slashes (/). The first number (on the left) is the number of messages in the mailbox. The second number tells you how much total disk space these messages take up, and the third number (on the right) tells you how much trash (wasted disk space) is in the mailbox. While Eudora is usually pretty good about cleaning up after itself regularly, you can force it to empty the trash by clicking this button.

Macintosh users will find a similar display in the bottom-left corner of a mailbox window. To empty the trash from this mailbox, hold down the Command key (⌘) and click this display.

Speaking of trash, the Trash button throws any messages you have selected into the trash, effectively deleting them.

The Reply button does the obvious—it lets you reply to any message(s) you've selected. It's probably wise just to select one message at a time to reply to. But if you love to have lots of windows open, Eudora will be happy to try to start up replies for as many messages as you've highlighted.

 **⊗<Caution>** | If you try to open too many replies at once, you can slow down and even crash your system. Worse still, because Eudora remembers the number of windows you had open when it quits and tries to reopen them all when you start it up again, you can find yourself crashing all over again the next time you start up Eudora.

The Reply All button starts up a reply to any marked messages in the mailbox, just like the Reply button, but in addition to sending a reply to the sender of each message, it also sends a reply to everyone else that message was addressed to.

Clicking the Forward button will forward the marked message(s) to someone else, just as if you'd chosen the Forward command from the Message menu. Note that if you select multiple messages, this will open up separate forwarding messages for each one—it will not forward all the selected messages to a single recipient, as you might think.

The Redirect button works much like the Forward button, only it "bounces" the selected messages to the recipients as though you'd never received them.

Clicking the Print button tells Eudora to print all of the selected messages in the mailbox.

Understanding message summaries

The bulk of a mailbox window consists of rows of **message summaries**, each of which has five columns to describe a message. The following sections look at each of these in detail.

Status/Priority column

The first column (from the left) contains a two- or three-character code that represents the status and priority level of the message. The first character represents the status and the second character represents the priority level. In the Windows version, a third character is used to indicate whether the message also has an attachment associated with it. The following table shows the status.

Status code	What it means
•	In the Out mailbox, this symbol means that the message can be queued to be sent, but hasn't been yet. In all other mailboxes, it simply means the message hasn't been read yet.
<blank space>	In the Out mailbox, this means that the message has no recipients, so it can't yet be queued to be sent. In all other mailboxes, it indicates that the message has been read.
-	A dash indicates that the message was moved to this mailbox from the Out mailbox before it was sent.
D	This code means that redirection has been selected for this message; when you choose to send it out, it will be sent as a redirection rather than as an original message.
F	Similar to the redirection code above, this code tells Eudora that this message should be forwarded when it's sent out.
R	This code means that you've chosen to reply to this message.
S	The S code only shows up next to outgoing messages; it indicates that the message has been sent.

The priority codes are shown in figure 14.4. Note that when you receive a message with a priority other than normal, the symbol for that priority will appear in the priority column for that message in the In box (see fig. 14.4). This column is blank for normal priority messages.

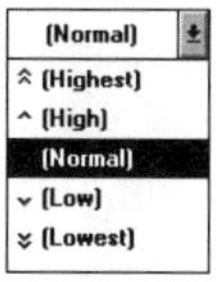

Fig. 14.4

This shows all of the available message priority codes.

[Normal]	⬍
⩘ (Highest)	
⌃ (High)	
[Normal]	
⌄ (Low)	
⩗ (Lowest)	

By default, the Status/Priority column only displays the first two character codes (status and priority level). To display the attachment code as well, you'll have to widen the Status/Priority column by moving the mouse to the vertical line between the first and second columns, holding down the left mouse button, and dragging the column divider farther to the right (see Adjusting column widths later in this chapter for more details).

Messages with attachments are shown with the Attachment icon (see fig. 14.5). This icon will be the same, regardless of how many attachments there are.

Fig. 14.5
The first message in this window has an attachment, the second one does not.

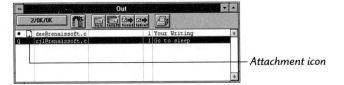

Attachment icon

If you want to change the status of a message in the mailbox window, select the message, and then open the Message menu and choose Set Status. After you've chosen the status you want for that message, release the mouse button and the Status/Priority code in the mailbox window should change accordingly.

Sender/Recipient column

For incoming messages, the Sender/Recipient column shows you the name of the person who sent you the message; for outgoing messages, this column displays the name of the recipient.

Date column

This is usually the date the message was sent. But in the case of timed messages (messages scheduled to be sent at a future time), this is the time the message *will* be sent. If you wish to change the format of the time or date, you can do this from the date and time configuration options in the Control Panel of your Macintosh or Windows system.

Size column

This column displays the size of the message in kilobytes, rounded up.

Subject column

This is the subject or title of the message, as entered by the sender.

Adjusting column widths

If you find you're not seeing as much information at a glance in your message summary lines, you can widen or shrink each of the columns to suit your tastes. You may find, for instance, that the Sender/Recipient column is excessively wide, and the Subject field seems too narrow. By shrinking the width of one and widening the other, you can make better use of your mailbox display.

To adjust the width of a column in a mailbox window, move the mouse to the vertical dividing line you'd like to move. The mouse pointer will change to a pair of arrows, one pointing left, the other pointing right (see fig. 14.6). Hold down the left mouse button and drag the divider in the direction you want to move it. When you've got it where you want it, let go and the mailbox window will redraw itself.

Naturally, you can only move a divider as far as the next divider in either direction. If you want to make changes to several columns, you're best to start from either the rightmost or leftmost column and work inward, moving the column dividers one at a time until they're all where you want them.

Creating a new mailbox or folder

After you've used Eudora for a little while, you'll soon find yourself wanting to organize all the mail you've accumulated into some kind of meaningful structure.

As hinted at earlier, you can use mailboxes to group together mail to and from a particular person, and then group some of these mailboxes together into folders to create an organized hierarchy.

To do any of these things, you first have to become familiar with the Mailboxes Window. Don't confuse this with mailbox windows covered in the previous section; the Mailboxes Window (see figs. 14.6 and 14.7) is a utility that allows you to create and manipulate mailboxes and folders.

Fig. 14.6
The Mailboxes Window (Macintosh).

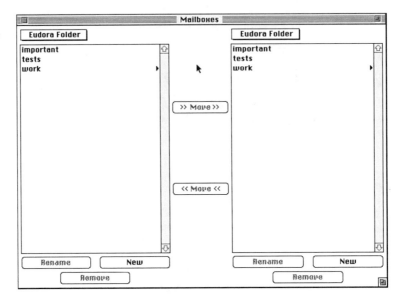

Fig. 14.7
The Mailboxes Window (Windows).

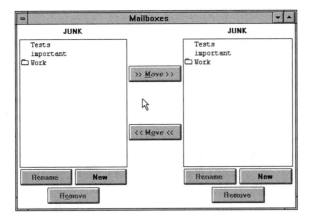

Let's take a closer look at this window. At a glance, it consists of two separate column listings that look very similar. The items in both lists are the names of mailboxes and folders. Folders are indicated on Macintosh systems by a right-pointing triangle to the right of the name; on Windows systems, a small folder icon is displayed before the name. Between the two listings there are a pair of Move buttons, one pointing in either direction, for moving items from one listing to the other. Beneath each listing are the buttons Rename, Remove, and New, which will be explained shortly. Lastly, above each listing is the name of the folder whose contents are displayed in that list.

You can think of the Mailboxes Window as a kind of file and directory browser similar to that used by Macintosh and Windows systems. If there are more mailboxes and folders than you can see in a listing, you can use the scroll bar to the right of the listing to navigate up and down through the complete list. Likewise, double-clicking a folder opens that folder and changes the display in that listing to show the contents (see figs. 14.8 and 14.9). Double-clicking the name of a mailbox opens up a mailbox window for that mailbox, allowing you to manipulate the mail within it.

Fig. 14.8
Double-clicking a folder opens it ...

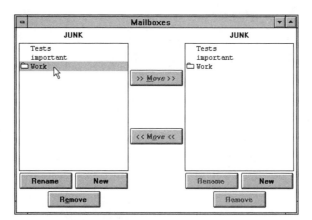

Fig. 14.9
... and displays its contents.

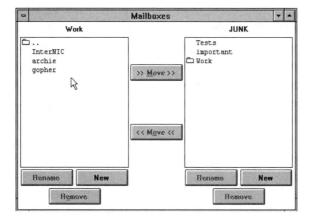

To create a new mailbox or folder, you only need to use one of the two listings in the Mailboxes Window (it doesn't matter which one you choose).

1 Choose either the left or right listing and navigate through the folders until you come to the folder you want to create your new mailbox or folder in (if your listing doesn't show any folders at all, you'll have to create your new mailbox or folder where you are, namely in the folder named above the listing, usually "Eudora Folder").

2 Click the New button below the listing. You should see the New Mailbox Dialog (see figs. 14.10 and 14.11).

Fig. 14.10
You can create a new mailbox or folder from the New Mailbox Dialog (Macintosh).

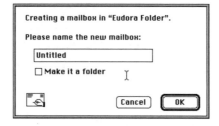

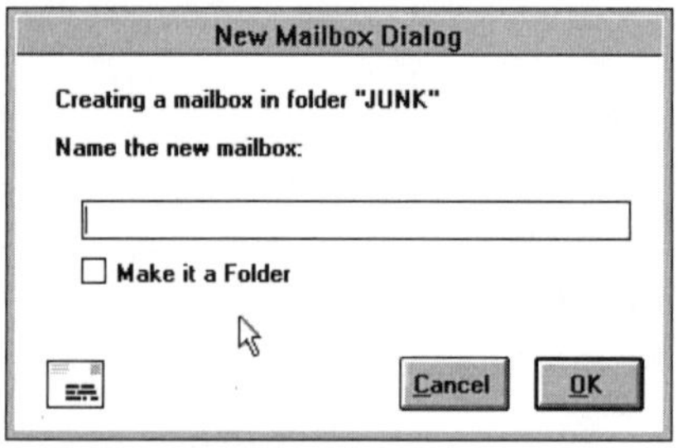

Fig. 14.11
You can create a new mailbox or folder from the New Mailbox Dialog (Windows).

3 Enter the name of the new mailbox or folder (yes, you can use spaces and punctuation marks too). By default, Eudora will assume you want to create a new mailbox; if you want to create a new folder instead, select the "Make it a folder" check box. (Remember: Mailboxes hold mail, folders hold mailboxes.)

4 Click on OK, and Eudora will do the rest. You should see your new mailbox or folder in the listing after the dialog box closes.

> There's another special way to create mailboxes and folders with Eudora that can be quite useful if you happen to be in a mailbox window at the time you realize the need for the new item. In particular, when you receive mail from someone new (for whom you don't have a mailbox), you may want to move his mail from your In mailbox to a brand new mailbox in one step.
>
> To do this, select the message in the mailbox window and open the Transfer menu. Instead of selecting another (existing) mailbox to move his mail to, choose New and enter the name of the new mailbox in the dialog box that appears.

Moving, renaming, and deleting mailboxes or folders

If you've ever used a telephone/address book for any length of time, you probably have dozens of scratched-out entries and margin notes for new phone numbers, name changes due to marriage, and changes of address. You may not even want to have anything to do with some of the people in your address book anymore. Fortunately, Eudora makes changes like this relatively painless when it comes to dealing with mailboxes.

Moving a mailbox or folder

Unless you're one of those compulsive organizers referred to earlier, you're likely to find one day that you have a hundred mailboxes to scroll through to find the one you're looking for. If this starts to annoy you, it might be time to start separating your mailboxes into folders. Creating the new folders is simple; the previous section described how to do so. But how do you move the mailboxes into the folders you want?

1 Open the <u>W</u>indow menu and choose <u>M</u>ailboxes. The Mailboxes Window appears.

2 Use either the left or right listing to browse through your folders to find the mailbox or folder you want to move, and select it.

3 In the other listing (the one you didn't use in step 2), browse until you're looking at the contents of the folder you want to move the mailbox or folder into (the name of the destination folder should be displayed above the listing).

4 Click on the Move button that points in the direction you want to transfer the mailbox or folder (see figs. 14.12 and 14.13).

Fig. 14.12
You can move mailboxes and folders into other folders (Macintosh).

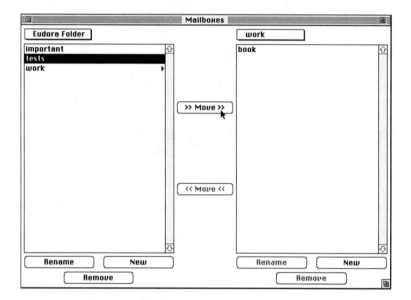

Fig. 14.13
You can move mailboxes and folders into other folders (Windows).

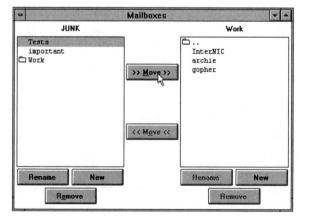

Renaming a mailbox or folder

It happens to just about everybody at one time or another. You start out naming your mailboxes with simple names like "john," "mike," "dawn," and "alex" and all is well, until you start writing to someone else named John. One popular solution is to differentiate between the two Johns by using an initial for their last names, such as "john r." and "john s." The problem is, you now have to rename the mailbox called "john."

1 Open the Window menu and choose Mailboxes. The Mailboxes Window appears.

2 Choose either the left or right listing and browse through the folders to find the mailbox or folder you want to rename, and select it.

3 Click the Rename button beneath the listing. This calls up the Rename Dialog (see figs. 14.14 and 14.15).

4 Enter the new name for the mailbox or folder in the Rename Dialog's text field.

5 Click the Rename button in the Rename Dialog, and your changes will take effect immediately. Clicking on the Cancel button aborts the procedure without making any changes.

Fig. 14.14
You can easily rename mailboxes and folders (Macintosh).

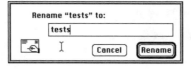

Fig. 14.15
You can easily rename mailboxes and folders (Windows).

Deleting a mailbox or folder

There are probably a thousand good reasons for wanting to delete a mailbox or folder. You might just be reorganizing your mail and throwing out old stuff you don't need anymore. You might be trimming things down to make your mail more manageable, or to save some precious disk space when things get tight. Or you might have just had the argument to end all arguments with your former best friend and never want to speak with him again, so you want to get rid of all your correspondence.

1 Open the Window menu and choose Mailboxes. The Mailboxes Window appears.

2 Choose either the left or right listing and browse through the folders until you find the mailbox or folder you want to delete, and select it. You can select multiple mailboxes or folders by holding down the Command key (⌘) (Macintosh) or the Ctrl key (Windows) and clicking the items that you want to select. To unselect a choice, just hold down this key and click the mailbox or folder again.

3 Click the Remove button below the listing. This will call up the Mailbox Removal Dialog (see figs. 14.16 and 14.17). The name of the first mailbox or folder you selected will be displayed with a prompt.

4 Click the Remove It button to delete the named mailbox or folder, or the Remove All button to delete all the items you selected. Clicking on Remove It deletes only the named item, and you'll be prompted to do the same for each of the remaining mailboxes or folders you selected. Clicking the Cancel button exits the dialog without performing any further deletions.

Fig. 14.16
Eudora confirms your intent to delete a mailbox or folder (Macintosh).

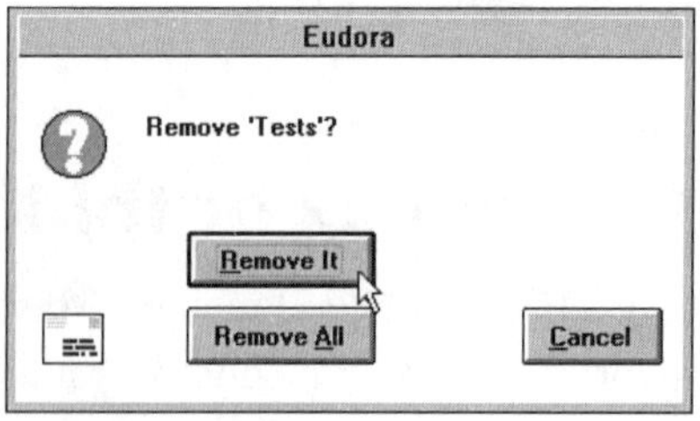

Fig. 14.17
Eudora confirms your intent to delete a mailbox or folder (Windows).

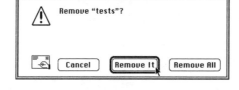

If you're about to delete a mailbox which still has messages in it, or a folder that contains mailboxes with messages in them, Eudora will send you a warning message (see figs. 14.18 and 14.19). If you choose Remove It or Remove All in this warning box, all of these messages will be deleted. Once these messages are deleted, they can't be recovered, so think carefully before doing this.

Fig. 14.18
Eudora warns you if you're about to delete a mailbox or folder with messages left in it (Macintosh).

Fig. 14.19
Eudora warns you if you're about to delete a mailbox or folder with messages left in it (Windows).

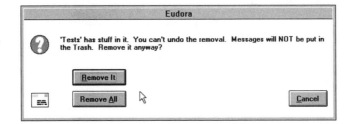

Making room in a mailbox

Macintosh users are accustomed to the concept of a "trash can" deletion system, where discarded items can be recovered as long as the trash can hasn't been emptied. For Windows users, this is a new idea; items they delete are generally considered "lost" and unrecoverable.

Eudora uses a Macintosh-like trash system in both its Macintosh and Windows versions. This means that when you delete a message, it goes into a kind of temporary holding bin; it doesn't actually get deleted until you open the Special menu and choose Empty Trash. Meanwhile, all of the messages in the trash can are still taking up space on disk.

In any mailbox window you can see just how much space is being taken up by trashed items (see the previous graphics page) by looking at the Mailbox Size display. On Macintosh systems, this is the set of numbers in the lower-left corner of a mailbox window; on Windows systems, it's the left-most button on the icon bar. The last of these numbers is the number of kilobytes of space being taken up by trash.

Normally it's sufficient to let Eudora deal with "taking out the trash" as it sees fit, but if you find yourself getting short on disk space, you may wish to get rid of all this wasted space yourself. This process is called **compacting** a mailbox.

As we mentioned in the Mailbox Windows section at the beginning of this chapter, you can compact a mailbox by clicking the Mailbox Size button in a mailbox window (Macintosh users have to hold down the Command key (⌘) while doing this).

If you want to be thorough, you can compact all of the mailboxes on your system by opening the Special menu and choosing Compact Mailboxes.

Sorting mail

Just as you can use folders to keep your mailboxes organized, you can keep the messages within a mailbox organized by sorting them by their status, priority, sender's name, the date they were sent, or their subject. This can make it a lot easier to find a particular message when you open up a mailbox—or to find out the last time you got a letter from that cheapskate Uncle Mike!

1 Open the Mailbox menu and choose the mailbox you wish to open.

2 Open the Edit menu and choose Sort.

3 From the submenu choose the option by which you wish to sort your mail (see figs. 14.20 through 14.22).

Fig. 14.20
Eudora allows you to
sort your mail several
different ways
(Macintosh freeware).

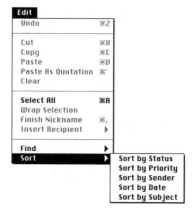

Fig. 14.21
Eudora allows you to
sort your mail several
different ways
(Macintosh
commercial).

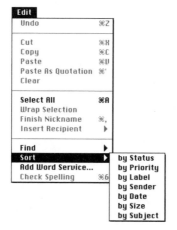

Fig. 14.22
Eudora allows you to
sort your mail several
different ways
(Windows).

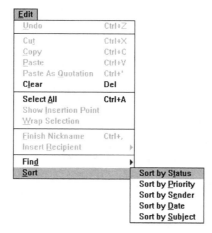

Eudora sorts items from lowest to highest (ascending order); if you wish to sort in reverse order (descending order), hold down the Option key (Macintosh) or the Shift key (Windows) while making your selection.

You can use Eudora's sorting features to sort based on more than one criterion, if you like. Suppose you want to organize your mailbox by sender, and within that you'd like to sort the messages by date, from the most recent to the least recent. The trick here is to work backwards; start by doing the sort by date. Since this is a reverse sort (latest date to earliest date), hold down the Option or Shift key while opening the Edit menu and choosing Sort, Sort by Date. After your mailbox is reordered, go back to the Edit menu and choose Sort, Sort by Sender. Now you can see at a glance when the most recent letter from Uncle Mike was sent.

15

Working with Mail

After a while, your In and Out mailboxes get pretty big and you get tired of sifting through them. At that point, it's time to start moving your mail to other mailboxes.

After a while, your In and Out mailboxes get pretty big and you get tired of sifting through them. If you selected Keep Copies when you were configuring Eudora, every piece of mail you send out is saved. You also may save a lot of the mail you receive for one reason or another. Eventually, you could have mailboxes so huge that they're awful to wade through.

All you ever wanted to know about saving mail

There's an important piece of advice that anyone who does a lot of work on computers will give you: *SAVE OFTEN!*

You never know when the power might go out, or you might hit a few keys accidentally and mess up everything you've done. One day, a calamity will strike in the middle of some four-page piece of e-mail you were writing. If you pause every few minutes to save what you're working on, then you've only lost a few minutes of work at worst. Don't be like the many college students who are almost finished writing the ten-page paper that's due tomorrow when the power goes out in the computer lab, and then they suddenly remember they never bothered to save their work.

❷Q&A

Should I keep backups of my e-mail messages?

If you've got important information in your e-mail, don't trust that it will always be there for you on your computer. Hard drives crash, disks go bad…it's amazing how many ways we manage to lose our data. This is why it's important to do two things: back up, and keep hard copies.

Backing up your e-mail can be done by saving it to floppy disks, to another computer on your network, or to a backup unit such as a tape drive. If you save it to floppies, make sure to keep those floppies in a separate place from your computer, such as in a disk box in your file cabinet or on a bookshelf on the other side of your office. You don't want the same catastrophe (theft or a lightning strike) that takes your e-mail from you to take your backup disks too!

Don't forget to label those disks so you'll know what's on each one. It's pretty daunting to look at a box of 20 disks and realize that somewhere, in there, is the backup of that file you need for a meeting that is only three hours away.

For that *really* important information, you'll want to keep hard copies too. That way, if all else fails you have a printout to look back on.

How do I save my mail while I'm working on it?

No matter what kind of window you have open, whether it's a new mail message, a reply, a forward, and so on, you can save a message by going to the File menu and selecting the Save option. Your composition window won't close, but you'll have a copy of the mail on disk exactly as it was when you selected Save. The file will be saved to your Out mailbox.

How do I save my mail to come back to it later?

Sometimes you're in the middle of a note and realize that you don't know some vital piece of information you need. No problem. There's no law that says you have to send out a piece of e-mail the same hour, day, or even week that you write it.

Just as we mentioned in the previous section, you go to the <u>F</u>ile menu and select the <u>S</u>ave option. Then, to close the message, just click in the close box in the upper-left corner of the composition window.

Later, when you want to reopen the message, go to the Out mailbox, find the message in the list, and then double-click on it.

✷ **{Note}** _____ | If you try to close a composition window without saving your work, a dialog box appears asking you if you want to save or discard the message. Be careful. If you discard it, you've just erased it. Figures 15.1 and 15.2 show you what you'll see on Macintosh and Windows systems.

Fig. 15.1
Macintosh Save/
Discard dialog box.

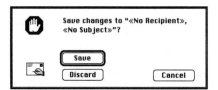

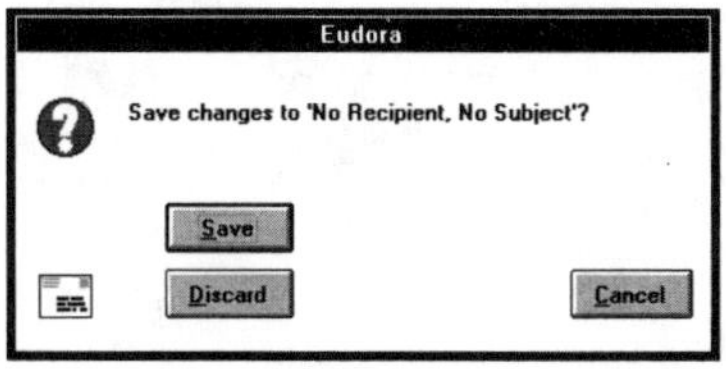

Fig. 15.2
Windows Save/
Discard dialog box.

How do I save my mail to a file instead of a mailbox?

Sometimes it's necessary to save mail to a normal text file. For example, you can put that mail on a disk and work on it somewhere else, even if you don't have Eudora where you'll be.

To save a mail message to a file, choose the File menu and select the Save As option. Figures 15.3, 15.4, and 15.5 show you what you'll see in various versions of Eudora.

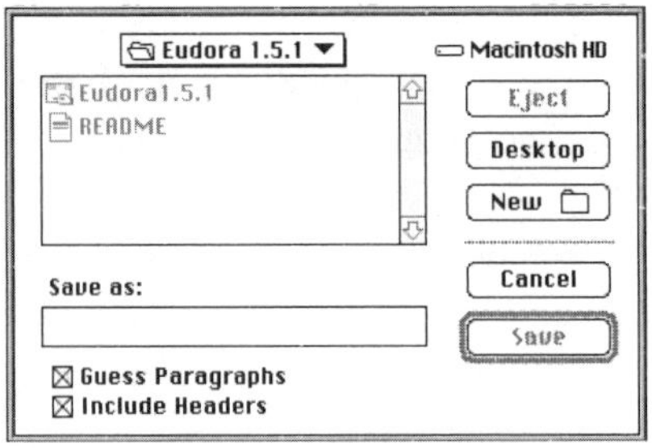

Fig. 15.3
Macintosh Freeware
Save As dialog box.

The death of a hard drive

During a recent move, Rob's eight-year-old Atari ST hard drive finally crashed, never to live again. Years of his work on personal projects were stored there, so it was a somewhat painful experience. Things became even more painful when we suddenly needed to refer to some of the things he'd had on it for a current project.

Fortunately, he had floppy backups of most of his work. We booted up the ST with a floppy and then spent about an hour going through the disks (which weren't well labeled) and managed to find what we were looking for. If he hadn't had those backups it would have taken us hours, maybe days, to reproduce that work. We were lucky it wasn't something that might have taken us weeks.

After that harrowing experience, we took some time to properly label the backup disks. This type of problem is what inspired us to invest in a tape backup drive.

Fig. 15.4
Macintosh
Commercial
Save As dialog
box.

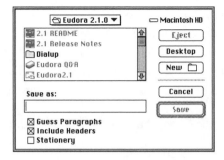

Fig. 15.5
Windows Save As
dialog box.

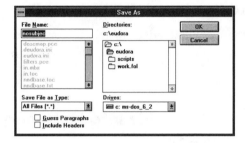

Choose a filename that will mean something to you when you look back at it later, and choose a directory you'll readily find it in (you don't have to keep it in your Eudora directory). Once you've chosen the filename and directory, select Save.

Most of the dialog box is familiar to you already. However, you have some extra options to choose from.

Saving without using Word Wrap

If you turn on the Guess Paragraphs switch, Eudora will remove all carriage returns from your message except the ones at the end of paragraphs. Now, you're probably thinking that those are the only carriage returns you put in there if you're using Word Wrap. What Word Wrap really does is find out where the end of each line will be on the page without breaking a word up, and then insert a carriage return in front of the word that needs to go down to the next line to stay in one piece. When you end a paragraph, however, Eudora inserts two carriage returns so it can tell the difference between a paragraph and a normal line end. Using the Guess Paragraphs switch tells Eudora not to save the Word Wrap carriage returns.

Turning on the Guess Paragraphs switch also turns multiple spaces into tabs. That means that if you used the spacebar to indent things, those spaces will become one big space, the same thing that happens when you use the Tab key. The problem is that to get multiple indentations, Eudora needs to know how many spaces to look for to assume you want more than one tab.

If you don't turn on the Guess Paragraphs switch, Eudora will just leave everything like it is.

Saving headers along with your mail

If you turn on the Include Headers switch, Eudora saves the header information and the body of your message in the file. If you don't, only the body of your message is saved.

Making a saved mail file into Stationery (Macintosh commercial version only)

If you turn on the Stationery switch, the current piece of mail will be saved to an icon instead of a normal file. There are two different uses for the Stationery switch.

Stationery for lists and form e-mail letters

You can use stationery as you use canned messages, creating lists and form e-mail letters you frequently have to send out. Just leave the "To:" header blank. Then, when you want to use the stationery later, double-click the icon for the one you want.

Stationery for all outgoing messages

You can also use stationery to create a template to use when sending out all of your e-mail. If the message you're saving consists only of what you want to have in every piece of mail you send out, turn on the Stationery switch and name the file "Stationery."

 **❌<Caution>** Be careful spelling it. "Stationary" won't work!

Now, every time you open a new message Eudora will use your Stationery file.

 **{Note}**

You're not stuck with your Stationery. If you don't want a particular message to use the Stationery format, you can change the format once you've opened up the new message.

How do I tell Eudora what application I want my saved files to belong to? (Macintosh versions only)

As discussed in the configuration section in chapter 5, you can tell Eudora what application you want to use to work on mail you save to a file. This lets your computer know what program to use when you double-click on the file later to work on it. If you don't want to use something as an attachment, it's best to leave it in TeachText or SimpleText.

How do I save copies of all of the mail I send out?

It's a good idea to select Keep Copies of outgoing mail (found by going to the Special menu, selecting Settings, and selecting Sending Mail). That way, if you forget what you said to someone in some e-mail you sent last week, you can just look at the note instead of having to ask him or faking it. Also, sometimes mail gets lost out there in the vast expanses of the Internet. If someone says he never got the e-mail you sent him, you can just open up your copy of it and "bounce," or redirect, it to him.

How do I delete mail from a mailbox?

It's just as easy to be a packrat with your files as it is to be a packrat with your worldly belongings. Either way, you end up wasting a lot of space with things you really don't need to keep.

Eudora knows how imperfect we humans are, so the program makes it difficult to accidentally delete something we were going to send out. Not selecting Easy Delete (Windows versions, found by going to the Special menu and selecting Switches) or selecting Require Confirmation for deletes (Macintosh versions, found by going to the Special menu, selecting Settings, and selecting Miscellaneous) makes sure Eudora checks with you before it deletes something from the Out mailbox.

To delete the current message, go to the Message menu and choose the Delete option. Figures 15.6 and 15.7 show you what you'll see in the Macintosh and Windows versions if you try to delete something in the Out mailbox and your options are set as discussed previously.

Fig. 15.6
The Macintosh Delete dialog box.

Fig. 15.7
The Windows Delete dialog box.

Doing this just moves the message to the Trash mailbox. Messages aren't really deleted until you go to the Special menu and choose the Empty Trash option.

As mentioned in the previous chapter, if you select the Empty Trash on Quit option, the Trash mailbox is cleaned out when you exit Eudora. This option can be found in the Windows versions by opening the Special menu and selecting Switches, and in the Macintosh versions by opening the Special menu, selecting Settings, and then selecting Miscellaneous.

How do I move mail between mailboxes?

If you want to move the current message from the mailbox it's in now to another one, go to the Transfer menu and select the name of the mailbox you want to move it to. Figures 15.8 and 15.9 show an example of having a Transfer menu open plus a mailbox submenu in the Macintosh and Windows versions.

Fig. 15.8

Example Macintosh Transfer menu and mailbox submenu.

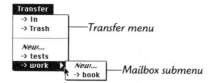

——Transfer menu

——Mailbox submenu

Fig. 15.9

Example Windows Transfer menu and mailbox submenu.

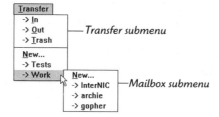

——Transfer submenu

——Mailbox submenu

(!)(Tip)

> If you want to transfer a lot of files from one mailbox to another, you can do them all at once. In the Windows versions you can do this by holding down the Ctrl key while you select the messages. In the Macintosh versions, hold down the ⌘ key while you select the messages to transfer. Then, use the Transfer menu like you would if you were just moving one message.

Only in the commercial versions of Eudora can you transfer a message to the Out mailbox. If you try to transfer a message out of the Out mailbox and with the Easy Delete switch off or the Require Confirmation for deletes switch on, you'll get the same dialog boxes shown in figures 15.10 and 15.11.

(✱){Note}

> You can undo a mail transfer in the commercial versions by going to the Edit menu and selecting the Undo option.

How do I copy mail from one mailbox to another?

Sometimes you have so many special mailboxes that a mail message has to go in more than one of them. There's nothing worse than spending ten minutes searching for a particular message when you want to read it again, and not being sure of exactly where you saved it. That's when you want to just copy a message over instead of transferring it so you can keep it in more than one mailbox.

To copy a message, do the following:

1 Select the message you want to copy.

2 Hold down the Option key on a Macintosh or the Shift key on a Windows system and go to the <u>T</u>ransfer menu.

3 Keep your finger down on the Option or Shift key while you select the mailbox you want to copy to.

4 Release the Option or Shift key once the message is copied.

All you ever wanted to know about searching for text

Sometimes you're sitting there looking at a five-page piece of e-mail thinking that you only want to know whether Shannon said she can make the meeting Monday or Tuesday. Or you can't remember which mailbox her message is in in the first place. You're staring at your list of mailboxes and see four or five possibilities but really don't feel like taking the time to go through all of them. Don't worry, all is not lost. Eudora lets you search through a message for a text string, or search through a bunch of messages and mailboxes for a text string.

 *{Note}* A **text string** is a group of text. It doesn't have to be a whole word or sentence, it's just a few characters strung together. A few examples are:
- and then he
- Four score and s
- meeting

How do I search inside a message?

To search inside a message, do the following:

1 Open the message you want to search through, or make it the current one.

2 Go to the Edit menu and pull down to the Find option.

3 Drag over to the Find command in the side menu. Figures 15.10 and 15.11 show you the dialog box that will appear in the Macintosh and Windows versions.

Fig. 15.10
The Macintosh Find dialog box.

Fig. 15.11
The Windows Find dialog box.

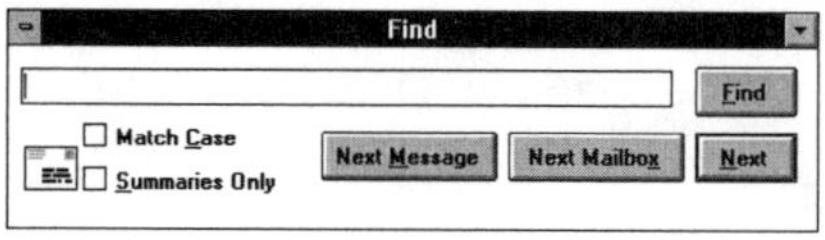

4 Enter the text string you want to look for in the text box. The switches are discussed later in this section.

5 Select Find.

If Eudora doesn't find the text you were looking for you'll get the Not Found dialog box. Figures 15.12 and 15.13 show you what you'll see in the Macintosh and Windows versions.

Fig. 15.12
The Macintosh Not Found dialog box.

Fig. 15.13
The Windows Not Found dialog box.

If Eudora does find the text you were looking for, the message is scrolled to the first place the text occurs (after all, it could be in there a few times). The Find dialog box is still open in case that's not the particular place you were looking for, and clicking the Find button again tells Eudora to keep looking after the first time the string appears in case it's in there more than once. If you close the Find box before you realize that's not the one you were looking for, you can go to the File menu, drag down to the Find option and drag over to the Find Again command in the side menu. Just choosing Find once again means Eudora will start looking from the beginning of the message instead from right after the first occurrence of your text string.

In the Macintosh versions you can use Cmd+F for Find and Cmd+G for Find Again. In the Windows versions it's Ctrl+F and Ctrl+G.

How do I search in more than one message or mailbox?

You have a few options if you want to search more than one message.

Continuing to Search within the message and mailbox

Clicking the <u>N</u>ext button in the Find dialog box, or choosing the <u>N</u>ext command from the Fin<u>d</u> submenu, tells Eudora to look for the next time your text string shows up even if it has to go to the next message. Eudora will keep looking until it reaches the end of the mailbox.

If you have a mailbox open and have more than one message from that mailbox open, Eudora will start looking in the first message you opened. Also, if you have a mailbox open with no messages open, Eudora will search all
of the messages in the mailbox and then move to the next mailbox until it finds what it's looking for.

Starting the search again with the next message

Clicking the Next <u>M</u>essage button in the Find dialog box, or choosing the Next Message command from the <u>F</u>ind submenu, tells Eudora to start looking in the message that's next in the mailbox after the one you're currently looking at. Eudora will keep looking for the text string in message after message, opening new mailboxes when it needs to until it reaches the end of the mailbox folder.

Starting the search again with the next mailbox

Clicking in the Next Mailbo<u>x</u> button in the Find dialog box, or choosing the Next Mailbo<u>x</u> command from the <u>F</u>ind submenu, tells Eudora to skip the rest of the current mailbox and start looking in the next one. Eudora will keep looking for the text string in message after message, opening new mailboxes, mailbox folders, and mailbox subfolders. Eudora will even search the In, Out, and Trash mailboxes when you use this option.

Eudora determines which mailbox is next by looking in the Mailbox menu. The search continues until Eudora has gone to the end, gone back to the top, and come back to the current mailbox.

When Eudora finds the character string on a Windows system it opens the message where it first finds the string. When Eudora finds the character string you're looking for on a Macintosh system, it puts a check next to the name of the mailbox containing the message in the Mailbox menu and also opens the message where it found the string.

!)(Tip)

> Windows users: If you want to open the mailbox containing the message Eudora found the text string in, hold down the Ctrl key and double-click the message title bar.

How do I abort a text search?

Sometimes a search is taking too long, or you suddenly remember exactly where the item is that you're searching for. No matter what the reason, it's simple to abort a search. Just hold down the ⌘ key and type a period (.) on a Macintosh system, or hit the Esc key on a Windows system.

What do those search options mean?

The Find dialog box has a few switches you can turn on or off.

Telling Eudora to pay attention to case

If you don't turn on the Match Case switch before you begin your search, Eudora will ignore whether the letters you're looking for are capitalized or lowercase. If you turn it on, Eudora will look for exactly what you typed in, case and all.

Telling Eudora to search only message summaries

If you turn on the Summaries Only switch, Eudora will search only the Sender and Subject fields of your messages.

Part V:

New Features of Commercial Eudora

Special Features of Eudora 2.1 for Macintosh

There are two ways you can go with Eudora. You can get the freeware version off the Internet or from someone you know, or buy the commercial version.

In this chapter:

- Mail features
- Getting assistance
- Spell-checking
- Mail management features
- Technical features

To help you decide which way you want to go, in this chapter we'll introduce you to the features Qualcomm added to the commercial version. We'll also show you how to use these features in case you decide to buy the commercial version, or already have it.

Filtering messages

There are a lot of things you can do with a message filter. You can tell the filter to watch for e-mail from particular users and mark it as high priority, or shuffle it off to a mailbox called "Flames." You can tell it to look for specific words in the body of the messages and put those messages in individual folders.

How to fill in the Filters window

To use message filtering, first go to the Window menu and choose the Filters option. Figure 16.1 shows you what you'll get.

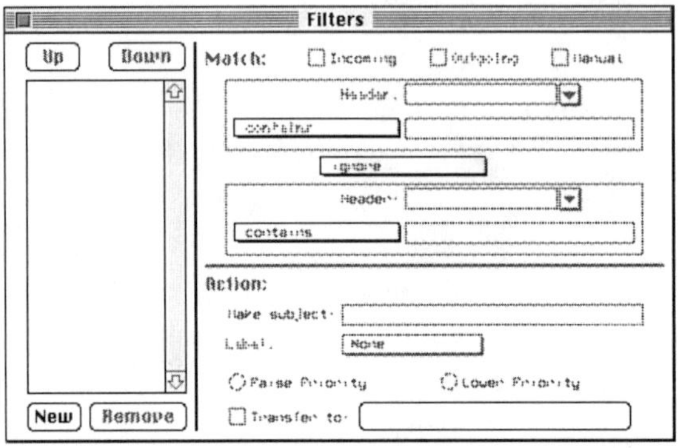

Fig. 16.1
The Filters window.

To create a filter, the first thing you need to do is select New. Figure 16.2 shows what the Filters window looks like once you've done this.

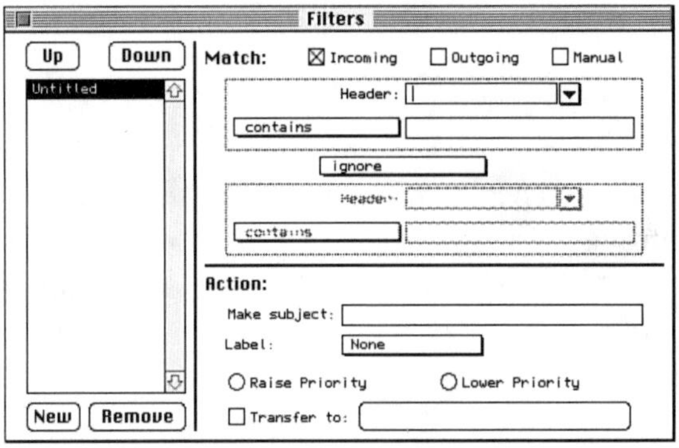

Fig. 16.2
The Filters window, ready to create a new filter.

How to fill in the Match area

The Match area is the upper-right section of the Filters window. It's where you'll tell your filter what to look for. Figure 16.3 shows the Match area.

Fig. 16.3
The Match area.

First, you need to tell Eudora when to apply this particular filter. If you want it to look at only incoming files, select Incoming. If you want it to look at only outgoing files, select Outgoing. If you want to filter Incoming and Outgoing, select both. If you select the Manual switch, the filter is only used when you go to the Special menu and select the Filter Messages option.

Now, you need to take a moment to decide what you'll select for the Header box, telling the filter which part of your messages to look through. Keep in mind that you can pick two terms with a conjunction between them if you want, or only pick one term. Figure 16.4 shows the options available in the Header pull-down menu.

Fig. 16.4
The Header
pull-down menu.

Next, go to the Match Term pull-down menu (the box with the word "contains"). Figure 16.5 shows the options available in this menu.

Fig. 16.5
The Match Term
pull-down menu.

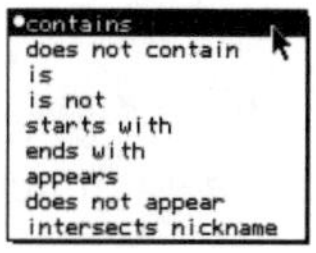

Table 16.1 lists the match terms and explains what each one does.

Table 16.1 Match Terms and Their Functions

Match Term	Action
contains/does not contain	If the portion of the message you chose with the terms contains or doesn't contain the contents of the Matching Text field, the filter does what's specified in the Action area.
is/is not	If the portion of the message you chose with the terms is or is not an exact match of the contents of the Matching Text field, the filter does what's specified in the Action area.
starts with/ends with	If the portion of the message you chose with the terms starts with or ends with the contents of the Matching Text field, the filter does what's specified in the Action area.
appears/does not appear	If a message header field is one of your terms and that field appears or does not appear in the message header, the filter does what's specified in the Action area. The filter does not use the Matching Text field for this option.
intersects nickname	If any address in any header matches any address in the nickname entered in the Matching Text field (very useful for a nickname that stands for a whole group of people), the filter does what's specified in the Action area.

Once you've selected the match term, move to the text box to its right and fill in the text you want the filter to look for.

 (Tip)

> Try to keep the contents of the text box short and to the point. The longer and more complicated the phrase the filter has to look for, the less likely it is that it will find anything.

If you want only this first item in your filter, leave the Conjunction box with "ignore" selected. Otherwise, you can choose a conjunction and add a second thing for the filter to look for.

Figure 16.6 shows the Conjunction pull-down menu.

Fig. 16.6
The Conjunction
pull-down menu.

Table 16.2 lists the conjunctions available and what they do.

Table 16.2   Conjunctions and Their Functions

Conjunction	Action
ignore	The second term is irrelevant, action is taken if the first term is matched.
and	The action is taken if both terms are matched.
or	The action is taken if either term is matched.
unless	The action is taken only if the first term is matched and the second term isn't matched.

If you want a second match term, go through the same process again, filling in the lower section of the Match area.

As an example, we'll fill in the Match area here. We'll filter Incoming messages. The first match term will be <<Any Header>> that contains qualcomm. The second match term will be <<Body>> that contains eudora. We only care that one of these terms is in the message, so for a conjunction we'll use "or". Figure 16.7 shows what the Match area filled in with these options looks like.

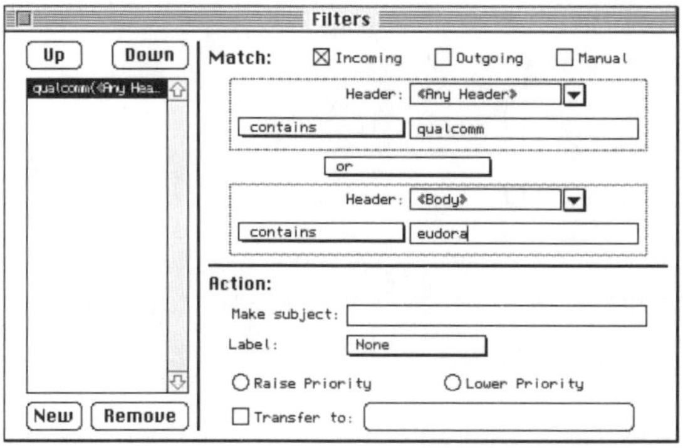

Fig. 16.7
Example of filled-in
Match area.

How to fill in the Action area

Now we move to the lower-right portion of the Filters window. Here's where you tell the filter what to do with the items it selects. Figure 16.8 shows the Action area.

Fig. 16.8

The Action area.

```
Action:
  Make subject: [                          ]
  Label:           [None        ]
  ○ Raise Priority        ○ Lower Priority
  ☐ Transfer to: [                        ]
```

Sometimes you want to make triple-sure that you notice mail immediately when it comes from a particular person or place, or is about a certain subject. One thing a filter can do is change the subject of a message to something you'll notice quickly. Filters can also add labels to messages, raise or lower priority, and transfer them to whatever mailbox you choose.

In the Make subject text box, you can tell the filter to change the subject of the messages that match everything in the Match area. This changes everything in the Subject field of the message. If you just want to change part of the subject area you use the & symbol where you want the original subject to be.

You can add a label to a message using the Label pull-down menu. Figure 16.9 shows the Label pull-down menu.

Fig. 16.9

The Label pull-down menu.

You can tell the filter to raise or lower the priority of a message by selecting Raise Priority or Lower Priority.

Finally, you can tell the filter to automatically transfer a message to a particular mailbox instead of putting it in the In mailbox. To do this, select the check box next to Transfer to, and then select the empty oval on its right.

As the box says, go to the Transfer menu and select the mailbox to which you want to save the messages chosen by this filter, or create a new mailbox for them. Figure 16.10 shows you the dialog box that will appear.

Fig. 16.10
The Filters Window
Transfer pop-up box.

Please choose a mailbox from the transfer menu.

Click elsewhere to cancel.

To continue the example, we'll fill in the Action area and go a little overboard to make sure we *really* notice the messages the filter chooses. We'll change the subject from what it originally was to work! (&), which will show up as work! (original subject). We'll choose a label of In Progress, select Raise Priority, and transfer the message to a mailbox named important.

Finally, we have a completely defined filter. Figure 16.11 shows you the filled-in Filters window.

Fig. 16.11
Filled-in Filters
window.

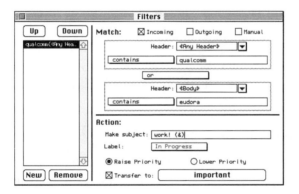

Notice that the filter has a name now, which Eudora determined by looking at the options you filled in.

How to remove a filter

Removing a filter from your filter list is easy. Just select the one you want to get rid of and select Remove.

 **<Caution>** When you select Remove, Eudora doesn't ask you if you want to delete the filter, it just does it.

How to save filter changes

You can save changes to your Filters window two different ways. You can go to the File menu and select Save, or you can close the Filters window. If you try to close the Filters window without saving the last changes you made since opening it, you get the dialog box shown in figure 16.12.

Fig. 16.12
Save Filters dialog box.

To save, select Save. To ignore the changes and exit the Filters window without saving, select Discard. To stay in the Filters window, select Cancel.

How to order your filters

Eudora uses filters in the order in which they appear in the list in the Filters window, top to bottom. Because you may have messages that fit the criteria of more than one filter, this is important. To move a filter up or down in the list, select the filter name and click the up or down button as many times as it takes to put it in the order you want it.

How to receive filtered messages

If you selected Open "In" Mailbox while configuring Eudora, all mailboxes that receive a message because of a filter transfer are opened when the message arrives.

If you didn't select Open "In" Mailbox, Eudora gives you a Filter Report that tells you which mailboxes in addition to the In mailbox received new mail.

Getting additional technical support

An 800 number is available to those who buy the commercial version of Eudora and need technical support. This phone number is found in the documentation you receive along with the program. This is in addition to the various forms of e-mail support mentioned in chapter 8.

Automatically opening attachments

You can open an attachment without having to leave Eudora to do it. To automatically open an attachment using the commercial version of Eudora, just double-click anywhere in the attachment title in the message body (the line that starts with Attachment Converted, not the one that starts with X-Attachments). If you have the application the attachment was created in (such as Microsoft Word), the application launches and the attachment is opened.

Getting online help

It gets annoying if you need to look something up but don't have your manuals handy. The commercial version of Eudora has a help menu that adds itself on to the Balloon Help menu.

Miss using a spell-checker?

Miss being able to spell-check your documents? No problem. The commercial version of Eudora supports the Word Services suite, which means you can plug a spell-checking program like Spellswell into Eudora and they look like they're both part of the same program.

For more information on Spellswell take a look at the next chapter.

Undoing transfers

There's nothing like the annoyance of transferring a message and then realizing you really wanted to transfer the one right next to it. Especially because you have to put the first one back before you can move the one you wanted to move in the first place.

The commercial version of Eudora has a feature that enables you to undo a transfer. To use this feature after you transfer something and want to "take it back," go to the Edit menu and select the Undo option.

Having multiple nicknames files

Sometimes you would rather have more than one file for your nicknames. For example, you want to have your normal nicknames file, but you also want to have separate ones for the people who are in the group you're working with on a project, or some other group that is temporary or changes frequently. Otherwise, everyone gets jumbled together in your main file and you have a bunch of extras later and have to stop and remember where they came from.

Setting up multiple nicknames files

To do this in the commercial version of Eudora, go into your System folder, then into the Eudora folder inside that, and create a folder called Nicknames Folder.

You'll put your different nicknames files all in this folder.

 **{Note}**_____ | Leave your main nicknames file where it is. Don't move it into the new folder. | Just move the other ones.

When you open the Nicknames window, all of your nicknames are displayed, no matter what file they're in. For those of you who use Eudora from your home and office, this means that you can keep your friends in one nicknames file and the work nicknames in another, bringing home occasional updates for the work nicknames file without having to sit down and figure out which are new and have to be added to the master list, and which are old.

How to put new nicknames in different files

When you have multiple nicknames files, creating a new nickname pulls up a dialog box letting you tell Eudora which file your new nickname belongs in.

Uuencoding a data fork

Often, when you send someone a file that needs to be encoded, that person isn't using a Macintosh. When this is the case, using BinHex doesn't help much. Instead, you want to use Uuencode. It's a problem in the other direction too. Many people on the Internet assume you have access to software that lets you Uudecode things.

To Uuencode or Uudecode something when you're using the freeware version of Eudora, you have to save the attachment to a file and get the software to let you do what you need to do. The commercial version has Uuencode/Uudecode included as one of the Attachments options, so it takes care of it for you.

Using Drop features

Eudora offers some of the Drop features available in System 7. With the commercial version of Eudora, you can use them to do the following:

- Start Eudora
- Open stationery files

- Open mailboxes

- Open plain text files

- Attach files to messages

To use Drag and Drop, you select a file and drag its icon over to the Eudora application icon until the Eudora icon is highlighted. Then, you let go of the mouse button. The file actually stays where it was originally, but doing this tells Eudora you want to use that file without having to wade through menus. If Eudora wasn't running when you "dropped" the file on it, the program starts up automatically.

If you want to drag and drop more than one file, go for it. Eudora reads them in this order:

- Settings

- Stationery files

- All other files

Also, if you want all of the files you're dropping to be considered Attachments, hold down the ⌘ key as you drag and drop.

Dropping stationery files

If you want to send a new message using one of your stationery files, just drag and drop the stationery file icon onto the Eudora icon. This opens up a new message using the stationery format you chose.

Dropping mailbox files

You can open a mailbox by dragging and dropping it onto Eudora. This is especially useful if you have some mailboxes that you don't keep in the Eudora folder. The folder then stays in the Mailbox and Transfer menus until you quit Eudora and start back up.

Dropping plain text files

If you want to open a plain text file, just drag and drop its icon on the Eudora icon. This opens a text window in Eudora containing the file.

Dropping attachments

To attach a file to the current message, or to create a new message that has the file as its attachment, drag and drop the file's icon on the Eudora icon. You can attach more than one file by doing this again with the same message still current.

Using stationery messages

Sometimes you just get tired of duplicating the same format for your e-mail over and over. In the commercial version of Eudora, you can create "stationery" that saves a "blank" piece of e-mail with all of the formatting and then go back to it whenever you need it and fill in the blanks.

Creating and using stationery is covered in chapter 15, as is creating stationery that you use for all outgoing mail.

Using Return Receipt

Sometimes you wonder if someone really got that important piece of e-mail.

The commercial version of Eudora has a Return Receipt option in the composition window. If you select this option for a piece of outgoing mail, the computer that receives the mail sends you back a notice saying the mail was delivered. The problem is that the computer needs to know how to deal with Return Receipt, and not all mailer programs support that option.

⊛ **{Note}** | Getting a return receipt back means your mail arrived in the recipient's
account, not that he read your mail.

However, if you happen to know that someone's mailer supports the Return Receipt option, it's a great way to make sure something gets there.

Keeping the Nicknames window in the foreground

When you're trying to add multiple nicknames to a message, it's easier not to have to constantly switch between windows.

In the commercial version of Eudora, you can keep the Nicknames window in the foreground by holding down the Shift key as you select nicknames for the To:, Cc:, and Bcc: fields.

Opening a mailbox using message titles

Having to always fish through menus gets really old when you want to open mailboxes. The commercial version of Eudora gives you a shortcut to opening mailboxes. If you have a message open and want to open the mailbox the message is in, you can double-click in the title bar of the message to open the mailbox.

Using multiple signatures

Sometimes you want to have two signatures files. Maybe one for friends and one for people you talk to professionally. With the commercial version of Eudora, you can do that.

You already know how to create a signature. Creating a second one is really easy. Just go to the Window menu and select the Alternate Signature option.

When you're working on a piece of mail, you can select which signature you want, or none at all.

Telling Eudora to open the next unread message

You shouldn't have to fish through menus just to read your mail.

If you turned on the Easy Open switch when you were configuring the commercial version of Eudora, deleting or transferring a message opens the next unread message in the mailbox.

Automatically deleting attachments

It's awful to realize that you have an attachment folder full of files that were attached to messages you got rid of months ago. A big waste of space.

If you turned on the Tidy att'ment folder switch when you were configuring the commercial version of Eudora, attachments are deleted at the same time as the message they were attached to.

Changing message status

Sometimes you've read a piece of mail but want to remind yourself to go back to it later. Aside from writing it down on a post-it note, there aren't many ways to do that.

In the commercial version of Eudora, you can change the status of a message. Just select the message summary in the mailbox window, go to the Message menu and select the Set Status option. You can then set the message back to "unread" status, or change the status to whatever you want it to be.

Saving message status

Sometimes you don't even need to read a message. You just want to save it and move on. The problem is, you're still stuck having to open it to get rid of it.

In the commercial version of Eudora, if you choose Save As to save a message or messages to a file, the message(s) status changes from unread to read.

Grafting mailboxes from outside Eudora

There are times when you want to keep things outside the Eudora folder. The commercial version of Eudora allows you to do this by using aliases.

Grafting mailboxes

If you move a mailbox outside the Eudora folder, move its .toc file with it. Then, use the system File menu to make aliases for both the mailbox and the .toc, and move those aliases into the Eudora folder in your System folder.

⊛ {Note}_____ You can make a subfolder in your Eudora folder for aliases if you don't want to save mailbox and .toc aliases with the other mailboxes and .toc files.

To open these mailboxes later, go to the Mailboxes menu and choose the Others option.

Grafting mailbox folders

Sometimes you want to move an entire mailbox folder outside of the Eudora folder.

The commercial version of Eudora lets you do that, too. It works the same way mailboxes do. Just create an alias for the folder you want to move out of the Eudora folder and put that alias in its place.

Getting a No New Mail alert

You get tired of always having to look in your In mailbox and see if you've got new mail.

The commercial version of Eudora gives you a dialog box letting you know you don't have any new mail so you don't have to waste the time checking.

Saving all open messages at once

It gets tiring having to save every open message and mailbox one at a time.

The commercial version of Eudora lets you save all open message and mailbox windows at once. Just go to the File menu and select the Save option while holding down the Option key.

POP3Post compatibility

It's a good idea to keep up with the times.

The commercial version of Eudora is doing that by being compatible with the newest version of POP.

New... in Mailbox menu

Less menu hopping is a good thing.

In the commercial version of Eudora you don't have to use the Mailboxes window to create new mailboxes. Instead, creating a new mailbox is as easy as going to the Mailbox menu and selecting the New option.

Compacting mailboxes

Sometimes you need to clear some disk space.

Mailbox compacting in the commercial version of Eudora helps you do that. Mailbox compacting is covered in chapter 14.

Transferring messages to the Out mailbox

Sometimes you want to transfer a message out of a special mailbox and into the Out mailbox.

You can do this in the commercial version of Eudora.

Replacing nicknames

You may stop using or forget you have some nicknames and then try to name something else the same thing.

The commercial version of Eudora gives you some options. If you try to save something to a nickname that already exists, Eudora asks if you want to add the new nicknames to the old one of the same name (making a group nickname with all of them in there), or just replace the old one with the new one.

17

Spell-checking E-mail with Spellswell

Spellswell works hand-in-hand with Eudora, so you can spell-check your outgoing mail without having to leave Eudora.

In this chapter:

- What Spellswell can do for you
- How to order Spellswell
- How to install Spellswell to work with Eudora
- How to use Spellswell from within Eudora

W e all make mistakes. We accept that as a part of life. But isn't there anything we can do to cut down on those embarrassing typos and spelling mistakes? Most word processors today come with spell-checking features, so why shouldn't a program like Eudora—which lets you compose letters—include one too?

The good news is that a company called Working Software has written a program called Spellswell that meets this need quite nicely. It works hand-in-hand with Eudora, installing itself as a new option at the bottom of Eudora's Edit menu. That way you can spell-check your outgoing mail without having to leave Eudora.

The bad news (for Windows users) is that Spellswell is currently only available for Macintosh System 7 users. The remainder of this chapter deals with Spellswell 1.0 as it relates to Eudora for the Macintosh.

An introduction to Spellswell

Most spell-checkers cross-check words in a document against words stored in a spelling dictionary. Spellswell is no exception. However, it has a number of exceptional features that are worth noting.

The standard dictionary that comes with Spellswell consists of over 93,000 words and abbreviations, and there are numerous add-on dictionaries available for specific fields, such as medicine, law, scientific applications, and business.

In addition to simple spelling mistakes, Spellswell also does its best to catch mistakes such as punctuation, capitalization, repeated words, and abbreviations, not to mention those tricky homonyms discussed in chapter 4, "E-mail Writing Style." It may not tell you when to use "whom" instead of "who," but it goes a long way toward helping you polish up your letters.

Product ordering and technical support

Spellswell may be available where you purchased Eudora. If not, you can order it directly by calling Working Software at (800) 229-9675, or by writing to:

Working Software

P.O. Box 1844

Santa Cruz, CA 95061-1844

Working Software also can be reached for technical support by electronic mail at the following addresses if you're a registered Spellswell user:

Internet: 76004.2072@compuserve.com

America Online: WORKINGSW

CompuServe: 76004,2072

AppleLink: D0140

Installing Spellswell and Eudora

Spellswell can be used as a stand-alone spell-checker for use with most popular word processors and text editors. But for our purposes, this chapter is limited to integrating Spellswell with Eudora. If you're interested in the stand-alone uses of Spellswell, the program documentation should be able to help you.

Copying the needed Spellswell files

1   Create a new folder for Spellswell on your hard disk. Go to the desktop, open the File menu, and choose New Folder. Name the new folder Spellswell 7 Folder.

2   Click and drag the new folder from the desktop to your hard disk and place it where you want it. The Eudora folder is a good choice, but you can put it anywhere.

3   Insert the Spellswell disk into a floppy drive and wait for the floppy icon to appear on your screen.

4   Double-click the icon to view the contents of the disk, and then copy the following files to the Spellswell 7 folder you just created on your hard drive (note that the exact filename of the Spellswell program may vary somewhat with version changes):

- Spellswell 7

- Dictionary 93000+

- Word Choices

- Check This Document

The remaining files on the Spellswell disk aren't needed for a basic installation, but if you think you might want to add another Spellswell dictionary to the main dictionary in the future, you might also want to install the Dictionary Merge Utility package. In addition, a rather comprehensive manual can be found on the Spellswell disk.

5 Eject the Spellswell disk. If you don't eject the disk, the disk is the first place Eudora will look for Spellswell.

Making Spellswell and Eudora work together

1 Start Eudora.

2 Open the Edit menu. If it isn't available, open the File menu and choose New Text Document to open up a blank document, then try to open the Edit menu again.

3 From the Edit menu, select Add Word Service. The Word Services dialog box should appear.

4 Use the dialog box to browse through the files and folders on your hard drive until you find the Spellswell 7 program, and select it.

5 Click Open. This closes the dialog box and tells Eudora where Spellswell can be found in the future, so you'll only have to do this once.

⊛ {Note}

At this stage you have the opportunity to configure some of Spellswell's options by opening the File menu and selecting Options. If this is your first time using Spellswell, however, you should probably leave these alone for now until you're more familiar with what they do.

Have no fear, though, you can always change these settings at a later date by starting Spellswell on its own (rather than from Eudora) and opening the File menu to select Options. This set of options is also accessible from within the Spellswell dialog box that appears when you spell-check documents.

6 Open the File menu and select Quit to exit Spellswell and return to Eudora.

When you return to Eudora's main menu, take a look at the Edit menu again. At the bottom, you should see the new option Check Spelling, which is just Spellswell in disguise. From now on, you won't have to go through any of this hassle to use Spellswell within Eudora; the Check Spelling menu option will remain a part of Eudora, even after you exit the program.

Fig. 17.1
Selecting Spellswell as
your Word Service
application.

Fig. 17.2
After installing
Spellswell, the Check
Spelling option is
added to the Edit
menu.

Using Spellswell from Eudora

The fact that Spellswell installs itself so nicely within Eudora makes it very easy to use; in fact, it's all too easy to forget that Spellswell is actually a separate program.

The most common use for a spell-checker is for proofing documents you write before sending them to others. In the context of Eudora, this makes a lot of sense—it's nice to be able to have your outgoing letters checked before you mail them. The following example illustrates how you can use Spellswell from Eudora.

To spell-check a mail message, follow these steps:

1 Open or create the mail message you want you check.

2 Open the Edit menu and choose Check Spelling. A few messages will pop up briefly to tell you that Spellswell is busy scanning the letter. After a few moments, if your letter contains any spelling errors you should see the Spellswell dialog box (see fig. 17.3).

Fig. 17.3
Spellswell flags a
spelling mistake.

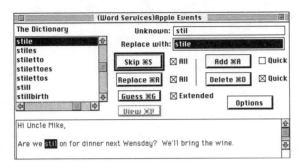

3 Use the View and/or Guess buttons to help you find the correct spelling for the misspelled word.

4 Click the correctly spelled word from the Dictionary/Guess window, or manually type the correct spelling in the Replace With field.

5 Click the Replace button to replace the misspelled word in your document with the correct one. If the All check box next to the Replace button is checked, this will replace all instances of the misspelled word in your letter.

If you select the All check box next to the Replace button, be sure to deselect it after you've made your replacements, so that you don't unintentionally replace all later on another word.

6 Repeat steps 3-5 as necessary for all the misspelled words in your letter that Spellswell has flagged.

7 Open the File menu and select Quit to exit Spellswell and return to Eudora.

8 Send your spell-checked letter as usual.

Using the Dictionary to identify misspelled words

By clicking the View button in the Spellswell dialog, the Dictionary/Guess window switches to Dictionary mode. When Spellswell has flagged a misspelled word, the Dictionary can show you where that word should appear in an alphabetical listing, along with a few of the words that would come before it and after it.

For example, if your misspelled word were "disketes," you'd see from the Dictionary window that this word isn't known to Spellswell, but that "diskettes" is. This not only helps you figure out whether your word is misspelled, it can also sometimes reveal the correct spelling.

Using Guesses to let Eudora figure out what you meant

Clicking the Guess button in the Spellswell dialog box sets the Dictionary/ Guess window to Guess mode, where Spellswell tries to figure out what you *meant* to type. This can be particularly useful if you haven't got a very good idea how a word is spelled.

For instance, let's say your letter contained the word "weazill" as your attempt at writing "weasel." Clicking the Guess button sets Spellswell to work trying to come up with a word that's spelled much the same and perhaps even sounds similar.

If you like, you can help Spellswell out a bit by supplying as much information as you know and filling in the rest with a wildcard. Go to the Replace With field and type **wea?l**, and then click the Guess button again. In the Guess window, Spellswell suggests some solutions. Click "weasel" and then the Replace button to make the replacement in your letter.

Adding unknown words to the dictionary

When Spellswell flags a word in your letter as suspicious, it doesn't necessarily mean you've misspelled anything. Spellswell's basic dictionary contains more than 93,000 words, but this is by no means exhaustive; you're likely to use a few words in everyday language that aren't found in the dictionary, and specialized, technical terms are often not found there either.

If you only use these words occasionally, you can simply tell Spellswell to ignore the word by clicking the Skip button. On the other hand, if you find yourself using a particular word often, it may well be worth your while to add this word to the dictionary.

Let's suppose you're fond of the word "whatchamacallit"—a bit of slang. When Spellswell flags this word in one of your letters, select the Quick Add check box (so that you'll only be adding "whatchamacallit," and not suffix variations as well) and then click the Add button. That's all there is to it! From now on Spellswell will accept "whatchamacallit" as a valid word.

The Spellswell dialog box

From within Eudora, virtually all of your interaction with Spellswell takes place through the Spellswell dialog box. Therefore, it's worth taking a little time to familiarize yourself with its features. To make the Spellswell dialog box appear, open the Edit menu and choose Check Spelling. Note that this menu option will only be available when you have a document open; if you're not already editing a document, open the File menu and choose New Document or Open. This will cause Spellswell to scan the current document. Then you should see something similar to figure 17.4.

⊛ {Note} The Spellswell dialog box will only appear if the spell-checker finds an error in your document.

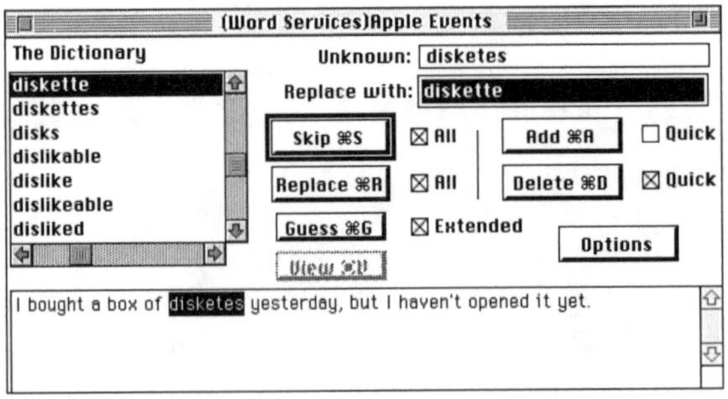

Fig. 17.4
A first look at the
Spellswell dialog box.

The Spellswell dialog box can be broken down into four main sections:

- The Dictionary and Guess window

- The Context window

- The Unknown and Replace With windows

- The command buttons

Using the Dictionary/Guess Window to find the right word

On the left side of the dialog box is the Dictionary and Guess window. This window can display either a list of words from the dictionary or a list of guesses—Spellswell's attempt at figuring out what you meant to type. Clicking the View button selects the dictionary for viewing, while clicking the Guess button turns the window into a list of suggested replacements. When the Spellswell dialog box first opens up as you're checking a document, it starts out in Dictionary mode.

The vertical scroll bar allows you to move up or down through the listing one word at a time, while the horizontal scroll bar moves through the list in increments of about 150 words.

In practice, this window can be useful for helping you find an unknown word in context. When Spellswell flags a word as unknown, it also calls up that portion of the dictionary where the word should have been found, including a number of words before and after it alphabetically. If you happen to spot the word you were looking for in the dictionary listing, clicking it will copy it to the Replace With window, and double-clicking it will go ahead and replace it in the document as well.

Using the Context Window to see the whole picture

The Context window, at the bottom of the Spellswell dialog box, shows a portion of the document surrounding the currently highlighted unknown word. The idea is to show you the context in which the word occurs so that you can decide whether or not you *meant* to spell it that way.

Using the Unknown and Replace With fields to correct words by hand

In the upper-right corner of the Spellswell dialog box, you'll find two small text fields; one contains the unknown word and the other contains a suggestion for a replacement. You can edit both fields manually if you like, but often this isn't necessary; Spellswell is pretty clever when it comes to figuring out what you intended.

The command buttons

The remainder of the Spellswell dialog box consists of command buttons. Each of these also can be accessed through a Command+key combination.

Making substitutions with the Replace button (⌘+R)

Clicking the Replace button replaces the unknown word in the document with the word in the Replace With field. Normally this only replaces a single instance of the word in the document. However, if you select the All check box, the Replace button will make replacements throughout the document.

Ignoring Spellswell: The Skip button (⌘+S)

If you find that Spellswell has flagged a perfectly valid word as unknown (which can happen quite often if you use obscure or technical terms in your writing), you can click the Skip button to make it take no action and move on to the next questionable word in the document. If you select the All check box next to this button, this will tell Spellswell to ignore all future occurrences of this word in the document.

Making educated guesses: The Guess button (⌘+G)

Clicking the Guess button makes Spellswell guess what you probably meant the current unknown word to be, and display its suggestions in the Guess window. Its guesses are based on common spelling mistakes, typos caused by hitting the wrong nearby keys, and words that sound similar.

If you want Spellswell to take more time and put more thought into its guess, you can select the Extended check box next to this button. If a guess seems to be taking too long, you can always abort the process by pressing ⌘+'.'.

Another way to use the Guess button is to enter as much of the word as you know in the Replace With window, using a wildcard (?) to substitute for the parts you're unsure of. Click the Guess button and Spellswell displays all the words that match your wildcard pattern. For instance, if you know the word starts with "s" and ends with "ynx," you could enter **s?ynx** and Spellswell would list all the words it knows that fit that pattern.

Looking a word up in the Dictionary: The View button (⌘+V)

The View button turns the Guess window into the Dictionary window; it displays the portion of the dictionary surrounding the unknown word.

Adding an unknown word to the Dictionary: The Add button (⌘+A)

You can use the Add button to add an unknown word to the dictionary, if you're certain it's spelled correctly. Clicking this button calls up the Add dialog box, where you can decide which suffix variations of the word you'd like to add to the dictionary. For instance, if you were adding the word "help," you would be offered the chance to add "helps," "helped," "helping," and so on. By checking the Must Capitalize box next to each item, you can insist that the word (or variation) for things such as proper nouns, is always capitalized when it appears in the dictionary.

If you select the Quick Add check box next to the Add button, you won't be prompted with the Add dialog box when you want to add items to the dictionary in the future; instead, only the unknown word itself is added, without any variations.

❶ (Tip)

> If you want to add a lot of words to the dictionary at once, the easiest way to do this is to enter them all into a text file and then have Spellswell check the document. Be sure to check the Quick Add box before you start adding. Then all that you have to do is click the Add button as each word gets flagged.
>
> You may find this feature especially handy as a means of expanding your dictionary with "add-to-dict" text files available at many Mac FTP sites. Text files containing proper names, holidays, computer terms, medical and legal terms, and so on can save you from having to buy additional dictionaries.

Removing a word from the Dictionary: The Delete button (⌘+D)

The Delete button lets you remove a word from the dictionary. Enter the word you want to remove in the Replace With window and click the Delete button. Normally, you'll be asked to confirm your deletions. However, if you check the Quick Delete box next to this button, this confirmation is bypassed.

Setting your preferences: The Options button (⌘+O)

The Options button calls up a dialog box that allows you to customize the rules Spellswell uses to determine whether a word is questionable or not. Each option is a simple check box that can be either selected or deselected to turn it on or off, respectively.

Capitalize after period

If this option is selected, Spellswell will expect the first word following a period, question mark, exclamation mark, or carriage-return to be capitalized. If you use carriage-returns to mark the ends of lines instead of just the ends of paragraphs, you might want to leave this option unselected.

Capitalize proper nouns

If this option is selected, Spellswell expects all proper nouns to be capitalized.

Fig. 17.5
The Options dialog
box lets you customize
the way Spellswell
works.

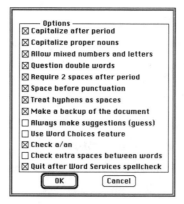

Allow mixed numbers and letters

Normally, a word like "32nd" would be flagged by Spellswell as questionable. But if you select this option, you can mix letters and numbers in a word. If you do this, just be careful with zeroes and Os, and ones and ls, which can look very similar.

Question double words

If this option is selected, Spellswell will flag any words it finds repeated consecutively, such as "on on." Most of the time, this is an error on your part, but bear in mind there are exceptions to nearly every rule (for example, "What's going on on Friday?").

Require two spaces after period

Purists like to have two spaces after every period, question mark, and exclamation mark. If this matters to you, select this option to have Spellswell warn you when you slip up.

Space before punctuation

Punctuation is supposed to follow a word directly, without any intervening spaces. If you select this option, Spellswell will cry foul when you leave a space before a comma, period, question mark, or exclamation mark.

Treat hyphens as spaces

Hyphenated words pose a dilemma for spell-checkers. Should they be checked as a single word (such as "off-road") or as two separate words, as though the hyphen were really just a space (for example, "Lieutenant-Colonel")? Spellswell lets you decide with this option.

Make a backup of the document

If you select this option, Spellswell will try to make a backup copy of the current document (with a *.sbk extension) before it makes any changes to it. This would seem the prudent thing to do, though it steals a few more precious seconds of your time.

Always make suggestions (guess)

If this option is selected, Spellswell assumes that you always want it to guess what you probably meant to type whenever it encounters an unknown word. This can be a handy thing, but it also can be time-consuming.

Use Word Choices feature

Spellswell comes with a text file called Word Choices, which is essentially a special dictionary of homonyms and frequently misspelled words. You can edit this file in any word processor or text editor to add your own favorite typos and spelling weaknesses.

By selecting this option, you tell Spellswell to check an unknown word against the Word Choices file as well. Unless your Word Choices file is really large, this shouldn't make Spellswell take any more time than usual to check your documents.

Check a/an

Selecting this option makes Spellswell perform a simple usage check whenever it encounters the articles "a" or "an," so that mistakes like "a otter" and "an house" can be avoided.

Check extra spaces between words

If you select this option, Spellswell will flag any instances where two or more consecutive spaces appear between words (other than after a period, question mark, or exclamation mark, of course).

Special Features of Eudora 2.0 for Windows

This chapter introduces you to the features that Qualcomm added to the commercial version of Eudora for Windows, and it shows you how to use these features.

In this chapter:

- Mail features
- Getting assistance
- Spell-checking
- Mail management features
- Technical features

You have two options with Eudora. You can get the freeware version off the Internet or from someone you know, or you can buy the commercial version. You've already seen some of the differences earlier in the book, but there are many more.

To help you decide which version you want to use, this chapter introduces you to the features that Qualcomm added to the commercial version of Eudora. It also shows you how to use these features in case you decide to buy the commercial version or already have it.

Filtering messages

There are a lot of things that you can do with a message filter. You can tell the filter to watch for e-mail from particular users and mark it as high priority, or shuffle it off to a mailbox called "Flames." You can tell it to look for specific words in the body of the messages and put those messages in individual folders.

How to fill in the Filters window

To use message filtering, open the Window menu and choose Filters. Figure 18.1 shows you what you'll get.

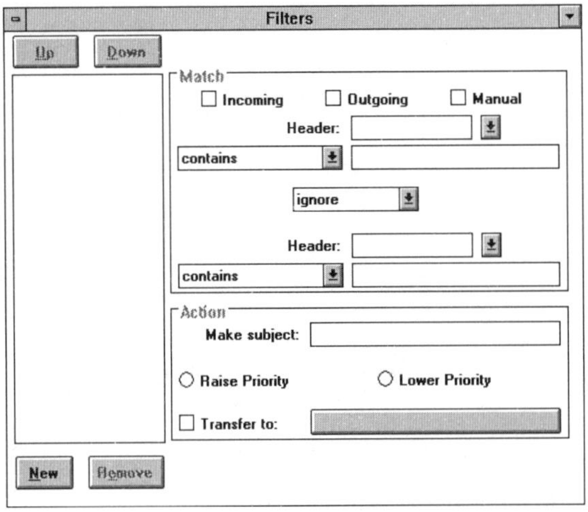

Fig. 18.1

The Filters window.

To create a filter, the first thing you need to do is select New. We'll do this now for our example.

Filling in the Match area

The Match area, in the upper-right section of the Filters window, is where you tell your filter what to look for. Figure 18.2 shows you the Match area.

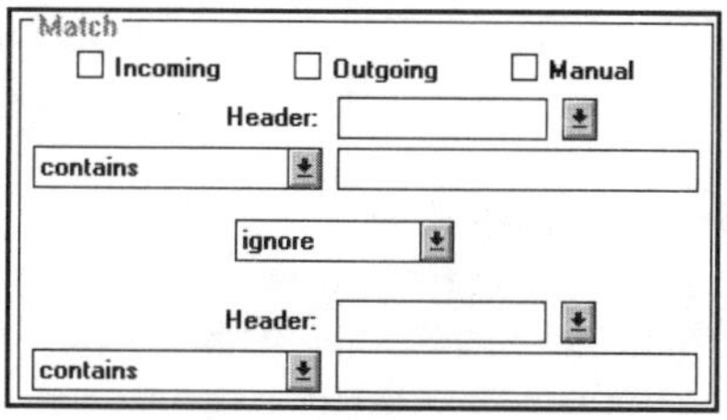

Fig. 18.2
The Match area.

First, tell Eudora when to apply this particular filter. If you want it to look at incoming files only, select Incoming. If you want it to look at outgoing files only, select Outgoing. If you want to filter Incoming and Outgoing, select both. If you select Manual, the filter is only used for current messages when you go to the <u>S</u>pecial menu and select the Filter <u>M</u>essages option. In the following example, you'll filter incoming messages, so select Incoming.

Now, take a moment to decide what you'll select for the Header box, telling the filter which part of your messages to look through. Keep in mind that you can pick two terms with a conjunction between them if you want, or only pick one term. Figure 18.3 shows the options available in the Header pull-down menu.

Fig. 18.3
The Header pull-down menu.

Next, go to the Match Term pull-down menu (the box with the word "contains"). Figure 18.4 shows the options available in this menu.

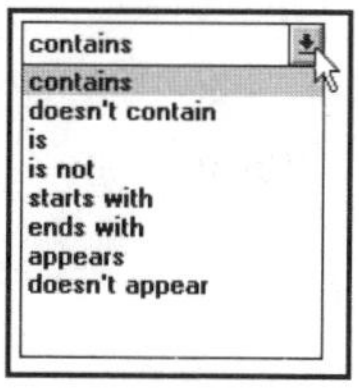

Fig. 18.4
The Match Term pull-down menu.

Table 18.1 shows the match terms available and explains what each one does.

Table 18.1 Match Terms and Their Functions

Match Term	Action
contains/does not contain	If the portion of the message you chose with the terms contains or doesn't contain the contents of the Matching Text field, the filter does what's specified in the Action area.
is/is not	If the portion of the message you chose with the terms is or is not an exact match of the contents of the Matching Text field, the filter does what's specified in the Action area.
starts with/ends with	If the portion of the message you chose with the terms starts with or ends with the contents of the Matching Text field, the filter does what's specified in the Action area.
appears/does not appear	If a message header field is one of your terms and that field does or does not appear in the message header, the filter does what's specified in the Action area. The filter does not use the Matching Text field for this option.
intersects nickname	If any address in any header matches any address in the nickname entered in the Matching Text field (very useful for a nickname that stands for a whole group of people), the filter does what's specified in the Action area.

Once you've selected the match term, move to the text box to its right and fill in the text you want the filter to look for.

> **(Tip)** Try to keep the contents of the text box short and to the point. The longer and more complicated the phrase the filter has to look for, the less likely it is that it will find anything.

If you only want this first item in your filter, leave the Conjunction box with "ignore" selected. Otherwise, choose a conjunction and add a second item for the filter to look for.

Figure 18.5 shows the Conjunction pull-down menu.

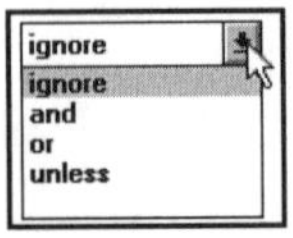

Fig. 18.5
The Conjunction
pull-down menu.

Table 18.2 lists the available conjunctions and what they do.

Table 18.2   Conjunctions and Their Functions

Conjunction	Action
ignore	The second term is irrelevant; action is taken if the first term is matched.
and	The action is taken if both terms are matched.
or	The action is taken if either term is matched.
unless	The action is taken only if the first term is matched and the second term isn't matched.

If you want a second Match term, go through the same process again, filling in the lower section of the Match area.

As an example, we'll fill in the Match area here and filter Incoming messages. The first match term will be <<Any Header>> that contains qualcomm. The second match term will be <<Body>> that contains Eudora. We only care that one of these terms is in the message, so for a conjunction we'll use "or". Figure 18.6 shows what the Match area filled in with these options looks like.

Fig. 18.6
Example filled in
Match area.

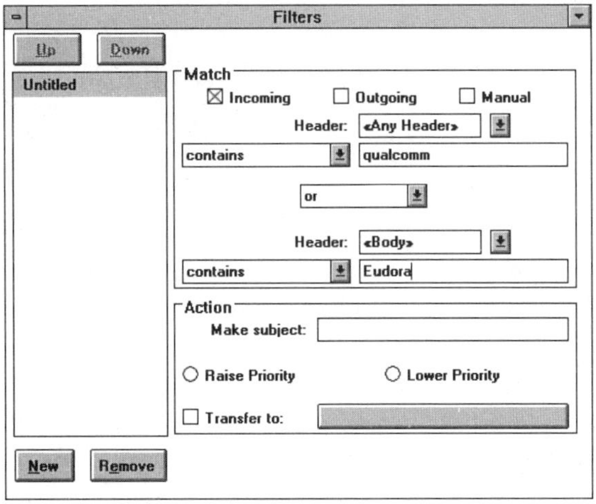

Filling in the Action area

Now move to the bottom-right portion of the Filters window. This is where you tell the filter what to do with the items it selects. Figure 18.7 shows the Action area.

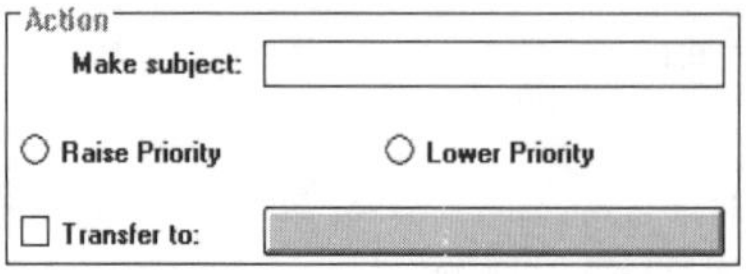

Fig. 18.7
The Action area.

Sometimes you want to make triple-sure that you notice mail immediately when it comes from a particular person or place, or is about a certain subject. One thing a filter can do is change the subject of a message to something you'll notice quickly. Filters also can add labels to messages, raise or lower priority, and transfer them to whatever mailbox you choose. In the box next to Make subject, tell the filter to change the subject of the messages that match everything in the Match area. This changes everything in the Subject field of the message. If you just want to change part of the subject area, use the & symbol where you want the original Subject to be.

You also can use the filter to raise or lower the priority of a message by selecting Raise Priority or Lower Priority.

Finally, you can tell the filter to automatically transfer a message to a particular mailbox instead of putting it in the In mailbox. To do this, select the check box next to Transfer to, and then select the empty oval on its right.

As the box says, go to the Transfer menu and select the mailbox you want to save the messages chosen by this filter to, or create a new mailbox for them. Figure 18.8 shows you the dialog box that will appear.

To continue the example, we'll fill in the Action area and go a little overboard to make sure we *really* notice the messages the filter chooses. We'll change the subject from what it originally was to work! (&), which will show up as work! (original subject). We'll choose a label of In Progress, select Raise Priority, and transfer the message to a mailbox named important. Finally, you have a completely defined filter. Figure 18.9 shows you the filled-in Filters window.

Fig. 18.8
The Filters window
Transfer Selection box.

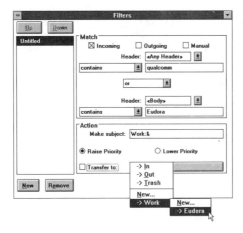

Fig. 18.9
The filled in Filters
window.

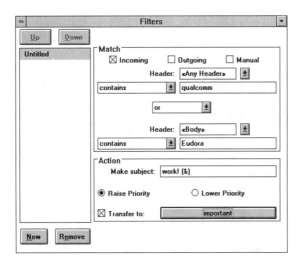

Notice that the filter has a name now, which Eudora determined by looking at the options you filled in.

Removing a filter

Removing a filter from your filter list is easy—choose the one you want to get rid of and select Remove.

 **<Caution>** | When you select the Remove button, Eudora doesn't ask you if you want to delete the filter; it just does it.

Saving filter changes

You can save changes to your Filters window two different ways. You can open the File menu and choose Save, or you can close the Filters window. If you try to close the Filters window without saving the last changes you made, you get the dialog box shown in figure 18.10.

Fig. 18.10
The Save Filters dialog box.

To save, select Save. To ignore the changes and exit the Filters window without saving, select Discard. To stay in the Filters window, select Cancel.

Putting your filters in order

Eudora uses filters in the order that they appear in the list in the Filters window, from top to bottom. Because you may have messages that fit the criteria of more than one filter, this is important. To move a filter up or down in the list, select the filter name and click the Up or Down button as many times as it takes to put it in the order you want it.

Receiving filtered messages

If you turned on the Open "In" Mailbox switch while configuring Eudora, all mailboxes that receive a message because of a filter transfer are opened when the message arrives.

If you didn't select Open "In" Mailbox, Eudora gives you a Filter Report that tells you which mailboxes, besides the In mailbox, received new mail.

Using Multipurpose Internet Mail Extension (MIME)

Using attachments on the Internet is a lot easier if you have MIME, because most other people on the Internet do, no matter what kind of program or computer they use.

The commercial version of Eudora has MIME support. MIME is covered in chapter 13.

Getting additional technical support

An 800 number is available to those who buy the commercial version of Eudora and need technical support. This phone number is found in the documentation you receive along with the program. This is in addition to the various forms of e-mail support mentioned in chapter 8.

Using direct serial dialup

It's helpful to have the flexibility of being able to get mail using a modem without needing SLIP or PPP. Some areas have limited kinds of Internet access available and only offer dialup accounts; others are just way too expensive for anything but the basics.

The commercial version of Eudora now supports this option, which is covered in chapter 7.

Automatically opening attachments

It's a lot quicker to open an attachment when you don't have to leave Eudora to do it.

To automatically open an attachment using the commercial version of Eudora, double-click anywhere in the attachment title in the message body (the line that starts with Attachment Converted, not the one that starts with X-Attachments). If you have the application that the attachment was created in (for example, Microsoft Word), the application launches and the attachment opens.

Getting online help

It gets annoying if you need to look up something but don't have your manuals handy. The commercial version of Eudora has a help menu that you can use to answer most of your questions.

Undoing message transfers

There's nothing like the annoyance of transferring a message and then realizing that you really wanted to transfer the one right next to it. Especially since you have to put the first one back before you can move the one that you wanted to move in the first place.

The commercial version of Eudora has a feature that lets you undo a transfer. To use this feature after you transfer something and want to "take it back," open the Edit menu and choose Undo.

Using Uuencode

Many people on the Internet assume you have access to software that lets you Uudecode things.

To Uuencode or Uudecode something using the freeware version, you have to save the attachment to a file, leave Eudora and use another piece of software. The commercial version of Eudora, on the other hand, has Uuencode/Uudecode included as one of the Attachments options, so it takes care of it for you.

⊛ {Note}⎯⎯⎯WinCode, a program that also handles file encoding/decoding, is discussed in detail in chapter 13.

Drag and drop

It's nice to be able to avoid fishing through menus. The commercial version of Eudora lets you attach documents to mail messages by dragging them into the message.

To drag and drop, open the message you want to attach a file to. Then, open the Windows File Manager, select the file you want to attach, and drag it from the File Manager to the mail message. This way, Eudora knows which file you want to attach without having to wade through dialog boxes. To attach more than one, select them all at once and drag them together. You can also select and drag them one at a time until you're finished with the attachments.

Getting a return receipt

Sometimes you wonder if someone really got that important piece of e-mail.

The commercial version of Eudora has a Return Receipt option in the composition window. If you select this option for a piece of outgoing mail, it tells the computer that receives the mail to send you back a notice saying the mail was delivered. The problem is that the computer needs to know how to deal with Return Receipt, and not all mailer programs support that option.

⊛ {Note}⎯⎯⎯Getting a return receipt back means your mail arrived in the recipient's account, not that they read your mail.

However, if you happen to know that someone's mailer supports the Return Receipt option, it's a great way to make sure you know it got to them and didn't get lost.

Opening mailboxes using message titles

Having to always fish through menus gets really old when you want to open mailboxes.

The commercial version of Eudora gives you a shortcut to opening mailboxes. If have a message open and want to open the mailbox the message is in, you can double-click in the title bar of the message to open the mailbox.

Using multiple signatures

Sometimes you want to have two signature files, such as one for friends and one for people whom you talk to professionally. With the commercial version of Eudora, you can do that.

You already learned how to create a signature in chapter 9. The second one is really easy. Just open the Window menu and choose Alternate Signature.

When you're working on a piece of mail, you can select which signature you want, or choose None at All from the Signature menu.

Changing message status

Sometimes you'll read a piece of mail and want to remind yourself to go back to it later. Aside from writing it down on a Post-It note, there aren't many ways to remind yourself.

In the commercial version of Eudora, you can change the status of a message. Just select the message summary in the mailbox window, and open the Message menu and choose Set Status. You can then set the message back to unread status, or change the status to read, replied, forwarded, or redirected.

Automatically deleting attachments

It's awful to realize that you have an attachment folder full of files that were attached to messages you got rid of months ago. This is a big waste of space.

If you select Tidy Attachment Directory when you are configuring the commercial version of Eudora, attachments are deleted at the same time as the message to which they are attached.

Getting the no new mail alert

Do you get tired of always having to check to see if you have new mail?

The commercial version of Eudora gives you a pop-up window saying you don't have any new mail so you don't have to waste your time looking in your In mailbox to check.

Saving unread messages

Sometimes you don't even need to read a message—you just want to save it and move on. The problem is, you're still stuck having to open it to get rid of it.

In the commercial version of Eudora, if you choose Save As from the File menu to save a message (or messages) to a file, the message's status changes from unread to read.

Saving all open messages at once

It gets tiring having to save every open message and mailbox one at a time.

The commercial version of Eudora lets you save all open messages and mailbox windows at once. Just open the File menu and choose Save while holding down the Shift key.

Finishing nicknames

Most people want to reduce the amount of typing they have to do as much as possible. Therefore, it's nice to have the option of not having to type everything out.

The Finish Nickname command in the Edit menu allows you to type in only parts of nicknames. How to use this feature is explained in chapter 9.

Using POP3Post

It's a good idea to keep up with the times.

The commercial version of Eudora is doing that by being compatible with the newest version of POP.

Transferring to a new mailbox

Less menu hopping is a good thing.

In the commercial version of Eudora, creating a new mailbox when you want to transfer a file is as easy as opening the Transfer menu and choosing New.

Compacting mailboxes

Sometimes you just need to clear some disk space.

Mailbox compacting in the commercial version of Eudora helps you do that. This feature is covered in chapter 14.

Showing all headers

It's helpful to be able to look at the full headers for a piece of mail because it's a good way to track down network problems.

If you select the BLAH,BLAH,BLAH icon in the incoming message window, you'll see the full headers for that message.

Transferring to the Out mailbox

Sometimes you want to transfer a message out of a special mailbox and into the Out mailbox.

You can do this in the commercial version of Eudora.

Replacing nicknames

Over time, you stop corresponding with some people and end up with a pile of nicknames you don't use. Then, when you're adding new nicknames, you accidentally try to replace one you'd forgotten about.

The commercial version of Eudora gives you some options. If you try to save something to a nickname that already exists, Eudora asks if you want to add the new names to the old nick or want to replace the old nick with the new nick. If you add the new nick to the old one, Eudora makes a group nickname of the two of them so sending e-mail to that nickname means you send e-mail to everyone you assigned to it. If you tell Eudora to replace the old nick, then Eudora deletes the old nickname and saves the new one in its place.

Inserting and expanding nicknames

Sometimes you want to insert the entire list of nicknames associated with a group nickname instead of just the group nickname itself. This means that the To line will contain all of the individual nicknames belonging to the group, instead of just the group's nickname.

The commercial version of Eudora lets you do this. Just hold down the Shift key when you select a group nickname and the entire list is inserted in the field instead.

{ Index }

Symbols

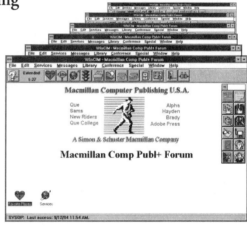